Deviant Knowledge

For Georgina C. Thomas

And in memory of Barrie H. Walters

Deviant Knowledge
Criminology, Politics and Policy

Reece Walters

WILLAN
PUBLISHING

Published by

Willan Publishing
Culmcott House
Mill Street, Uffculme
Cullompton, Devon
EX15 3AT, UK
Tel: +44(0)1884 840337
Fax: +44(0)1884 840251
e-mail: info@willanpublishing.co.uk
website: www.willanpublishing.co.uk

Published simultaneously in the USA and Canada by

Willan Publishing
c/o ISBS, 920 NE 58th Ave, Suite 300,
Portland, Oregon 97213-3786, USA
Tel: +001(0)503 287 3093
Fax: +001(0)503 280 8832
e-mail: info@isbs.com
website: www.isbs.com

First published 2003

ISBN 1-84392-030-1 (cased)
ISBN 1-84392-029-8 (paper)

British Library Cataloguing-in-Publication Data
A catalogue record for this book is available from the British Library

Project management by Deer Park Productions
Typeset by GCS, Leighton Buzzard, Beds
Printed and bound by T.J. International Ltd, Padstow, Cornwall

Contents

Preface

What are the dangers of a 'market-led criminology'? How have new modes of governance in contemporary society influenced the production of criminological knowledge? What is the future of the critical voice in these changing political and economic landscapes? Are there politics involved in the processes and production of criminological knowledge? If so, what form do they take and what impact, if any, do they have on contemporary criminological scholarship?

This book addresses the above questions through a sociology of knowledge, which examines the extent to which criminological knowledge, both historical and contemporary, has been shaped by processes and practices of governance. It explores the factors behind the nexus between criminological endeavour and government and analyses the ways in which criminology's legitimation as a scientific specialism has been influenced by its technocratic and policy-directed orientations. It argues that whereas postwar social welfare agendas emphasized the production of pragmatic, disciplinary expertise, and accordingly sanctioned prescriptive criminological truths in defense of society, contemporary conservative politics have created competitive, managerial and risk-based governmental rationales for criminological knowledge, which favour technocratic forms of knowledge to the virtual exclusion of critical research. In doing so, it further argues that critical criminological voices have, in many instances, become 'deviant knowledges' within neo-liberal political frameworks.

In addressing the above issues, this book examines the 'political' dynamics and the details of conducting criminological research on a day-to-day basis. As Michel Foucault has pointed out, the 'art of governing' or 'to govern' involves not only the protection of principality but also the governing of 'things', the daily events that influence, or are capable of influencing, the economy of the state (Foucault, 1978: 89–91). The book examines the difficulties that criminologists sometimes endure when conducting research and charts the ways in which criminological scholarship is influenced, shaped or governed. It explores the role of government and commercial contracts in contemporary criminological scholarship as well as the various obstacles that criminologists must negotiate prior to, during and after the completion of a research project.

This book further examines the criminological implications of the ways in which academic environments are changing under new managerialist philosophies. The commercialization of criminological knowledge provides a useful mechanism for developing strategic approaches to risk populations. These developments have promoted intense competition within universities to access resources. Funding sources, both internal and external to universities, have become hotly contested as governments calculate budgets on research activity. The increased competition for grants has resulted in criminological researchers seeking funds through commercial sources. The emergence of consultancies and other forms of private work places the researcher in a relationship of service-provider to a client, where there is a responsibility to deliver a product by a said date.

Finally, this book examines the ways in which notions of 'critique' have become subordinate to, the politics of existing governing rationalities. As a result, criminology must begin to re-examine critical scholarship within frameworks that focus on the politics and rationales of new modes of governance. In doing so, it explores new possibilities for the deployment of future criminological knowledge.

Acknowledgements

I would like to acknowledge and express my deepest gratitude to Professor Kit Carson who has taught me the importance of turning over all stones and seeing all possibilities. I am indebted to him for his provocative and insightful comments, his collegial support and for signposting areas worthy of closer scrutiny.

I would also like to acknowledge all the scholars (listed in the appendices) who gave their time to be interviewed by me or to discuss their views about the content of my book. Moreover, special thanks are owed to several academic colleagues who have provided personal support and intellectual input into this project: in alphabetical order, Pat Carlen, Dag Leonardsen, Allison Morris, John Muncie, Pat O'Malley, George Pavlich, David Pearson, Laura Piacentini, Mike Presdee, Phil Scraton, and Jackie Tombs. Such acknowledgment is made with the usual caveat that any errors, inconsistencies or theoretical flaws in this book are in no way a reflection of their input.

Thanks to Brian Willan, a most efficient publisher, who continues to promote diverse and critical criminological narratives, and who has diligently and promptly dealt with various issues associated with this book's development and production.

Finally, thanks to Georgie, Genevieve, Lachie and William for trekking from Australia to New Zealand and now to Scotland. Thanks for your love and support and for much more.

Chapter 1

Questions, contours and methods

It is not only to the poets therefore that we must issue orders requiring them to portray good character in their poems or not to write at all; we must issue similar orders to all artists and craftsmen, and prevent them portraying bad character, ill-discipline, meanness or ugliness in pictures of living things, in sculpture, architecture, or any work of art, and if they are unable to comply they must be forbidden to practise art among us. (Plato, *The Republic*, translated by Desmond Lee: pt. 3, bk. 3, para 401)

Introduction

In 1979, at the seventh conference of the European Group for the Study of Deviance and Social Control in Copenhagen, Professor Manfred Brusten raised serious concerns about what he called the 'social control of criminology and criminologists in West Germany'. Brusten's paper generated widespread reaction, and the following year, in Leuven, the conference convenors devoted the entire programme to debating the state control of criminological knowledge. In his address, Professor Brusten identified the various ways in which 'deviant knowledge' (that which is critical of the state crime-control apparatus or challenges the existing social and political order) was systematically neutralized or marginalized by what he called 'offensive' and 'defensive' social controls of criminological research (see Brusten, 1981). The offensive social controls included state-controlled research institutions and state-controlled research funds that initiate, finance and organize 'scientific research to achieve better administrative control and legitimation'. The defensive mechanisms referred to the ways in which agencies of social control were able to defend themselves against critical research through various forms of passive resistance, all intended to 'obstruct whenever possible research that is disliked' (Brusten and Van Outrive, 1981: 18).

This book broadens the scope of Brusten's initial analysis by focusing on the sociology of criminological knowledge. It questions how knowledge about crime and criminal justice comes into being and examines the ways in which deviant knowledge (criminological knowledges that are unfavourable to, and/or critical of, agents of power) are regulated by new modes of conservative governance. In doing so it asks whether there are politics and governing practices that influence the processes, contours and production of criminological knowledge? If so, what forms do these practices take, and what impact, if any, do they have on contemporary criminological scholarship?

In order to address such issues, it must be acknowledged that criminological research does not take place in a social or political vacuum. It is a genre of knowledge, which has the potential to question the role and management of the state, structures of power and governance, as well as notions of social order. It is an eclectic discipline and is capable of touching those who govern 'on a raw nerve' as it attempts to unearth and locate new knowledges within contested discourses of power, human behaviour and social relations. Whether challenging underlying and established notions of social order or confronting government policy and practice, criminological research may provide views unwelcome to governments seeking reassurance about their political ideologies and agendas. The extent to which criminologies have realized their potential as knowledges challenging existing structures of power and governance will be a major focus of this book.

As Brusten noted almost 25 years ago, criminological researchers who question regulatory practices in society may risk conflict with the officials and authorities that govern such practices. Modalities of power (Foucault, 1980a) seek to regulate the production and utility of knowledge. Governmental practices, contextualized within broader notions of regulation and not confined to definitions of 'state' and bureaucratic authority (Foucault, 1977a), continue to evolve and hybridize in late modernity. These emerging forms of governance (private industry, state and local authorities, and regulatory bodies) are central to understanding the production, content and direction of criminological research. As Hogg points out: 'The production and circulation of criminological knowledge and programmes are also governed practices, dependent on and relative to particular institutional, technical and normative conditions and frameworks' (Hogg, 1998: 146–47).

The production of criminological knowledge may present a site of contestation and conflict. Governments may attempt to stifle, suppress and regulate dissenting views of official policies and practices. The unwillingness of governments to entertain criticism is of major concern, given the changes occurring in academic institutions. O'Malley (1997) argues that neo-liberal political ideologies requiring a cost-effective public sector have placed pressure on universities to be both business- and profit-centred institutions. Criminological research is becoming more commercially and market driven. Many criminologists are finding themselves working in environments that demand greater efficiency and output, where tenure is difficult to secure and where university 'managers' are placing pressure on academics to seek out and engage in commercial research (O'Malley, 1997: 270). We are witnessing an unprecedented volume of 'private criminological research' or consultancies, where the researcher enters into a transaction as service-provider to a designated client. These contractual arrangements continue to blossom as government and private industries seek expertise or aim to demonstrate accountability, and with them they bring a range of regulations covering the scope of the research as well as legal controls over the way the research findings are reported and disseminated. This phenomenon is not unique to criminological discourses. The promulgation of New Right ideologies is affecting the production of new knowledges across a variety of disciplines as well as altering the traditional role and autonomy of academic institutions, although it is on the governance of criminological knowledge and research that this book will focus. It will analyse the ways in which 'deviant knowledge' is policed and/or censured by regulatory agents.

Therefore, this book explores the politics of criminological research. Those often unwritten events or struggles (such as negotiating access to information, copyright and intellectual freedom, difficulties over publishing results, seeking ethical approvals and pressure to alter findings) that seem to have become 'part-and-parcel', in one way or another, of contemporary criminological endeavour are factors that barely receive attention in the final product of publication (Jupp, 1989; Hughes, 1996) but are integral to understanding the nature and content of criminological knowledge. We need to examine the genealogy of these struggles as both independent and singular events (Foucault, 1977b) as well as within the broader historical contours and contexts of criminological thought. Such explorations require us to journey within academic institutions and examine the ways in which university management, driven by neo-liberal ideologies, are influencing the genesis and progress of research projects through methods that are challenging traditional notions of academic freedom, as well as redefining the centrality of academe as the 'critic and conscience' of society. This excursion examines the regulations of university ethics committees as well as exploring the new managerialist policies driving university research.

The 'booming industry' of criminology

Is this a topic worthy of detailed analysis? Why ask questions about the production of criminological knowledge? Surely criminology with its increasing student numbers, its new degrees and journals and its flourishing commercial opportunities are signs of a discipline in a healthy state? In their introductions to the second and third editions of the *Oxford Handbook of Criminology* (1997 and 2002), Maguire *et al.* refer to the growth of criminological studies as 'an explosion in academic activity… a boom in criminological research', an 'enterprise' seen to be flourishing in teaching and research and influencing criminal justice policy and practice. They point out that the expansion of the number of criminological centres, teaching institutions, journals, funding bodies and criminal justice professionals accelerated in the postwar years in tandem with increases in reported crime and government rhetoric about law and order. So extensive is the expansion in criminological knowledge that Maguire *et al.* (2002) argue that 'it is no longer possible, as it once was, for individuals to keep abreast of all this activity and output' (2). Moreover, Jewkes and Letherby (2002: 1) assert that criminology has been 'one of the fastest-growing subjects for university study' throughout the past decade. Similar increases in student numbers and memberships of criminological societies have also been reported in North America (see Laster, 1994; Adler, 1996; Dantzker, 1998). Morgan (2000) points out that this 'criminological enterprise' is attributable partly to law-and-order politics and the growth of 'evidence based policy', notably in the United Kingdom. Do these developments in criminology signal or define a discipline in a healthy state?

Nowadays, the success of a policy or programme is often determined by its level of acceptance or its subsequent proliferation. When a business, government sector or 'community' is seen to be embracing a concept, this is presented by governments or managers as evidence of its value, often without any critical appraisal of its origins, theoretical underpinnings or application. If it is consistent with the organization's 'strategic objectives', is cost-effective and widely embraced, then it must be worthwhile and/or successful. The expansion of criminology as a 'booming enterprise' and references to it as a discipline in a 'healthy state' must also be critically examined. The litmus test for assessing a discipline's achievement must be its content and not its popularity, political versatility or pragmatic relevance. Toffler (1965) critiqued the 'culture boom' in the United States during the postwar years, described as a cultural revolution or renaissance (Grana, 1964). As Americans began to crowd the theatres and art galleries during the early 1960s, many began to question what the emergence of 'art affluence' meant for contemporary society. The 'art elitist' referred to it as the vulgarization of art; others saw it as a cultural revolution. Toffler citing Mannes, argued that the booming industry of art was insufficient to conclude that American society had become more cultured.

> I know people who have gone to concerts every week of their lives and say they love music, but most can't tell Bach from Haydn or know what a grace note is … Attendance, then, at a cultural event is alone not evidence of culture. (Toffler, 1965: 12)

Nor is the growth of criminological centres, journals, programmes, student numbers or contract research necessarily evidence of a discipline in a healthy or productive state. It is evidence of the market value of criminology but such value requires a critical examination. For some, such as Hillyard *et al.* (2003), this expansion in criminology 'mystifies a range of perverse and … deeply disturbing trends in the content of criminology', namely a 'ceaseless chatter' or noise about criminal justice practices driven by the political rhetoric of 'evidence-based policy' (1). At the same time, they argue that criminology fails to engage critically with the state or with notions of social and political order, while remaining silent about crimes of the powerful. This Foucauldian position of 'garrulous discourse' suggests that criminological knowledges have, thus far, been dominated by a self-serving or state-serving noise of narrowly defined notions of crime and criminality.

Criminology – and the need for a sociology of knowledge

Criminology as a viable and constructive knowledge or as a healthy discipline has been the subject of rigorous intellectual debate for decades. There have been several positions suggesting the 'failure' and crisis of criminology (see Taylor *et al.*, 1973; Cohen, 1988; Braithwaite, 1989a; Smart, 1990; Daly and Maher, 1998 and so on). Chan (1994: 25) argues that the criminological research agenda is dominated by a pragmatic or applied element: '[I]s criminology losing its critical edge or have we fallen victim to the lure of relevance'?

5

This is an important question and one that this book examines. It is a question that requires a reflexive analysis of criminological discourses as well as one that demands an investigation of the notion of critique. What is the critical edge that criminology may be losing? And has 'relevance' become a key factor for the production and consumption of criminological knowledge? To address these questions, Pavlich (1998) argues that we must examine the ways in which criminology has developed within narrowly defined discourses of critique. He charts the lines of descent, or the genealogies, that have informed the development of various strains of thought within criminology and contends that critical genres within criminology are unreflexive, limited and historically fragmented. If we are to assert that critical commentary by criminological researchers may bring unwelcomed responses from governing authorities, we must ask why this is so. What does it mean to be critical within new modes of governance? This book will examine these questions through the lens of a sociology of knowledge. Inspired by the works of Michel Foucault, it examines how criminological knowledge comes about and takes form. What counts as knowledge? What is important and what is not? Why are certain forms of knowledge upheld as sophisticated, relevant and useful and others marginalized, neutralized, dismissed and disregarded – in what this book refers to as 'deviant knowledge'.

In doing so, it emphasizes the importance of criminology's intellectual history and its contemporary politics, in what Barbara Hudson (2000) refers to as 'critical reflection as research methodology' (176–77).

The initial impetus for this book came from my previous and current experiences as a criminological researcher working at universities in Australia, New Zealand and Scotland. These experiences have involved the coordination of research under contract with various government agencies and the submission of written reports, as well as the provision of short-term, paid and non-paid, consultancies for verbal and written advice. Therefore, many of the questions that this book raises have emerged from my 12 years of conducting criminological research under various forms of 'agreement' with governments. Naturally, it would be insufficient to develop a book based solely on the above personal experience, and, therefore, the theoretical and analytical framework in this book has been informed by a series of 36 semi-structured interviews with scholars from Britain, the United States, Australia and New Zealand (see Appendix A and C).

I make no claims to be value-free in the creation of my argument. In the spirit of 'standpoint epistemology' I agree that 'the creation of objective, value-free knowledge … is unrealistic' (Hudson, 2000: 184), and while my ideological persuasions are influenced by critical social theory I have nevertheless approached this topic without prejudice and with careful attention to ideological perspectives, narratives and discourses. I recall reading Thucydides' *Pelopennesian War* as a student of Greek history and remember his grappling with the issue of providing an unbiased account. He wrote:

> I have made it a principle not to write down the first story that came my way, and not even to be guided by my own general impressions; either I was present myself at the events which I described or else I heard them from eye-witnesses whose reports I have checked with as much thoroughness as possible. Not that the truth was easy to discover: different eye-witnesses gave different accounts of the same events, speaking out of partiality for one side or else from imperfect memories (Thucydides, 1, 22, cited in Warner and Finley, 1972: 11).

I'm not claiming to have been as thorough as Thucydides. His account of the Pelopennesian War was a *magnum opus*, which took him 27 years to research and write. That said, his above statement acted as a working principle for this book, namely, not to reach conclusions too early, but to investigate as thoroughly as possible the veracity of a given theme before making definitive statements.

Structure and Content

This book will use the terms 'criminological research and/or knowledge', 'criminologies' or 'criminology' interchangeably throughout. 'Criminology' was adopted as a unifying and neutral term in the late nineteenth century (Radzinowicz and Hood, 1986) in preference to value-laden and demarcating phrases such as 'criminal biology', 'criminal psychology' and 'criminal sociology' (Garland, 1997). Nowadays, some scholars speak of 'criminologies' in preference to 'criminology' in order to encapsulate the various narratives, which include a variety of 'distinctive brand names' (Carlen, 1998: 64), such as 'Marxist', 'feminist', 'postmodernist', 'republican', 'administrative', 'realist' and so on. This book argues that all criminologies are susceptible to differing degrees of governance. These regulations often take different forms and this book will distinguish between the different modes of governance that operate against specific forms of criminological knowledge.

This book uses the label 'criminologist' to identify those scholars engaging in criminological research, while recognizing that it is a term fraught with stigma and unwanted connotations. Interestingly, the title 'criminologist' is selectively used within academia. Academics working within schools of criminology often express resentment when referred to as 'criminologists', and individuals may opt for the more generic referents of 'sociologist' or 'historian', 'feminist' or 'social theorist'. The origins and constestations within the discipline of criminology may provide valid explanations for an unwillingness to be constrained by what many interviewees in this research refer to as a 'limiting title'; namely, one that fails to recognize the various levels or 'metadebates' (Cohen, 1998: 119) within studies of crime, knowledge, power and social order. As Ericson (1996) argues, academics working in criminological roles 'cringe when they are asked by acquaintances who are not insiders to explain what criminology is. They cringe because they find it uncomfortable to be so unclear about the boundaries of Criminology' (Ericson, 1996: 16). Perhaps this statement is somewhat hyperbolic; yet it serves to illustrate the ambiguous, disparate and expansive nature of criminological discourses. As such, criminology has been described as a 'hotly contested terrain full of turf wars' (Ericson, 1996: 17; cf. Nelken, 1994). The term 'criminologist' is, therefore, reluctantly used throughout the book and should be interpreted broadly to include those scholars who cross disciplinary boundaries to analyse discourses on crime, law and order, and deviance.

Throughout the book terms such as 'governmentality', 'governance' and 'government' appear. Inspired by the works of Foucault (1977a, 1978), researchers from various disciplines have examined new methods or technologies of rule in what is broadly referred to as discourses in governmentality. Governmentality, therefore, reflects an approach that seeks to understand how individuals and groups are governed or administered (Rose, 2000). This book adopts Garland's (1999) definition of governmentality and how it relates to criminological thought. Garland (1999) argues that the governmentality thesis intersects with criminology to explore power/knowledge complexes: that is, 'a frame-work for analyzing how crime is problematised and controlled' (15). This framework is aided by understanding processes and practices of governance. Throughout the book the term governance is used in a broad sense to examine criminological knowledge. As Rose (2000) argues, governance refers to 'tactic, process, procedure or programme for controlling, regulating, shaping, mastering or exercising authority over others in a nation, organisation or locality' (15).

The term 'government', moreover, is used throughout this book in a broad sense, beyond notions of the 'state' or the executive to bodies of regulation and control. In this sense, the book aims to explore the 'capillary forms' of power (Foucault, 1980b) or, as Donzelot (1979) has argued, power in the form of dispersed and complex technologies both public and private (see also O'Malley, 1992). Unless otherwise stated, references to government will imply a range of governing technologies, such as private security, the insurance industry, and risk management through the practices of a variety of industries and agencies.

Chapter Two charts the origins, processes and events that have shaped the directions of criminological discourses, notably in Britain, Australia and the United States. As Williams has noted when discussing the evolution of culture:

> When the concepts, as it is said, from which we begin – are suddenly seen to be not concepts but problems, not analytic problems either but historical movements that are still unresolved, there is no sense in listening to their sonorous summons or their resounding clashes. We have only, if we can, to recover the substance from which these forms were cast (Williams, 1977: 11).

Chapter Two, therefore, explores those 'substances' or movements from which criminologies were cast. It will examine theoretical developments in the late nineteenth century, including the influence of social defence, and trace the impact of events following World War II as well as specific developments within the United Nations that have, arguably, shaped the directions of criminological research and its relationship to government. Carson and Ditton (1979) have argued that criminological research in post-war Britain 'became directed towards empirical work as a guide to social policy, while theoretical and methodological questions were relegated to peripheral status' (cf, Wiles, 1976). We need to explore the unresolved movements around this period that gave rise to certain forms of criminological knowledge and the influence such movements have had on the development of subsequent discourses within criminology. This chapter will, therefore, assess the extent to which criminological knowledge has been historically governed by a focus on 'crime' as an ontological category and explore the extent to which contemporary criminological research is haunted, to use Derrida's (1994) analysis (see also Pavlich, 1998), by a spirit or legacy of pragmatism and/or state regulation or control. In that sense, the key question is: is the governance of criminological knowledge a new phenomenon?

Chapter Three traces the emergence of criminological 'bureaucracies' and centres as well as the rise of contract research. It argues that research-producing bodies, such as the Home Office Research, Statistics and Development unit in London, the National Institute of Justice in Washington D.C., the Institute of Criminology at Cambridge University, the Australian Institute of Criminology and others, have indeed created important sites for the production of criminological knowledge. But what informed their development? How have they been funded, and how have their research agendas been determined? If these central criminological bodies have, in the main, been sites for the production of relevant or applied knowledge to be used and/or discarded by governments at their discretion (see Radzinowicz, 1988; Pratt, 1996), we must explore why this is so; and we must ask what effects this has had for the production of alternative or critical genres within criminological discourses.

Chapter Four provides an analytical overview of the various ways in which criminological knowledge is governed. Bell and Newby (1977) have described criminological research as a 'deeply political process'. What is the nature of this political process? This chapter explores whether or not criminological research is often a negotiated process, whereby findings are sometimes compromised. If so, why does this occur? It also examines how criminological research may often be 'policed' by funding and/or governing authorities through a range of methods. Some of these 'political' processes include: the politics of winning contracts and grants; restricted and proceduralized access to information; negotiating or bargaining for independence; the use of contracts to legalize control and restrict academic freedom; censorship of written work; failure to publicly release research findings, and so on (see Barnes, 1979; Jupp, 1989; Hughes, 1996).

The chapter explores the extent to which these processes operate at different levels towards different forms of research. For example, 'administrative' criminological research may be critical of government policies and practices and, as a result, the researchers may be subject to a range of interventions, all geared towards rearranging or softening the findings or perhaps stalling the production of the report. Alternatively, research that challenges fundamental features of the social order itself, and state-defined notions of crime or consensus, may bring about widespread smear campaigns by government or even total rejection. Chapter Four explores these themes with published illustrations of such regulatory practices as well as drawing upon experiences obtained from the interviews conducted.

Chapter Five explores further the broader political and economic dimensions that influence the production of criminological knowledge. As Foucault (1977a) has so persuasively argued, power/knowledge complexes create and legitimate 'regimes of truth'. Modalities of knowledge are informed by power relations, which operate through various forms of governance. The chapter uses examples from the current Bush administration's 'War on Terror' to establish this broader context of governance, in which criminological knowledge is funded and developed.

It argues that techniques of neutralization and governance within criminology must be contextualized within broader political frameworks. It uses the War on Terror as a case-study to show how governmental technologies of power suppress critical knowledge. In doing so, it examines the suppression of dissent and explores concepts of free speech within governmental regimes of intolerance. It suggests that criminological agendas are increasingly shaped and funded by governments and this chapter aims to bring into focus some of the discourses and rationales that inform the power/knowledge nexus in the production of criminological scholarship.

Chapter Six analyses further the interconnected discourses of knowledge, power and governance (Foucault, 1980a; Miller and Rose, 1990; Malpas, 1996). Criminological discourses often pivot on modalities of power. As late modernity moves further towards a 'market society', these modalities of power, such as crime-control industries, private security and state and local authorities, are becoming increasingly blurred within contested sites of the public and private. The centrality of risk management within modern forms of government puts critical forms of criminological knowledge to the outer margins. Cohen (1994), writing a postscript to a discussion on the 'lure of relevance', suggests that criminologists 'have to remain vigilant and [have] to retain our critical faculties and our theoretical integrity' (104). The chapter explores notions of critique. If critical knowledge is to be defined, silenced and regulated by the political vagaries of late modernity, where will the critical voices in criminological discourses be, and what form will they take? And how should criminological knowledges respond to existing forms of governance?

Furthermore, the chapter examines broader political trends within Western democratic societies and explores how these shifts are influencing the production of knowledge. It examines how political structures premised on neo-liberal rationalities are challenging the autonomy of academe as well as its role as 'critic and conscience' of society. More specifically, Chapter Six explores how new modes of governance are influencing the production of criminological research, or, as O'Malley (1996) argues, how such changes are influencing the production of 'post-social criminologies'.

Braithwaite (in Smellie, 1996) has further argued that criminologists should always be in a state of constructive tension with regulatory bodies, and has called on criminological researchers to be 'buccaneers' and not allow funding bodies 'carte blanche' with research findings. There may be consequences, however, for researchers who take the approach urged by

Braithwaite, and the chapter further explores some of the struggles, contestations and political dimensions involved when conducting criminological research.

Chapter Seven provides a concluding argument and draws together the key themes identified throughout the book. It emphasizes the importance of a reflexive revision of criminological knowledge as well as proposing potential routes beyond existing modes of governance.

Finally, governments have regulated or silenced critical voices for thousands of years, and even Plato (quoted in the opening of this chapter), who has been described as something of a visionary, subscribed to suppression and/or censorship of those ideas considered contrary to the state's best interests. This book aims to open up for debate the various ways in which criminological knowledges are governed; to explore the political dimensions in the production and consumption of criminological research; to ask why and how criminological research is governed; and to address what the potential dangers inherent are in these governing practices.

Chapter 2

Contours of criminological knowledge: haunted by a spirit of pragmatism?

> History becomes essential to an understanding of the modern criminological enterprise. If we are to understand the central topics which criminology has marked out as its own, if we are to understand the discipline's relation to institutional practices and concerns, if we are to understand some of the key terms and conceptions which structure the discourse, then we will have to ask genealogical questions about the constitution of this science and examine the historical processes which led to the emergence of an accredited disciplinary specialism (Garland, 1997: 13).

Can genealogical questions about the origins of criminology help us to understand why criminologists today experience various forms of regulation or governance? Does criminology have a critical history? Or has it been a government-based project tied to the policy processes of the state? If so, what influence has the discipline's past had on the production of criminological knowledge? This chapter aims to provide a reflexive analysis of criminological discourses; to deconstruct some of the accepted theoretical positions within criminology and to locate specific forms of knowledge within underlying social and political contexts; and to recover those substances, events and struggles from which the forms of criminology were cast (Williams, 1977). In doing so, it draws on Foucault's position in *Discipline and Punish* (1977a) that criminology emerged as knowledge entangled in processes of power, government and the administration of individuals. The aim here is to disentangle the dynamics of specific sites and objects of power and governance that have created criminological furrows. Therefore, this chapter recognizes that we should trace, as Cohen (1988), Garland (1997) and many others urge us to do, those shifts and events that have shaped the developments of modern criminological inquiry.

Criminologies are socially constructed knowledges (Cohen, 1988) and, as such, require an examination of the social and political conditions that give rise to their genesis and promulgation. Such an account seeks to demonstrate that certain historical movements are central to under-standing the contours of criminological research and its relationship to government.

It is not my intention here to rehearse, in detail, an historical account of criminology's origins; such contributions have been made elsewhere (see, for example, Mannheim, 1960; Cohen, 1988; Rock, 1988; Jones, 1986; Beirne, 1993; Garland, 1994; Maguire *et al.*, 1997, and many others). How-ever, it will be necessary to chart specific intellectual and political currents and to explore how such movements have influenced the direction of criminology. It attempts what Foucault referred to in his 'Questions of Method' (1980) as 'eventalization', seeking to isolate specific historical developments as 'events' and to analyse the various processes and pieces that create them. This approach provides new ways of understanding what is often identified as a historical constant and of further appreciating a broader picture – in this instance, the production and governance of criminological knowledge.

First, this chapter aims to enrich existing debates concerned with the development of criminology within political and government contexts by illustrating that the doctrine of social defence, as presented by and through the United Nations, constituted certain areas as objects of knowledge (Foucault, 1977 a and b), which required the involvement of 'criminological experts' while paving the way for technocratic and policy-oriented criminal justice research. Areas such as 'delinquency', outside existing legal frameworks, were isolated by the United Nations as areas that required a social defence strategy. This chapter explores the extent to which power-knowledge complexes associated with the United Nations influenced the governance of criminological discourse in the initial postwar years.

Second, this chapter examines the definition of critical criminological research and how it has evolved within criminological discourses. This analysis necessitates charting the developments of various critical criminological genres and examining their effect on the production of knowledge about crime and deviance. It begins to explore some of the rifts and schisms that occurred within criminological discourses, notably in the late 1960s, and how these developments influenced the contours of criminological research. Again, it is not the intention here to produce a comprehensive account of the rise and development of 'critical' discourses, but to demonstrate that 'radical' departures have become a 'splinter' group within a fragmented criminology, which temporarily asserted themselves in dominance or perhaps popularity, but which have in more recent years been overwhelmed by a criminological retreat to pragmatism.

Early Criminological Developments

The birth of 'criminal science' during the late nineteenth century was to have profound implications for future criminological research (Muncie *et al.*, 1996). The Italian school of criminologists, more commonly referred to as the 'positivists', argued that the cause of criminal behaviour could be empirically explained through the unity of the scientific method (see Lombroso [1876], Ferri [1878], Garofalo [1882], in Muncie *et al.*, 1996). The 'criminal' was to become the object for distinct examination, and 'criminology' (a term first coined by the French anthropologist Topinard in 1879; see Mannheim, 1972) was the science for explaining the causes of criminal behaviour (Garland, 1985). This was a position that rejected earlier notions of free will, arguing that individuals were propelled into criminal lifestyles by a diversity of determining factors (whether individual or social).

Earlier explanations for crime had pivoted on concepts of offenders' rationality and free will. The offender was viewed as a rationally calculating individual who violated the social contract by freely choosing the perceived gains of law breaking against the proposed penalties (Carrara [1874] in Muncie *et al.*, 1996). These earlier 'classicist doctrines', informed by Enlightenment philosophers, which focused on jurisprudence and law reform (Beccaria, 1764), were debunked by positivists in favour of a naturalistic science, which endeavoured to isolate the causes of crime within deterministic factors of undersocialization or abnormalities in human pathology (Ferri, 1901; Young, 1981).

While the early positivists can legitimately lay claim to being the first 'criminologists', they were preceded by a vast amount of scholarship concerning the nature of punishment, the measurement of crime and the administration of law (Rousseau, 1644; Beccaria, 1764; Quetelet, 1842) as well as a large body of work on penal reform (Howard 1777; Romilly, 1806;

Bentham, 1879). Indeed, the science of criminology has been described as a 'secondary evolutional consequence of the study of penology' (Smithers, quoted in Mannheim, 1972; see also Rose, G., 1961). Moreover, it is important to note that philosophies of punishment date back to antiquity: Plato wrote: 'whoever does wrong does not do so of his own free will' (Plato, *Laws* V).

While it may be possible to disentangle ideologies within earlier movements and juxtapose them within later theoretical developments, it is clear that earlier works on justice, law and punishment did not demarcate a 'science of crime'. Positivism carved out a specialism for itself by centering on the question of 'what in fact is the criminal?' (see Garland, 1985).

The early positivists were influenced by the writings of Darwin, Spencer and Broca who sought to explain the origins of human society with scientific method, and who argued, furthermore, that it grew out 'of an anthropological concern to study man and his natural varieties' (Garland, 1988: 1). Mannheim's edited collection (1972) on the pioneers of criminology examines in detail the biographies of earlier criminologists and alerts readers to the importance of the sociopolitical contexts that influenced their writings. Mannheim refers to William Bonger's critique of Carlyle's concept of 'the great man' theory to explain intellectual develop-ment in favour of 'mass movements', those underlying social and political conditions that stimulate and nurture the growth of new knowledges. 'Movements', as mentioned earlier, are important for understanding the developments of intellectual episodes. Bonger (1916) was influenced by the social and economic circumstances of his time, including World War I and widespread unemployment. He argued:

> Production is carried on for profit exclusively; if greater profits can be made by stopping the production it will be stopped – this is the point of view of the capitalists ... The present economic system and its consequences weaken the social feeling (Bonger [1916] quoted in Muncie *et al.*, 1996: 42).

It is important here to recognize that positivism emerged during a period of social and political turmoil in Italy. In 1870, after 50 years of internal and external conflict, Italy was unified as a republic. Rome was declared the capital of the new nation and the Papacy was granted spiritual independence and authority. For half a century, Italy had been marked by periods of revolution, civil conflict between the north and south, wars with France and Prussia, and political and religious instability (Berkeley, 1932; Bosworth, 1979). The events following 1870 provided the country with much-needed stability. Whyte (1950) summarizes this period in Italian history: 'a new Italy had arisen, free, independent and united, under a constitutional government with her King in the Eternal City'(180).

During the 1870s, notably after the fall of the right-wing Minghetti government in 1876, the new left-wing government, led by Prime Minister Depretis, introduced a range of domestic policies (for example, road and railway construction and industrial development) to deal with the growing number of social problems (Whyte, 1950). It is during this period in Italy that we see the origins of 'social defence' (discussed below), a doctrine that promoted the protection of society (or, as is the case with Italy, the protection of a newly formed nation) and which evolved with and through a positivist science of criminal behaviour (Ancel, 1965).

Lapis (1981) argues that the 'new Italy' was not united at all but was characterized by a political economy of 'class warfare'. The bourgeoisie of the north monopolized the growing industrial economies and actively asserted policies of southern suppression in the name of 'social reclamation'. The construction policies of the Depretis government, he argues, were merely supporting the industrial imperatives of middle-class northern capitalists and alleviating widespread social inequities. For Lapis, the early positivists were politically important for asserting a northern hegemonic plan, in that:

> It attributed the low level of life in the South to the supposed inferiority of the Mediterranean race. They were therefore biologically unable to sustain the competition levels given by the new middle-class economy ... Positivism was used to justify, scientifically, social inequalities, considering them as natural differences (Lapis, 1981, 157–58).

It is important to recognize, therefore, that a social-defence or social-reclamation strategy was an amalgam of anthropological and sociological sciences. It was a politically motivated policy in late nineteenth-century Italy by a middle-class northern government, one that sought to suppress the southern regions from rebelling against a biased and unjust economic policy (Lapis, 1981; Pavarini, 1982). This is the bedrock upon which a social-defence theory is developed in the early twentieth century.

The development of social-defence theory has been accredited to the Belgian jurist, Adolphe Prins, following the publication of his book *La Défense sociale* in 1910 (see Ancel, 1965). As a penological concept, however, its origins are to be found in the early nineteenth century. In 1830, the Italian jurist, Camignani, argued that the rigid administration of crimes and punishments should be replaced with a new penal theory based on the concepts of 'social offence' and 'social defence' (see Pasquino, 1980). Its origins are clearly European, notably Italian, German, French and Belgian. Camignani's vision of a social-defence doctrine gathered momentum and acceptance during the positivist revolt of the late nineteenth century. Radzinowicz describes the place of social defence within positivist ideology:

> It was not the business of the criminal justice system to assess and to measure the moral guilt of an offender but only to determine whether or not he was the perpetrator of an act defined as an offence and then to apply to him one of the measures of 'social defence' so as to restrain him from committing further crimes (Radzinowicz, 1961: 17).

'Social defence' is a phrase that has been subject to widespread interpretation and distortion (Ancel, 1965). In the first half of the twentieth century, it received much attention among European lawyers and social theorists. Despite its shifting emphasis, however, 'social defence' refers to the protection of society against crime. While some interpretations have emphasized that social defence refers to the repression of crime by the criminal law and the administration of 'stern' punishment (Signoral [1912] in Ancel, 1965), thus reflecting classicist doctrine or principles of the *ancien régime*, the weight of opinion would suggest that social defence, at least when adopted into criminal-science rhetoric in the late nineteenth and early twentieth centuries, centred on the protection of society by the neutralization and resocialization of the offender, whereby fixed penalties were set aside for 'individualized' punishment (see Ancel, 1965). In a slight variant, the phrase was used by Ferri in the late nineteenth century to explain the purpose and justification of punishment as an indeterminate treatment reflecting the needs of the individual rather than moral culpability and retribution (Ferri, 1895).

The Italian positivist school at the end of the nineteenth century referred to the failures of social defence ('la difesa sociale') expressed through repressive criminal law and deterrent-based punishments. In its place, they argued that a doctrine of social defence should no longer focus on individual and moral responsibility but be replaced with 'mesures de surete', or preventative measures, which would address the criminal's 'dangerous condition' (Ancel, 1962: 498). Pratt (1997) argues that a 'new penality' emerged in Europe in the late nineteenth and early twentieth centuries, one that classified criminals into categories (insane, habitual, degenerate, weak-minded and the like) and subsequently tailored punishment on an individual basis. For Pratt, 'the individualisation of punishment' served a broader social purpose. He argues, '[the penal process] would now be a form of social defence, providing insurance against the risks that the habitual criminals presented, alongside the other strategies that the emerging welfare state had introduced to protect its citizens from risk, and ensure their security' (Pratt, 1997: 47). This Foucauldian argument asserts that the criminal anthropologists of the late nineteenth century emphasized that criminal sanctions or penalties need not be seen as 'punishment but, rather, a mechanism for the defense of society', which necessitated a 'knowledge system' that would be capable of measuring and assessing the risk and dangerousness of criminals (Foucault [1978] cited in Faubion, 2000: 193–94).

As a concept, social defence in the first half of the twentieth century received much criticism because of its suppression of the individual in favour of social protection or, as Radzinowicz (1999) has argued, 'social defence [sliding] into social aggression'(38). Individual freedoms were viewed as subsidiary to those justified measures that aimed to protect the moral and legal fabric of society (Hall, 1947). Social defence has also been interpreted as a form of social hygiene. The International Union of Penal Law, founded in 1889, comprised an alliance of European penal reformists. It adopted an interventionist approach to penology and interpreted social defence to mean 'social hygiene', involving the 'mopping-up of the social breeding grounds of crime' (Pasquino, 1980: 24). Social-defence theorists viewed habitual criminality as a social phenomenon and not solely as an anthropological characteristic (Pasquino, 1980). Marc Ancel describes the more extreme applications of social defence expressed through repressive governmental regimes such as Communist Russia, Nazi Germany and Fascist Italy, where social defence was viewed as a form of 'community protection' completely eroding human rights and civil liberties (Ancel, 1965).

The earliest usage of the term 'social defence' is, therefore, founded on broad and changing interpretations. Its 'modern' definition and application is, however, applied with greater consistency. The United Nations resurrected the term in 1948 as 'the prevention of crime and the treatment of offenders' (Ancel, 1965: 17–18). This definition focused on positivist explanations of criminality and on penal solutions that served to protect society while addressing the criminogenic circumstances of the offender. Mannheim (1972) argues that classicism and positivism comprised the nineteenth-century 'schools' of criminology and that 'social defence' is a potential 'twentieth-century Third School' (35). Nowadays, social-defence theory is rarely used within criminal justice rhetoric. However, its underlying principles of protecting society through individualized punishment (for example, indeterminate sentences, preventative detention) have remained central facets of penal and criminal justice policy throughout the twentieth century. That said, it has been applied consistently as a penal philosophy that would protect society. Moreover, social defence established a knowledge-system that could assess and predict risk. As a result, Foucault argues that the responsibility of 'crime' was removed from the sole jurisdiction of the judges to 'experts in psychiatry, criminology and psychology'. I shall return to the social-defence movement shortly and chart its influence through the United Nations after World War II.

Here, however, it is important to explore how the positivist movement cemented 'the criminal' as an ontological or absolute category for analysis. 'Crime' defined by the state emerged for the first time as a legitimate object of scientific analysis and throughout the early years of the twentieth century criminology was closely aligned to government institutions. Radzinowicz (1961) describes the opening of the Institute for the Study of Criminal Sciences in the School of Law at the University of Rome in 1912 as an event attended by the Prime Minister, ministers of justice and public education, as well as several other dignitaries who came to officially open a school that had been recommended by the Government's Supreme Council of Education. This opening sparked the establishment of other criminological centres, including the Institute of Criminal Anthropology at the University of Turin in 1912, the Institute of Studies in Criminal Science and Police at the University of Bologna in 1918 and others during the same year at Modena, Naples and Genoa (Radzinowicz, 1961). The study of crime and the criminal had blossomed as an academic science within a disciplinary boundary defined by the state. As Mannheim (1960) has pointed out, 'the state was at the heart of criminology as crime was defined by the criminal law' (Mannheim, 1960; see also Reiner, 1988).

Within its historical context, the positivist movement challenged existing ideologies, and as a result has been referred to as a 'revolution' or a revolt against traditional concepts of criminal behaviour (see Radzinowicz, 1961; Young 1981). Throughout the twentieth century it was characterized by a focus on state-defined notions of crime and criminal behaviour, seeking expression through correctional practices in the care and treatment of offenders (Taylor et al., 1973). Positivist criminologies, whether biological (Kretschmer, 1921; Sheldon, 1940), psychological (Trasler, 1962; Eysenck, 1970) or sociological (Merton, 1957; Ericson, 1962; Durkheim, 1964) dominated criminological endeavours for much of the first six decades of the twentieth century (Radzinowicz and Hood, 1986) and continue to play an influential role within contemporary criminological research. Yet as a paradigm, positivist ideologies have been subject to wide-scale criticism (Young, 1981; Cohen, 1988). Among these criticisms are arguments that positivism has denied authenticity to offending, and that it has ignored notions of human choice and rationality as well as failing to emphasize the political and cultural motivations of individuals and groups who rebel against repressive laws and state policies. Moreover, there is a view that positivism has created a substantial bias in how it shapes the contours of criminological research. As Fattah has noted:

> Since it emerged as a scientific discipline in the 19th century, criminology has exhibited and continues to exhibit a clear bias. Research and theory have focused on crimes by the powerless, not the powerful; crime in the streets, not crime in the suite; conventional crime, not white collar crime, crime by individuals, not crime by governments and corporations; disorganised crime, and not organised crime. Mainstream criminological theories are the product of this slanted approach (Fattah, 1997: 67).

Garland (1988; 1997) points out that British criminology did not evolve from a Lombrosian tradition (although influenced by its scientific imperatives); rather, it developed from a medico-legal science, 'sponsored by the penal and psychiatric establishments' (Garland, 1988: 1). He argues that British criminology prior to 1935 was institutionally based and arguably governed by the disciplines of medicine, psychiatry and law. Moreover, he highlights how these close institutional ties are important for understanding the uncritical nature of that earlier work, which he describes as 'generally modest in its claims, and very respectful of the requirements of institutional regimes and legal principles' (Garland, 1988).

Martin's (1988) overview of British criminology during the years 1948–60 emphasizes the 'scanty' amount of criminological literature and the dominance of state questions about penology and prevention. It is not until the latter part of this period that criminology in Britain witnessed the demise of psychoanalytical approaches to criminology, as well as the rise of journals, criminological centres and what Martin calls 'the beginnings of a home-grown sociological literature' (44). It is not until the 1960s that we see criminology blossom into a 'multi-institutional academic enterprise' (Rock, 1988) and thus move its development beyond that of a 'scholarly cottage industry' (Downes, 1988: 45).

These pragmatic and conservative roots have also characterized criminological developments in the United States. Universities in the United States did not offer courses in criminology until the 1930s, and the first department in criminology was not established until 1950, at Berkley (Petersilla, 1991). The American Society of Criminology was founded in

1941 where 'the discipline and ASC were strongly grounded in practical concerns of the criminal justice system' (Petersilla, 1991: 2).

Reckless (1970) points out that American criminology has always maintained strong sociological traditions. The sociologist Maurice Parmelee published the first criminological text for academic use in 1920 (Reckless, 1970). Moreover, US criminological traditions were significantly influenced by the classical sociological theories of Marx, Durkheim and Weber. Despite the sociological currents, Reckless (1970) argues that 'clinicians, mainly psychiatrists and psychologists'(9) were extremely influential in the direction of early criminology in the Unites States. The role of professionals from the medical and behavioural sciences in criminological research, during 1920–40 in particular, were influential for developing many areas of inquiry, notably the prediction of juvenile delinquency. Reckless (1970) concludes his history of American criminology by stating that:

'American criminology from 1940 until the present extended the interests and developments which took place in the period 1920–1940. It appears that more psychiatrists and psychologists are making contributions' (20).

This view of the origins of criminology in the United States is consistent with the arguments of Morris (1975) and Scarpitti (1985). In addition Jeffrey (1972) argues that the development of criminology in the United States was closely aligned with issues of prison reform:

Criminology has developed to a great extent as a branch of the penal reform movement in the United States. The major problems in Criminology have been derived from the needs of parole boards and prison administrators for tools with which to reform or manage criminals …. The development of criminology is limited by this interest in penal reform and prison problems (Jeffrey, 1972: 467).

Sociology in the United States has, however, a history of confronting mainstream criminological orthodoxy and ideology. Carson (1983) accurately points out that Edwin Sutherland in 1939 challenged the criminological fraternity in America by introducing his contemporaries to what he viewed as a widely neglected yet commonplace phenomenon, which he termed 'white collar crime'. Sutherland (1940) challenged positivist concepts of social pathology as inadequate for their inability to explain the harmful practices of professionals in the course of their daily business. His presidential address to the American Sociological Society of

1939, where he first voiced his theory of a 'white collar criminality', must surely have been received as radical for its time. He criticised positivist theory and challenged legal processes that systemically dealt with white collar crime as an administrative and not a criminal issue. Carson (1983) recognizes the pivotal nature of Sutherland's address for criminology in laying the foundations for radical scholarship, but suggests that Sutherland failed to pursue his thesis within his own discourses of the sociology of law, preferring to retreat into an alternative form of criminological causation: what is today referred to as sociological positivism.

Despite these strong sociological traditions in North America, particularly those that influenced radical deviancy thinking during the 1960s (discussed below), criminology in the United States has developed as in Britain, Australia, Canada (see Gladstone, *et al.*, 1991), New Zealand (see Robson, 1975) and elsewhere from narrowly construed discources of law, medicine and penology. Carson and O'Malley (1989) observe within the Australian context that the foundations of contemporary criminology were both conservative and pragmatic. They conclude that Australian criminology 'was nurtured as a university-based service discipline for state agencies, providing correctionalist technicians and knowledge' (Carson and O'Malley, 1989: 351). As a result, they assert that criminology has been subject to institutional controls, whereby theoretical and critical research has remained underdeveloped, and the discipline has been dominated by 'criminological commissions' (convened by the state) providing criminological knowledge and expertise to senior public officials.

The foundations of the criminological enterprise are those of a 'positive science'; it was a discipline that sought autonomy as an academic specialism by scientifically establishing the causes and prevention of crime: an academic project closely aligned with government institutions and the production of applied knowledge for state policy and practice (Roshier, 1989). Sociological theories of crime, notably those that developed in the late 1960s (discussed later), attempted to break away from 'mainstream' analyses by focusing on questions of deviance and social order. Earlier sociological contributions to criminological research from the University of Chicago Sociology Department and the works of Park (1915), Thrasher (1927), Shaw and McKay (1942) and others to Merton's contribution on anomie (Merton, 1957), Sykes and Matza's (1957) theories of techniques of neutralization and Hirschi's (1969) control theory were developments influenced by a positivist approach to understanding criminal behaviour (Downes and Rock, 1982). These forms of sociological positivism were also challenged by more radical or critical paradigms (Taylor *et al.*, 1973) and I shall discuss them shortly.

What follows is an analysis of criminological contours in the postwar period. What were considered the areas of criminological concern, and why? Which theoretical assumptions were underpinning the initiatives undertaken by governments in the postwar years to prevent crime, and why? And how and why is this period important for understanding the 'politics' and governance of contemporary criminological research?

International Reconstruction and Developments in Criminological Research Following World War II

The postwar years in Europe, particularly Britain, provide an important context for understanding shifts in the direction of criminological research. It is during these years of social reconstruction that we see the emergence of 'social justice' and the welfare state, where explanations for criminal behaviour, particularly juvenile delinquency, were to be explored within wider social parameters (cf. Mannheim, 1946, Morris, 1989). Radzinowicz (1999) argues that the disciplinary nature of criminology was more prominent in Britain than elsewhere, although he emphasizes the invaluable contribution of European scholars. I have interviewed criminologists from the United Kingdom, Australia, New Zealand and to a lesser extent from the United States, countries which share common criminological traditions: all were significantly influenced by European scholars throughout the early years of their development (Van Swaaningen, 1999). However, Britain was the first of them to establish academic teaching and scholarship in the field of 'criminology', as well as being the first to create criminological research within government. It is, therefore, worth examining the events that foreshadowed and arguably influenced the development of criminological scholarship in Britain.

In July 1945, Winston Churchill's re-election campaign failed. His 'finish the job' slogan and his ongoing attacks on the Labour Party's socialist agenda that would lead Britain into totalitarian rule by a 'British Gestapo' were rejected by the British public (Sked and Cook, 1993). The Labour Party leader, Clement Attlee, was elected prime minister with a commitment to restore Britain beyond the promises of the 1942 Beveridge Report. This report (agreed to by all three major political parties at the time) contained, *inter alia*, a commitment to ensuring full employment, reducing inflation and expanding existing health services. Labour's introduction of what would become the postwar welfare state based on Keynesian economic principles (Clarke, 1996) offered to develop further the social agenda with the provision of a 'social insurance', which included a set of policies that would care for the civilian population from what had been previously dubbed 'the cradle to the grave' (Pierson, 1996). Moreover, the state was to provide aid in the form of a social wage that would ensure improved standards of living. While many commentators argue that Attlee's administration was a 'gradual approach' to economic reconstruction (Grenville, 1994), others contend that the Labour government was more concerned with addressing the immediate needs of the people (food, housing and healthcare) and thereby bringing about social justice (Cole, 1956; Titmuss, 1962).

The United States – the postwar economic superpower – supported reconstruction efforts in Europe through the United Nations Monetary and Financial Conference, which met in Bretton Woods, New Hampshire, in July 1944 at the invitation of President Roosevelt (United Nations, 1947). While much of the Bretton Woods proceedings are peripheral to this book, it is important to recognize the importance of the International Monetary Fund for the reconstruction efforts in Europe, particularly in Britain, which attempted to bring about social justice and uphold social defence.

The Bretton Woods agreements focused on world trade and eliminating trade restrictions that had proven crippling during the 1930s. Bretton Woods forged agreements that would see all currencies regulated by an international body – the International Monetary Fund (IMF). This fund was constituted by an organization of member states, whereby the largest contributor of gold bullion to the fund (the United States) was given the greatest voting power (Scammell, 1975). Countries could access the IMF for loans towards social reconstruction. Britain's contribution to the IMF in the postwar years was negligible. Nearly all of Britain's financial reserves had been spent on fighting World War II. Domestic industry in Britain was slowly recovering and, as a result, British imports in the immediate postwar years were very high (Grenville, 1994). In Britain, unemployment was rapidly increasing with export levels less than one third of the pre-war trade figures, high inflation and a soaring national debt. Throughout the world, Britain's essential needs had been sustained through the American Lend-Lease programme, which was established in 1942. This loan scheme had accrued a substantial debt to the United States and in 1945 President Truman ended the programme. The decision increased Britain's current account deficit and forced it to borrow large sums from other countries (Cole, 1956).

Amid these financial crises in Britain, this period of social and economic reconstruction also witnessed a significant increase in reported crime. The economic struggles facing Britain were intensified by an internal threat to human life and safety. Society needed to be protected by the criminal law (Mannheim, 1946; Morris, 1989) as well as strategies of social defence. In a

25

similar fashion to Italy in 1870, Britain, having defeated the foreign enemies by military means, was now faced with internal conflicts that would be addressed by social means, or, as Titmus (1959) puts it, 'social administration in a changing society' (33). This internal or social focus was characteristic of several European nations in the decade following World War II. For many, the focus of war shifted from foreign enemies to domestic wars against poverty and social problems (see Wilson, 1953).

Financial support for social-reconstruction endeavours was to come from the IMF and the World Bank as well as other funds made available by the United Nations. More importantly, if countries like Britain were to take advantage of the expanding trade economies established after Bretton Woods, it would need to demonstrate internal stability. As Eichengreen and Kenen note:

> The establishment of welfare states and social-market economies created a web of domestic commitments and side payments that locked in cooperative behaviour. The result of political stability and support that governments enjoyed at home buttressed the credibility of their international undertakings (Eichengreen and Kenen, 1994: 6).

This became important when voting members of the IMF and World Bank determined financial aid for reconstruction initiatives. If a country could demonstrate political and social stability it would thereby enhance both its opportunities for aid as well as developing new trading partners (Kenen, 1994). Chan (2000) cites Bauman (1998) to provide a similar example of contemporary governments within globalized economies. She argues that 'the problems of insecurity and uncertainty brought about by (economic) globalisation into anxiety about personal safety is attractive for politicians, who "can be supposed to be doing something about the first two because being seen to be vociferous and vigorous about the third"' (Bauman, 1998: 117). Governments are, in this view, reduced to the role of fighting crime to provide 'safe environments' for market forces to operate in a global economy.

The prevention of crime and the maintenance of social order, therefore, became a political issue for economic prosperity. As in Victorian England during the mid-1840s, following a period of international conflict, crime was 'becoming a vehicle for articulating mounting anxieties about issues which really had nothing to do with crime at all' (Gatrell, 1990, cited in Sharpe, 1996: 137). Rising crime rates in the postwar years represented a threat to internal safety as well as to external aid and trade. In Britain, legislation was passed in the late 1940s that would see a crackdown on criminal behaviour (discussed later).

Not surprisingly, the greatest increases in reported crime in Britain during this period were for drunkenness (Struthers, 1952). Juvenile crime rose sharply and offences with substantial public visibility, such as disorderly behaviour, drunkenness and personal robbery, became targets of law enforcement. Moreover, it is during this time that we begin to see the harnessing of science to the practical affairs of government (discussed later). We shall see in the next chapter that criminological research gathered rapid momentum in the 1950s, resulting in the development of government and university research units and the expansion of funding to undertake research into crime causation and prevention (Sapsford, 1996). In order to understand the vastly expanding nature of criminological research during the 1950s and its relationship to the state, however, it is important to trace the events that led to widespread interest in crime as a 'social phenomenon'. In doing so, the following section charts the development of the social defence movement and emphasises how its influence on the United Nations in the late 1940s produced profound effects on the direction that criminological research would take.

United Nations, Criminological Discourse and Government(ality)

What follows is an examination of how crime was defined and problematized at an international level and the influence that organizations such as the United Nations had on the contours of criminological knowledge.

League of Nations

The postwar reconstruction efforts of the United Nations and its focus on crime prevention took direction from the earlier work of the League of Nations. The League of Nations, established in 1919, provided one of the first international forums for exploring issues relating to the prevention and suppression of crime (League of Nations, 1938). Much of its criminological work through its social and humanitarian committees focused on drugs, child exploitation, the unification of criminal laws, and penal and penitentiary issues relating to the treatment of prisoners (see League of Nations *Yearbooks*, 1920–35).

In 1930, the Economic and Social Council proposed that the Assembly of the Secretary-General should include penal administration on its agenda (League of Nations, 1938). On the issue of the prevention and suppression of crime, the League of Nations consulted with seven international organizations: the International Penal Law Association; the International Bureau for the Unification of Criminal Law; the International Criminal Police Commission; the International Penal and Penitentiary

Commission; the Howard League for Penal Reform; the International Law Association, and the International Penal Law Union. These organizations met in Geneva on 10 May 1932 and compiled a joint resolution to the Secretary-General on penal and penitentiary questions. That resolution, *inter alia*, called for the standardization of criminal laws across member states, international police cooperation and the setting up of 'ad hoc committees of experts' for the ongoing provision of research (League of Nations, 1933). While most countries rejected the unification of criminal laws, it was agreed that the League of Nations could play an active role in researching crime and developing strategies for crime prevention.

In the 1930s the League of Nations commissioned several studies into the number of prisoners in member states, the treatment of witnesses and persons awaiting trial, and minimum rules for the treatment of prisoners, and it continuously urged countries to study methods likely to reduce prison populations (League of Nations, 1938). In providing recommendations and commissioning research, the League relied upon those 'technical organizations' mentioned above for ongoing expertise. Their inclusion as consultants or advisors to the League was based on perceived scientific and technical knowledge of criminal behaviour. These organizations pursued a range of research topics, each with a clear positivist focus. For example, the International Penal and Penitentiary Commission provided the League with a 'scientific examination of prisoners in custody' and concluded:

There are not many countries with a systematic criminal anthropology or biology service, and it is hardly likely that such services will be established in the near future in other countries, chiefly on account of the economic and financial depression. The study of the problem is being continued with a view to preparing, if possible, an anthropological or biological dossier which could be generally applied (League of Nations, 1934: 8).

In 1933, the fifth Committee of the fourteenth Assembly of the League of Nations urged governments to undertake research into priority areas, including:

Criminal biology, the organisation of international penal and penitentiary statistics, the general limitation of the period of detention pending trial, certain international aspects of the problem of assistance to convicts, compulsory after-care and its extension to prisoners who have been fully discharged, the general and international regulation of prison labour, the placing of discharged prisoners in free industry by means of legislation and the systematic collaboration of representatives of Governments, industry and labour with a view to obviating the drawbacks of the possible competition of prison labour in the open market (League of Nations, 1934: 10).

The above areas were to dominate the criminological research agendas of the League of Nations throughout the 1930s, up to the outbreak of World War II. It is important to note here that the League of Nations was asserting an influential and prominent role in the international dissemination of crime research. Its research agenda was set by criminological experts (largely from medical and law schools), with an ideology that medicalized the causes and prevention of criminal conduct.

United Nations

The United Nations has historically played a role in the production of specific forms of criminological knowledge, and the vast majority of this research is found in the work of the Social Commission, a sub-committee of the Economic and Social Council. Nowadays, the United Nations remains active in the production of international crime and victim surveys as well as passing resolutions on issues such as children's rights, gun controls, and crime prevention (see Frate *et al.*, 1995; Zvekic *et al.*, 2000; Scherpenzeel, 2000). Many of these modern-day United Nations activities were discussed and pursued in the late 1940s, a period which, this book argues, was an important time for the development of a government-centred or policy-related criminological agenda.

On 29 March 1947, the Economic and Social Council recognized that crime was a substantial problem with widespread social ramifications and requested that the Secretary-General submit a report to the Social Commission 'on the question of the prevention of crime and treatment of offenders, showing which suggestions are suitable for international action' (United Nations, 1947). Moreover, the Economic and Social Council requested that the Social Commission consider:

... how effective machinery can be developed for studying on a wide international basis the means for the prevention of crime and the treatment of offenders [and to] undertake consultation with the International Penal and Penitentiary Commission, and recommend a scheme by which work on this whole subject can be fruitfully dealt with on a broad international basis in close association with other social problems (United Nations, 1947: 514).

As a starting point, the Social Commission selected a series of topics that had been explored by the League of Nations, and set about seeking reports on issues of juvenile delinquency, habitual offenders, and criminal statistics as well as pursuing a general inquiry into the role of the medical, psychological, and social sciences in dealing with the problems of crime (United Nations, 1948: 613). To assist its work in 'assuming leadership in promoting study in the field of prevention of crime and treatment of offenders' (United Nations, 1949a: 616) the United Nations convened a conference in Paris during 1948, inviting nine 'principal international organisations'[1] that would aid the Social Commission to achieve its crime-prevention objectives. It was viewed as a continuation of the efforts that had taken place under the auspices of the League of Nations between the two wars. Prior to this meeting, the United Nations established a Social Defence Section, with a mandate to assist the international organizations in achieving the goals of the Secretary-General.

Following the 1948 conference in Paris, Resolution 155(vii) on the prevention of crime and treatment of offenders was passed before the Economic and Social Council, which affirmed that the United Nations :

(a) assume leadership in promoting study in this field, on an international basis, having regard to the knowledge and experience of international and national organisations with interests and competence in this field, and requested the Secretary-General, subject to budgetary limitations,

(b) convene in 1949 a group of internationally recognised experts, to act in an honorary capacity and advise the Secretary-General and the Social Commission in formulating policies and programmes to the study on an international basis of this problem and to international action in this field (United Nations, 1949b).

In August 1949, in response to Resolution 155(vii), the United Nations convened a gathering of international experts at Lake Success in New York,[2] which recommended that the United Nations expand its Social Defence Section, commission a variety of scientific research projects, engage 'specialists' outside the United Nations to provide expertise on specific issues, commence a publication series and begin a regular conference programme to address issues of crime prevention and the treatment of offenders (United Nations, 1949c). Lopez-Rey (1974) argues that social defence at this stage had become subsumed within broader issues of socio-economic development. The emphasis on 'preventing crime' was slowly moving towards broader objectives of social change, and the United Nations began developing strategies which, Lopez-Rey argues, contained 'vague terms [that would] inevitably lead to confusion and generalities of no scientific or policy-oriented value' (492). One way of remedying this generalization of social defence, and of redirecting attention to specific 'crime problems', was for the United Nations to consult with 'elite organisations and recognised experts' (Lopez-Rey, 1974: 500). Therefore, at its October 1949 meeting, the Social Commission endorsed the recommendations of the International Group of Experts calling on the Economic and Social Council to provide 'special budgetary provisions' for governments to undertake research relating to the objectives of the Commission (United Nations, 1949c). The Social Commission also moved that the Social Defence Section should provide a clearing-house function, by collecting and disseminating 'the experience of different countries with respect to specific preventive measures' (United Nations, 1949e: 4).

This agenda, or 'program of research and action in the field' (United Nations, 1950), which had been informed by an established group of consultants to the United Nations and supported with resources, was to be a platform for international criminological research into the 1950s. The Social Commission's research agenda was divided into three categories. The first included subjects on which research was already 'in progress', such as: the problem of juvenile delinquency; medical, psychiatric and social examination of offenders as a guide to treatment; probation and related measures; and compiling criminal statistics in order to assess the state of crime. The second category of research included 'subjects which should receive top priority': pre-sentence detention and the use of short-term imprisonment; parole; habitual offenders; open correctional facilities; and the training of personnel for penal and correctional institutions. Finally, the United Nations listed a number of subjects 'which should be undertaken as soon as feasible'. These programmes included: police initiatives directed towards crime prevention; treatment in penal institutions designed for the resocialization of the offender; the role of prison labour; capital and corporal punishment; forfeitures and loss of civil rights; and 'collection of information with respect to the precise ways in which knowledge of, and training in, the behavioural sciences are at present being used in practice in the prevention of crime and the treatment of offenders' (see United Nations, 1949d: 1–6).

Here we begin to see the United Nations mobilizing resources during the postwar years for crime prevention – an important category within the United Nation's social reconstruction endeavours.

In 1950, the United Nations' work on the prevention of crime and treatment of offenders was subsumed within the title of 'Social Defence' – a title deemed to reflect a more comprehensive social programme, and a movement, as discussed earlier, with its roots embedded in a positivist doctrine of criminal behaviour. During 1950, the United Nations stepped up its dissemination of social-defence principles by sponsoring 15 'social defence observers' across member states to facilitate and promote research into crime and its prevention (United Nations, 1950). In late 1950, at the 12th and final gathering of the International Penal and Penitentiary Congress, the delegates discussed the need to address 'measures which are appropriate substitutes for punishment, taking into account the necessities of a humane social defence' (Commission Internationale Pénale et Pénitentiaire, 1951: 510).

The principles of social defence, promulgated through the United Nations, emerged as the cornerstone of criminological endeavours during the 1950s. The early works of influential British criminologists such as McClintock (see Garland, 1995), Wootten (1978) as well as Radzinowicz, particularly his writings on indeterminate sentences and habitual criminals (see Hood, 1997, and Radzinowicz's foreword to Ancel, 1965) were heavily influenced by social-defence doctrine.[3] Moreover, this was an important period, which defined and legitimized the role of the criminological 'expert', a time when credible consultants, identified by their affiliations with established scientific institutions, were called on to provide advice for the development of international directions on the prevention and treatment of criminal behaviour. These 'elite' individuals and organizations had their roots in disciplines such as medicine, psychiatry, psychology and law. They were nominated by the Secretary-General, 'but experience shows that such nominations are seldom made without previous official approval' (Lopez-Rey, 1974: 501). It was, therefore, a period that gave life to the role of the criminological expert, a time that professionalized 'government approved' elites for the development of international crime policies and the funding of crime-related research.

Wiles (1976), in turn, argues that criminological research in the years following World War II was an amalgam of government-funded projects geared towards producing solutions for pressing social problems:

> The exigencies of war fostered a situation in which research was firmly harnessed to the pressing problems of the day .... In the immediate post-war period, the organisation and use of research had itself become a subject for government policy .... Such, in brief, was the way in which the structure of criminological research developed in the wake of the Second World War and its lessons in the harnessing of science to the practical affairs of government (Wiles, 1976: 2–3).

The funds to sponsor policy-based criminological research were provided by central government organizations as well as through the United Nations and its affiliate institutions. This type of direct government funding often produces a specific type of knowledge, which, as Wiles (1976: 5) argues, 'is almost always bound to generate demands for investigations which have explicit relevance to policy issues'. Moreover, the United Nations established significant international resources through the establishment of the IMF and the World Bank, both influential in the postwar years, particularly (as mentioned) for those countries (like Britain) that relied on aid for social and economic rebuilding. Criminological research was an element of reconstruction, as crime became an internal threat to safety and prosperity. The United Nations continued to play a key role into the 1950s.

On 1 December 1950, the United Nations General Assembly passed Resolution 415(v) for 'the convening every five years a world congress on the prevention of crime and the treatment of offenders' (United Nations, 1954: 1). In 1955, the United Nations convened its first Congress on the Prevention of Crime and the Treatment of Offenders, in Geneva. This international gathering of 521 delegates from 62 countries was regarded as a 'continuation' of the International Penal and Penitentiary Commission, which had met 12 times (1950 being the final one) over a period spanning three quarters of a century (United Nation, 1956: 4–6). In his opening address, Mr Pelt, the then Director of the European office of the United Nations, identified the significant areas that encapsulated the United Nations' contribution to the field of the prevention of crime and the treatment of offenders: the organization of meetings, intended 'not to regard crime from the strictly juridical point of view, but to look at it rather as a social phenomenon, in the context of related social problems', and the United Nation's commitment to aid governments and individuals in 'solving the problems facing them in the field' (United Nations, 1956: 6).

Moreover, delegates to the Congress heard, during the opening session, Mr Lopez-Rey the representative of the Secretary-General at the Congress, outline the difference between this gathering and those previously convened under the auspices of the International Penal and Penitentiary Commission, stating that the first major difference was that the present Congress formed part of the 'extensive United Nations work programme on social questions' and that the prevention of crime and treatment of offenders should be viewed within the context of broader social issues.

Crime had clearly emerged within the United Nations' rhetoric as a social issue. Rising crime rates were a feature of the decade following World War II and as such posed a threat to the economic and social development of allied nations. Even though the causes of crime continued to be located within a medical framework, crime had become an impediment to social stability, an important factor, mentioned earlier, for establishing international trade. Crime, therefore, became a social danger with international consequences.

The agenda for this first congress included five areas: standard minimum rules for the treatment of offenders; selection, training and status of prison personnel; open penal and correctional institutions; prison labour; and the prevention of juvenile delinquency. The first four items concerned prison administration and penal policy, not altogether unfamiliar issues for such a forum; but the fifth item clearly paved a new direction for this international gathering. It received significant time for discussion and was presented at greater length in the published proceedings than any other item on the agenda. The congress proceedings assert that, in the area of 'Social Defence', 'juvenile delinquency has from the outset been the chief concern of the Social Commission of the Economic and Social Council' (United Nations, 1956: 40). The congress submitted a number of recommendations to address juvenile delinquency, among which were resolutions to address issues of community, family and school, the social services and, most importantly, a desire to further efforts at understanding and preventing delinquency, through research:

> ... directed both to the identification of the measures that are currently employed and critical evaluation of the effectiveness of such measures ... it may be possible to develop a highly promising new field of comparative criminology, based on research employing standard definitions and techniques (United Nations, 1956: 81–82).

During the postwar years and throughout the 1950s, governments in Western democracies were concerned, from a criminological perspective, about general issues of morality and the rise of the permissive society (Newburn, 1992). Yet the social danger presented by crime resonated in the growing problem of juvenile delinquency. The reported increase of juvenile crime (Struthers, 1952) was frequently used to identify a society in moral decline, requiring scientific inquiry and state intervention (Muncie, 1984). The politicization of youth crime and the resultant moral panics surrounding the demise of society's moral fabric were not twentieth-century constructs. Rather, they have been deployed by government officials for hundreds of years as justifications for increasing existing methods of maintaining law and order (cf. Pearson, 1994). That said, the postwar years, notably in Britain, witnessed a bipartisan expansion of the state's juvenile justice apparatus, with a prevention programme that emphasized punitive measures (Gelsthorpe and Morris, 1994).

Research into juvenile delinquency focused on scientific inquiry and was used to construct a state mechanism for dealing with what was perceived as a growing social problem. It was a period when government-funded research was intended to produce results that would be directly relevant for state policy and practice and not a time of sponsoring 'theoretical criminology'. Carson and Ditton (unpublished 1979) argue that theoretical criminology was peripheral in the postwar years as governments sought practical advice to deal with immediate social problems. They argue that criminological research 'became isolated from the mainstream of sociological thought within which historical analyses had retained a place, if not a central one, and the tyranny of the present became a criminological reality' (3). The tyranny they refer to is a legacy of criminology's development: a tyranny that comprises an ongoing emphasis on technocratic research that is specific, uncritical and 'relevant' for government while dismissing theoretical and historical research as a marginal knowledge.

In the postwar years, criminological research that focused on juvenile delinquency and penology was influenced and resourced by the United Nations as part of a unified programme of social reconstruction. Understanding and preventing crime became an important social-defence objective as countries attempted to maintain socio-economic stability for social and fiscal growth. Debates within the House of Commons in Britain reflect these international trends. Parliamentary debates in the late 1940s provide an advancing commitment to the doctrine of social defence as well as a compelling belief in searching for the causes of crime. For example, when debating the Criminal Justice Bill in 1947, the then Home Secretary Chuter Ede stated:

> The progress which has been made in the past generation in the attitude of society to offenders and to the problems of juvenile delinquency is surely a growing recognition of the fact that the offender is an individual, and that it is only by careful consideration of each offender as an individual that the aims of the protection of society and the reformation of the offender can be achieved. The recognition of this principle is the foundation of many of the principles in this Bill (*The Parliamentary Debates Official Report*, House of Commons, vol. 449: 1309).

Clearly by the end of the 1940s the work of the United Nations' Social Defence Section and its commitment to protecting society, preventing criminality and treating the habitual offender were common parlance within the criminal justice debate in Westminster. As one MP, Mr Rankin, stated when referring to the role and purpose of parliament in shaping criminal justice policy, 'First of all there is the protection of society, which is our business; secondly, the prevention of crime, which is also our business; and thirdly, associated with it, the treatment of the criminal (*The Parliamentary Debates Official Report*, House of Commons, vol. 468, Parliamentary Session 1948–49: 798). Here the postwar social-welfare agendas emphasized the production of pragmatic, disciplinary expertise and accordingly (as will be discussed in the following chapter) sanctioned prescriptive criminological truths in defence of society.

Criminological research was closely tied to the state and its programme of social and economic recovery. The topics or criminal behaviours for discussion, the employment of experts, and, as we shall see in the next chapter, the establishment of research centres and institutions were embedded in medico-scientific analyses of the causes of crime for the development of government policy. This relationship between criminological research and the state characterized the production of crime-related knowledge for much of the twentieth century, and it was not until the 1960s that we witness a new and critical genre of criminologies.

The Rise of Critical Genres

Mainstream or positivist criminologies were challenged in the late 1960s and early 1970s by a range of radical discourses, which focused on crime, deviance and social order. Young (1986) referred to this as a period of aetiological crisis within positivist criminology: a time when criminological research was questioned by policy-makers for its frequent retreat into inconclusive and ambiguous conclusions and when academics (notably within schools of sociology), influenced by a changing social world, critically denounced mainstream criminological ideology (Taylor, *et al*. 1973; Young, 1986; Cohen, 1988).

The rise of 'administrative criminology' within the Home Office in England (discussed further in Chapter Three), often referred to as a variant of 'Right realism' in the United States (see Walklate, 1998), emerged in response to the perceived failure of 'social democratic positivism' (Young, 1986). The term 'administrative criminology' was first coined by Young (1986) to describe the application of rational choice theory (Clarke, 1980; Cornish and Clarke, 1986) to specific criminal behaviours. Administrative criminology gathered momentum in the 1980s and continues to be sought after by Western democratic governments seeking specific cost-effective solutions to targeted crime problems. In consequence, criminological researchers have recently witnessed an unprecedented demand for their services as consultants, and I shall turn my attention to this growth area in criminological research in the following chapters.

The advent of 'critical' criminologies (labelling theory, new deviancy theory, conflict theory, Marxism and feminism) sparked intellectual debate and constituted a radical shift within existing criminological discourses. Criminology came to be recognized as an important part of the sociology of deviance and mainstream positivist theory was challenged for its political alliance with the state's crime-control apparatus (Cohen, 1988). 'Radical criminologies' rejected concepts of individual and social pathology in preference to a framework that examined crime and deviance in terms of the processes by which certain behaviours were defined, labelled and policed by the state (Scraton and Chadwick, 1991). To this extent, radical or 'critical' criminologies of the 1970s (see Taylor *et al.*, 1975) were positioned within the 'broader realm of political activism' (Muncie, 1998: 221). These 'young sociologists in Britain' (Cohen, 1988: 80), influenced by the works of American sociologists such as Becker, Lemert and Matza, rejected positivism by exploring areas of 'deviance' (such as drugs, sexuality, youth culture, and race relations) and argued how these behaviours were labelled and politicized by powerful groups as 'dangerous'. They formed an intellectual alliance through the National Deviancy Conference (NDC), first held in 1968, which proved a forum for developing libertarian ideals as well as discussing how this 'radical' agenda could change criminal justice policy (Cohen, 1988).[4]

One of the founding members of the NDC, who was interviewed for this book, acknowledged that the rise of radical criminology in the mid-1960s reflected a time of immense intellectual struggle: a period when positivist ideology in criminology was strongly supported in both government and the academy. Interestingly, academic criminologists involved in the 'critical uprising' of the NDC emphasized that contemporary university environments would probably prohibit, or at least restrict, them from developing the sort of criminology that they were involved in during late 1960s and early 1970s. One academic criminologist commented:

The pressure to bring in money nowadays is so intense, and the teaching demands are so much greater, that I doubt I could have got so involved in developing an alternative sort of criminology. Certainly not in the way that we used to get together so often and discuss what was happening in the field. Perhaps I still could have, but things have changed so much that there is really very little time or very little support for critical reflection and good critical scholarship.

While the late 1960s marked the beginnings of a radical criminology in a disciplinary sense, another interviewee acknowledged the critical contributions made by earlier writers and scholars when 'thinking about crime':

There is a history of the professional discipline of criminology … but there is a need for a complex history of 'thinking about crime'. That would include the debates around the rise of the positivist school … that would include the debates about social biology at the end of the nineteenth century, that would include the debates about the effects of the First World War, that would include interventions by Fabians, and H.G. Wells, and George Bernard Shaw, as well as other fields over time. If you look at it in this way, rather than in a disciplinary sense, then you conclude that there is a long history and debate about crime questions.

The intellectual currents of the late 1960s attempted to harness existing sociological debates in the areas of deviance and the sociology of law but also attempted to bring together an eclectic critical mass of 'thinking about crime' which moved beyond existing disciplinary boundaries. Did the form of critique that evolved during this period include concepts of Fabianism as well as various other social democratic narratives? Moreover, did it utilize the critical criminological voices of state punishment and penology to be found in, for example, George Bernard Shaw's *Crude Criminology*, and George Orwell's *A Hanging*? Pavlich (2000a and 2000b) suggests that these diverse narratives, alluded to in the above quotation, were of peripheral significance to the development of critical genres in criminology and, therefore, were not fully realized. The critique that developed from the NDC and the radical movements of the late 1960s coalesced around Marxist principles of class, power, the market and the political economy of crime (see Chambliss, 1975) as well as a vast amount of scholarship about the social and political construction of rules, norms and laws culminating to form conflict and new deviancy theories (see Taylor *et al.*, 1973).

These radical detours from the scientific approach became marginalized and, in some instances, disregarded by others who claimed that they represented a form of Left idealism (Lea and Young, 1984; Young, 1986). While Left realists challenged the proponents of neo-conservatism and Right realism (see Wilson, 1975), they also asserted that crime 'must be taken seriously' and embarked on a socialist based agenda that would address the 'realities' of crime at the local level (Lea and Young, 1984). This side of the schism within criminology's Left represented a return to pragmatic ideals: a realist agenda, which extricated itself from notions of crime as a socially constructed entity and focused on, in particular, questions of victimology. While left realism asserted a midway position between what it called 'Left idealism' and administrative criminology, many authors argue that Left realism compromised its 'radical' roots in favour of a pragmatic programme that diluted 'the new criminology's quest for radical criticism beyond correctional horizons' (Pavlich, 1999: 10).

Pavlich's important work on 'critical genres in criminology' traces the 'art of critique' by traversing broad philosophical terrain. It concludes that critique within criminological discourses has been narrowly expressed (see Pavlich, 1998; 2000a and 2000b). For Pavlich, critical criminology has demonstrated a technical lure, an involvement in a 'crime solving ethos' (Pavlich, 1999: 3), a condition that is symptomatic of criminology's origins and development – that is, an intellectual enterprise that has served the state by producing specific knowledges for government policy or which has focused on state-defined notions of crime and criminal behaviour (see also Taylor, 1995). Therefore, some radical departures have found themselves drawn back by the magnet of pragmatism in an attempt to be seen as 'useful' in preference to an idealistic and academic knowledge of little practical utility. For Pavlich, modern critical discourses within criminology[5] attempt to 'reorient critical criminology within epistemological tendencies' (Pavlich, 1999: 14). As a result, critical genres fail to question their historical and internal logics and thus continually run the risk of becoming fractured, fluid and susceptible to domination by conservative ideologies. Pavlich (2000a and 2000b) again argues that criticism, more broadly defined as 'accusation' and based on truth and authenticity, provides a more useful response to advanced liberal modes of governance than those based on Hegelian and Kantian notions of reason. I shall return to this discussion later.

This chapter concludes that criminology, throughout its development, has largely been a state-directed enterprise. Rock argues that there is a growing trend of governments shaping criminological knowledge as a pragmatic knowledge tied to the immediate needs of the state apparatus:

There is a growing influence of government and government money in shaping criminological work. Policies and politics have conspired to make rational choice theory, the criminological anti-theory, attractive to criminal justice agencies. Rational choice and control theories lay out a series of neat, inexpensive, small-scale, practicable, and non-controversial steps that may be taken to 'do something' about crime. Moreover, as theories that are tied to the apron strings of economics, they can borrow something of the powerful intellectual authority that economics wields in the social sciences. (Rock, 1997: 260).

I explore in later chapters the issues raised in the above quotation. The processes of governance, alluded to by Rock (1997), are not new. Criminology's origins reveal it as an intellectual project largely dominated by scientific empiricism to explain the causes of crime for the purposes of developing a more efficient state crime-control apparatus. Criminological research is, therefore, to use Derrida's (1994) analysis, haunted by a spirit of pragmatism: a spirit or legacy that has promoted a scientific and administrative criminology to aid the immediate policy needs of the government of the day.

Theoretical and historical contributions that question definitions of crime and social order have comprised boutique knowledges within a corpus of criminological work focused on the production of solutions to specific crime problems. Criminology's roots are embedded in the state crime-control apparatus and throughout its development it has served the needs of government for enhancing policy and practice. Theoretical and radical excursions into social order have been marginalized and have even themselves turned away from their own critical origins in favour of a pragmatic approach to address the realities of crime.

Social defence through the United Nations, as well as the international monetary policies of the late 1940s, provide important contexts for understanding the power-knowledge complexes of criminological research. The direction of criminological research in the postwar years (including the emergence of government and university-based criminology research centres discussed in the next chapter) were not driven by academic discussions of crime and the social order but by an international political concern for social defence. The United Nations reaffirmed 'crime' as an ontological category, one that should be explored within social parameters. It called upon and legitimized the use of criminological 'experts' from scientific disciplines at international gatherings as well as providing guidelines, at an international level, for the subsequent directions of key government and university-based criminology research units.

This chapter thus concludes that social reconstruction and the United Nations in the postwar years provide important insights into how crime was problematised at an international level, and how governmental rationalities within the United Nations (that is, the styles of reasoning that are inculcated into institutional practices – see Garland, 1999) categorized 'delinquent behaviour' and 'crime prevention' within a 'problem-solving ethos'. This, in turn, influenced the contours and production of criminological knowledge. Moreover, this chapter has identified what Foucault (1977) would regard as the 'distant roar of battle' (308), the historical contexts that illustrate how techniques of power (politics, discipline, supervision, management) are capable of producing self-serving knowledges. For Foucault, the most dangerous aspect of power is to view it as 'neutral' or 'politically invisible' (cf. Faubion, 2000). This chapter identifies that criminological contours in the postwar period were not created by a neutral-free politics, and it therefore attempts to unveil some of the political undercurrents that have shaped, and continue to influence, the production of criminological knowledge.

The following chapter argues that the pragmatic and state-oriented foundations of criminology discussed above are important for understanding the development and orientations of significant criminological centres and institutes as well as contextualizing the increasing amount of contemporary government-funded consultancies. Such developments, it will be argued, are providing 'specific' forms of knowledge often under the close regulation and control of governing authorities.

Notes

1 The meeting was held at the Palais de Chaillot, Paris, on 15 and 16 October 1948. The principal international organizations invited included: the International Association of Penal Law, the Nordic Associations of Criminologists, the International Bureau for the Unification of Penal Law, the International Penal and Penitentiary Commission, the International Criminal Policy Commission, the Howard League for Penal Reform, the International Institute of Statistics, the International Law Association and the International Union for Child Welfare. For a full report of this meeting, see United Nations Economic and Social Council, E/CN.5/104, 18 February 1949, pp: 1–31.

2 The gathering of the International Group of Experts on the Prevention of Crime and Treatment of Offenders included the following invited delegates: Mr Sanford Bates (United States), Dr Denis Carroll (United Kingdom), Professor Donnedieu de Vabres (France), Dr Kumarappa (India), Dr José Augustin Martínez (Cuba), Professor Thorsten Sellin (United States), Mr Alva Myrdal (Department of Social Affairs, UN Secretariat), Mr Delierneux (Division of Social Activities), Mr Amor (Social Defence Section), and Mr Litteria (Committee Secretary). See Economic and Social Council, E/CN.5/154, 1949, for a full report of the meeting.

3 The term 'social defence' has also been applied in more recent times. During the 1970s, conservative politicians in the Australian state of New South Wales were attempting to set up a ministry of social defence (see Maddison, 1971: 7). The phrase was used to define non-custodial correctional policies in Norway during the 1980s (see Evensen, 1973).

4   The critical alliance formed through the NDC was followed by a second and more Marxist uprising involving the scholars at Warwick University and the Birmingham Centre for Cultural Studies (see Sullivan, 2000).
5   Pavlich (1998) refers to anarchism and peacemaking (Ferrel, 1994), Milovanovic's (1994) semiotics, feminist perspectives (see Gelsthorpe and Morris, 1990; Naffine, 1997), state criminology (Barak, 1994), reflexive criminology (Nelken, 1994), and the contributions of modernism and postmodernism (see Maclean and Milovanovic, 1991).

Chapter 3

Criminology, government and public policy

The greatest danger of government research is that it may be insufficiently critical of the particular policy directions of the day, and it has often been argued that such research inevitably becomes subservient to short-term administrative and political concerns (Clarke and Cornish, 1983: 5).

The previous chapter argued that the study of crime has hinged historically on government-defined notions of criminal behaviour. It was further argued that the origins and contours of criminological discourses have been shaped by a state crime-control apparatus, where pragmatic-centred criminologies have served the immediate needs of government policy and practice.

This chapter examines the relationship between criminological research and government. It explores the rise of the specific government-based criminological centres that have emerged since World War II, and analyses the extent to which these organizations have been, and continue to be, influential sites for the production and promulgation of criminological knowledge. This discussion focuses primarily on those organizations that have brought criminology inside government, such as the Home Office in England and Wales and the Department of Justice in the United States. These government agencies have been influential in the funding and dissemination of criminological research and have provided organizational models followed in other countries, such as Canada and Australia.

What types of criminological projects have they pursued? And what, if anything, do they tell us about the governance of criminological research? This chapter also explores the rise of criminological research performed under government contract as well as discussing the increasing amount of paid consultancy work, or what has been referred to as 'jobbing criminology' (Loader, 1998). In doing so, it opens discussions about the increasing opportunities to undertake paid or privately contracted research. What types of research are privately contracted, and what becomes of the results of such work?

Criminology in Government

As discussed in the previous chapter, criminological research gathered momentum in the 1950s. Social surveys conducted between the wars identified increasing crime as a trait of city life (Bulmer, 1982). Crime and crime prevention, as discussed in the last chapter, also became issues of social and political importance, receiving international significance through the operations of the United Nations (cf. Mueller, 1983), as well as numerous domestic inquiries and commissions in Britain (see Rose, 1964). The rhetoric of the 'war against crime' was firmly implanted into political dialogue during the 1950s.

The development of criminology as an academic specialism at an international level, however, evolved slowly during the postwar years, notably within narrowly defined discourses of correctionalism and legal pragmatism (see Johnson, 1983). Yet the place of criminology within government asserted a firm footing. For example, in the British context, Cohen (1981) argues that criminology up until the late 1960s was dominated by four separate institutions: the Institute for the Study and Treatment of Delinquency, the Home Office, the Institute of Criminology (at the University of Cambridge) and the Department of Sociology at the London School of Economics. He characterized these criminological institutions as 'pragmatic', serving the correctionalist and positivist interests of the state (Cohen, 1981).[1]

The intersection of government with criminology requires a close analysis. Again, it is not the intention here to provide a comprehensive overview of the rise and development of criminology within state bureaucracies around the world. The examination will be limited to selective examples in England, America, and Australia. The intention, rather, is to demonstrate that specific sites of bureaucratic or government criminology have historically been, and continue to be, important places for disseminating and funding specific forms of criminological knowledge. Moreover, the development of government criminology provides an important context for understanding the rise of contract and 'expert' research and various modes of governance that will be discussed further in Chapter Four.

The Home Office, England and Wales[2]

In 1957, the British parliament brought criminology inside the operations of government by establishing the Home Office Research Unit. The academic and disciplinary nature of criminology was still in its infancy in Britain, with its only teaching posts at the London School of Economics, and at Oxford and Cambridge universities (Mannheim, 1970). The creation of a criminological research body within the Home Office during the 1950s was instrumental to the institutionalization of criminology (Cohen, 1981; Jupp, 1996), and thus a growth in bureaucratic or government led criminology.

The Home Office Research Unit, now termed the Home Office Research and Statistics Directorate (HORSD), continues to grow in size and influence. In 1959, it consisted of two Civil Servants; by 2003 its staff comprises around 400 members, with an estimated budget of £19 million (Home Office, 2002). Radzinowicz (1999) describes the (HORSD) as: 'The leading institution of its kind in the world, its appraisal ... based, as it should be, on its size, scope, quality of output and financial resources put at its disposal' (175). Moreover, Morgan (2000) has identified HORSD as the 'largest single employer of criminological researchers in the UK' where almost all its research is 'atheoretical fact gathering', 'narrowly focused', 'short-termist', 'uncritical' and 'designed to be policy-friendly' (70–71).

A review of HORSD's origins provides valuable insights into the shape and orientations of its criminological scholarship. The background and development of the Home Office Research Unit has been well documented (see Lodge, 1974; Clarke and Cornish, 1983). The Criminal Justice Act (1948) made provision for the establishment of government-sponsored criminological research deemed essential for the development of state policy and practice (Clarke and Cornish, 1983). Although, as Lodge (1974) notes, the provisions for criminological funding 'slipped into the Bill in a most casual way' (12) without parliamentary debate, they rapidly gathered political support and the unit became a significant outlet for the production of criminological knowledge.

The first move towards developing a criminologically oriented research unit within the Home Office occurred in 1949, following the Carnegie

Trust's funding of the Home Office to undertake extensive work on juvenile delinquency (Lodge, 1974). As mentioned in the previous chapter, juvenile delinquency became an area of social concern in the postwar years. World War II marked a watershed, and the return to peace in the late 1940s was greeted with an extravagant GDP deficit, soaring inflation, shortages in food, and rising unemployment. Social unrest among British people was widespread during this time and, as discussed in the previous chapter, access to international aid for social reconstruction was contingent on social and political stability.

The introduction of the 1948 Criminal Justice Act, as well as the Children Act in the same year, were seen as important mechanisms for restoring 'social order' (Morris, 1988). The Criminal Justice Act made provisions for a range of new offences as well as improving existing methods of quantifying rates of criminality. Section 77(b) of the Criminal Justice Act provided for the funding of criminological research 'in the conduct of research into the causes of delinquency and the treatment of offenders and matters connected therewith'. It is not surprising, therefore, that we see a steady rise of reported juvenile delinquency in 1949, a scientific fact responded to by the Home Office 'badly want[ing] research done on juveniles, and on various other subjects arising out of the examination of the criminal statistics' (Lodge, 1974: 17). Moreover, in 1947 the government implemented the recommendation of the Curtis Committee on the Care of Children – that one department be solely responsible for the administration of caring for children 'deprived of normal home life', as well as laws governing adoption, juvenile courts and delinquency prevention (Newsam, 1954). Therefore, in 1948, the Home Office became responsible for a range of juvenile dispositions relating to 'care and protection'.

Some of the earliest Home Office funding of criminological research, including the 'etiology of juvenile delinquency', was allocated to the Department of Criminal Science at Cambridge University, which would later become the Institute of Criminology (discussed below). Other major funding, also made available to academics, was for the study of 'prediction methods in relation to Borstal training' (see Mannheim and Wilkins, 1955). Galliher and McCartney (1973) argue that the increased levels of government funding for juvenile delinquency in the late 1950s promoted positivist and politically appealing research. They conclude that government-funded research led to 'simplistic and politically appealing theories such as Opportunity Theory, which still stresses the individual as the locus of the problem' (Galliher and McCartney, 1973: 86).

Clarke (1977) argues that there was a view in government in the early 1950s that universities were inadequately resourced to undertake the vast amount of criminological research required by the Home Office. As a result, he argued, the Home Office Research Unit was established because 'it was felt that a permanent internal unit would be better able to undertake the coordinated and long-term programme of work envisaged and, moreover, undertake it in the way the Home Office wished' (Clarke, 1977: 115).

B.N. Bebbington, Director of the Police Research and Planning Branch in 1968, stated that the Home Office had up until that year focused its attention on 'one side of the coin', namely crime causation, the social environment, and treatment of offenders, and that it would turn to the other side of the coin and examine law enforcement (Bebbington, 1968). This emphasis on the needs of the Home Office and the immediate political concerns of the day has remained characteristic of the HORSD.

The restructuring of the unit in 1981, under a new title of the 'Home Office Research and Planning Unit', furthered its role with the 'formulation and monitoring of policy' (Croft, 1982: 4). The type of research produced by the Home Office since the late 1950s suggests that its 'two-sided research coin' has consisted of a pragmatic and policy-oriented approach (Mair and Nee, 1990), or, as Jupp (1996) argues, one 'mainly designed to evaluate the efficacy of policies relating to criminal justice' (25). This is not surprising, given that HORSD is required by law to support Home Office ministers and the department in policy making. The aims and objectives of HORSD are outlined in a recent Home Office Annual Report (2002: 131):

> To improve policy making and decision taking and to help deliver Home Office policies successfully;
> To provide Parliament and the Public with the necessary information for informed debate about Home Office policies and their implementation.
>
> (Home Office, 2002: 131)

In 1995, internal management restructuring concluded that the Home Office needed:

> ... a radical culture change with more emphasis being given to service provided to ministers and to a more business-like approach to our work. RSD was criticised in a similar way: it was felt that RSD needed to be more outward-looking of policy and ministerial customers and more efficient in our internal organisations (Home Office, 1996 unpublished: 1).

Indeed, the Home Office has clearly stated that the long-term life of the HORSD hinges on its ability to provide data to ministers about political concerns of the day. Moreover, at a briefing meeting convened by the HORSD in late 1996 with academic researchers and other likely consultants, the Home Office stated that researchers should be mindful of the ways in which the objectives of commissioned research could change 'midstream' as a result of intervening political forces:

> For its long-term survival RSD will need to ensure that it delivers results customers need. RSD stakeholders will also have to produce results in a timely fashion responding to needs as specified today, which may be different from the needs stated when the research was originally commissioned. (Home Office, 1996: 4)

As a result of this one-day conference held by the RSD on 13 September 1996, the representative from the Institute of Criminology at the University of Cambridge, Dr Adrian Grounds, reported:

> Ministers are insisting that there are break points in research contracts, so that projects can be stopped if they are no longer useful or policy relevant. The Home Office will want to define the finished product more and there will be more pressure to deliver on time. The new contract will specify more clearly what constitutes a satisfactory final report …. Although there was expressed openness to external ideas about the research agenda, in practice the research unit and customer departments within the Home Office do not control what research is commissioned. There was a strong sense that decisions are increasingly being taken at a higher level and that they are more unpredictable (Grounds, 1996: 2–3).

Home Office criminology thus has a very clear purpose: to service the 'needs' of ministers and MPs. It is a politically driven criminology, one that provides policy-salient information for politically relevant crime and criminal justice issues. Its research agenda is motivated by outcomes deemed to have immediate benefit for existing political demands. As Grounds (1996) again reports, HORSD commissions research with an 'out-clause', allowing the Home Office to discontinue the project if the research is perceived to be of little utility. The Home Office, therefore, has considerable influence over the content and direction of research it commissions and I will return to this discussion shortly.

It is also important to recognize the influential role that the Home Office has played in developing criminology within British academia. The

Home Office was instrumental in the establishment of the Institute of Criminology at Cambridge University (see Butler, 1974; Radzinowicz, 1988). The institute continues to receive funding from the Home Office for course development; however, this occurs through successful tendering and not philanthropic sponsorship. As late as 1995, a postgraduate degree in applied criminology (police studies) was introduced, with two lecturers appointed, each on five-year contracts funded by the Home Office (University of Cambridge, 1998).

Despite its close association with the Home Office, the founding director of the Institute of Criminology at Cambridge, Sir Leon Radzinowicz, consistently argued that the institute was an independent source of criminological knowledge:

> With reference to its programme of research, I laid down six directives which should regulate the adoption and launching of the investigations carried out by senior members of staff. No topic of inquiry should be imposed on us by the Home Office, or by any other source from which financial support for the particular topic was expected to come .... The subject of crime is a highly sensitive and volatile political component and I was, therefore, particularly anxious that, from the very outset, the Institute should not be identified with any political parties or affiliations (Radzinowicz, 1999: 198–99).

Radzinowicz (1988) argues that the institute attempted to avoid 'causative research'; yet such work, notably its longitudinal studies on delinquency and its vast amount of quantitative research, characterized the bulk of its output, especially during its first 20 years (Cohen, 1981). Jupp (1996) concurs with Cohen (1981), arguing that the research conducted by the institute has been characterized by mainstream criminology, 'carrying out predominantly positivist, quantitative, survey-based research' (Jupp, 1996: 25).

There is no doubt that the Institute of Criminology has played an important role in the development of British criminology. A large number of academic criminologists working in British universities today were either educated at it or were in some way affiliated (as a researcher or postdoctoral fellow, or as a staff member) with it. The type of criminology taught and the sorts of knowledges produced there have influenced a large number of academic and government criminologists.

Several interviewees for this book argued that there was a 'Home Office legacy' attached to the work of the Institute of Criminology; that is, an unspoken and unwritten emphasis on research that would in some way directly influence policy and practice. Indeed, the previous director of the institute, Professor Anthony Bottoms, has reaffirmed the strong links between it and the Home Office in the early days. He has also referred to the institute's ongoing commitment to the production of policy-relevant research: 'the Institute has throughout its history sought to remain a strongly policy-relevant department, while maintaining the highest standards of independent academic scholarship' (Bottoms, 1996: 1).

Many interviewees were of the opinion that government departments have turned continually to the Institute of Criminology and to certain staff members to conduct specific policy-relevant research because of a prior relationship that has evolved over a long period of time. Several interviewees suggested that the institute has always been a reliable source of information for the Home Office. As one academic criminologist stated, 'Home Office staff don't use the *Yellow Pages* when they want something done; they just open their little black book and refer to several reliable and trusted sources at Cambridge'.

Sources internal to the institute and within government suggest that comments like the above are either an exaggeration or completely false and fail to recognize that the institute, like other criminology departments, is competitively tendering for research funding. However, the links between the Home Office and the institute are longstanding. Bottoms confirms that the bulk of research funding for the institute's projects has come from the Home Office. He states: 'historically, the major funder of the Institute's research has been the Home Office Research and Statistics Department, and its predecessor the Home Office Research and Planning Unit' (Bottoms, 1996: 13). In addition, some interviewees for this book reported that an 'institutional credibility' came with approaching the University of Cambridge, which was 'absolutely and ultimately safe' for government. Moreover, an analysis of research grants received by staff at the institute from January 1995 to December 1996 reveals that most projects continue to be funded by the Home Office. During this period a total of eight grants were received, totalling £826,048. Six of the eight (worth £599,636) were funded by the Home Office (see Bottoms, 1996).[3] This proportion reflects the institute's ongoing commitment to policy-relevant research as well as its desire to generate much-wanted revenue for the university.[4] As one academic criminologist commented:

> Money calls the shots. There is a consciousness that the department [Cambridge Institute of Criminology] has a responsibility to bring in money. And it does impact on the kind of research that gets done .... It undermines small-scale research that involves charitable

trusts and the kind of social end of criminology, as well as theoretical research. The Institute is certainly being pressured to do empirical research, like doing crime audits and local surveys to bring in money.

The above quotation points to the changing ethos within universities, one driven by new modes of conservative governance, which I will examine in Chapter Six.

The influence of the Home Office on the development of British criminology has been substantial. It has, and continues to be, a major source of funding for academic researchers (cf. Morgan, 2000). Ericson (1996) contends that the history of criminological research is closely associated with government funding through contracts – arrangements, he argues, that often produce sites of contestation:

Research funding in criminology has always been heavily dependent on contracts with government agencies. These contracts are enabling to the extent that the reform agenda of the sponsoring agency accords with the reform questions posed by the criminologist. They become more constraining when the criminologist wishes to ask research questions driven by a theoretical puzzle internal to the academy, or to seriously criticise the policy framework prevailing in the agency concerned (Ericson, 1996: 16).

The 'constraining' nature of contract research alluded to by Ericson as well as other 'political' dimensions will be explored further in the following chapter. It is important here to acknowledge that institutions like the Home Office have historically played an influential role in the funding and shaping of criminological research. Martin (1988) argues that 'from about 1953 onwards Wilkins [deputy statistical advisor to the Home Office] advised unofficially almost everyone doing empirical research in criminology in the country' (Martin, 1988: 41).

As funding for university research becomes more competitive there is growing dependence on government organizations for grants to conduct criminological research. All recipients of Home Office funding are required to sign a contract that binds the researcher to the conditions of the Official Secrets Act as well as prohibiting the contractee from publicly disseminating information emanating from the research without first receiving permission from the Home Office. The standard Home Office contract reads as follows:

You shall not communicate with representatives of the general or technical press, radio, television or other communications media unless specifically granted permission to do so by the Head of the Crime and Criminal Justice Unit, RDS, or an officer appointed by him.

In his address to the delegates of the 1993 British Society of Criminology Conference, Radzinowicz expressed concern that the independence of academic criminologists was under threat by government authorities wishing to control access to information and regulate the publication of research results. He argues that the freedom to interpret and publish research were 'prerequisites for any really incisive and honest research' (Radzinowicz, 1994: 103).

Government criminologists argued that Home Office contracts were necessary for the 'orderly release of research', stating that the contracts were not intended to 'control' the process but were designed to achieve two important objectives. The first was to ensure that research was not released and discussed prior to the Home Office's external refereeing procedures; to do so, one government criminologist stated, would be 'bad science'. The second reason for the contract was to prevent research reaching the public domain without the minister's knowledge. As one government criminologist stated:

> The Home Office doesn't want its ministers to be in a position where they are completely blind-sided about the results of Home Office-funded research. It does kind of irritate them. They should know about it before somebody else pops up or otherwise they are going to be interviewed on the *Today* show or something .... So what we are talking about with contracts is orderly release .... I know researchers get frustrated with Home Office contracts and they complain about the time that it takes to get their research out and I think there's a kind of irony here because if they were publishing with an academic journal it might take two or three years to come out.

Many interviewees for this book were tolerant of the delays in publishing research; however, they were frustrated about the proscriptions imposed on the research process by Home Office 'specs' and contracts, and the inability to speak about their research at conferences and seminars. While academic journals may often take time to be printed, it is common practice for academics to discuss their work at conferences while their research is in press. This ability, however, is often denied by Home Office contracts. Moreover, many interviewees identified Home Office contracts as prohibiting long-term investigation or social-scientific inquiry and as rarely permitting the opportunity to raise what Hillyard and Sim (1997) refer to as 'speculative and agnostic questions' (57).

Several academic criminologists (and senior ones at that) expressed a firm position of resistance about undertaking contract work for the Home Office, arguing that their own previous experience, or that of a colleague, had not only controlled the processes of publication but, more importantly, had regulated the intellectual direction of the scholarship to suit government policy. As one academic criminologist stated:

> I refuse to do work for the Home Office and to produce research that does nothing other than support a predetermined government policy .... I also strongly object to the ways in which the Home Office controls the entire research from start to finish .... There is nothing critical about Home Office research and academics who sell themselves to the Home Office have lost sight of the importance of independent academic scholarship.

Furthermore, many interviewees expressed grave concerns that academic criminologists had become subservient and, in some instances, completely dependent on government agencies for money to conduct research. One academic criminologist commented: 'You want to talk about the politics of criminological research. The sight of whole rows of British criminologists with their hands out to the government waiting for the money to be dropped into their hands is obscene.' Academic criminologists often attend seminars run by government agencies in an attempt to discover how they might successfully receive a government contract and what, if any, will be the conditions of the contract. Another academic criminologist, who had recently attended a Home Office meeting to discuss 'doing research for the Home Office', stated:

> I went to this Home Office meeting where the chair [HORSD Director] stated that 'this is where we start, we say what we want and you say that's not academic, and we negotiate that and you get a bit of what you want and we get a bit of what we want and we all go home happy'; it kind of ridicules the process of research. It's very cynical ... and they have the power.

The question about who gets funded from government money unveils a host of political dimensions about the governance of criminological knowledge, which will be examined in more detail in the following chapter. It is necessary in this chapter, however, to briefly identify that the *modus operandi* of 'who and what gets funded' has long been established within the Home Office. T.S. Lodge, former Director of Research and Statistics at the Home Office, diplomatically describes the 'unwritten' funding rules of the Home Office:

> The Home Office has been willing to give financial support to research if satisfied about the competence and integrity of the person or organisation who would be responsible, and if there seemed to be a reasonable chance that the research would produce a worthwhile result (Lodge, 1974: 23).

Academic criminologists interviewed for this book reiterated some of the comments above, arguing that the Home Office frequently appointed uncritical researchers who were able to meet a set of administrative requirements.

> What the Home Office wants is quick fix. Bicycle repair kits for the criminal justice system, they want patching devices. Although the rhetoric year on year of the Home Office is that they want major studies and major evaluations, and they want big overviews. When push comes to shove, when you see where the money is actually placed, it's placed usually with quite safe people. People who are going to produce on time, that's very important, they've got these schedules that fit in with governmental manifestos. Who can produce a competent piece of work that is statistically respectable and that doesn't really frighten the horses.

Some government criminologists, consulted for this book, echoed various aspects of the above sentiments, arguing that contemporary decisions over funding hinged on a range of unwritten criteria, that is,'in-house criteria', based on previous experience with outside researchers. Morgan (2000: 78) refers to the 'Home Office equivalent of the Chinese walls', whereby the process of awarding and negotiating the terms of Home Office research contracts are shrouded with mystery, uncertainty and bias. At a more insidious level, Morgan suggests that ex-HORSD staff now working in universities are often the recipients of the largest HORSD contracts, in what, he argues, is akin to 'insider-trading' (Morgan, 2000: 79).

This is not uncommon across the English public sector. Turpin (1989) refers to a 'procurement community' in some sectors of British government contracting. This involves a close association between government and select private industries. This relationship, he argues, is characterized by 'interdependence and shared interests'. Features of this relationship are a 'continuous exchange of information, migration of personnel, hard bargaining and search for a common ground' (Turpin, 1989: 263).

The Home office tendering process has changed in recent years. All 'large contracts' (amounts unspecified) must be advertised publicly. However, the HORSD has discretion to send some projects 'to single tender' (Home Office 1996: 4). While the Home Office acknowledges that a vast amount of their external research is sent out for competitive tender, often the competitors (not greater than five in number) are pre-selected by the Home Office. How are the selective tenders chosen? One government criminologist captured the Home Office tendering and selection process as follows:

> It can be difficult for new and young researchers to break into this market. After all this is public money, and sometimes quite con-siderable amounts of public money, and the Home Office has a public duty to get the best researcher. Now, we still have the problem in criminology of the lone researcher and I've been saying to young researchers that if you want to get into the market what you ought to do is become part of an experienced team so you build up the experience. We are taking past track record into consideration when deciding whether or not to give someone public money .... How do we judge quality? .... We are taking account of RAE scores and I'd be concerned if the Home Office wasn't giving a research contract to a department that had a 4 rating as an absolutely minimum.

On the one hand we have government criminologists urging junior academic staff to enter partnerships with more experienced academic colleagues from well-rated institutions; but on the other, we are seeing that senior academic criminologists are adopting a position of resistance – a position that rejects Home Office criminology for its failure to critically engage with government and other powerful actors in society. Moreover, this is a resistance formed by an unwillingness (on ideological grounds) to have knowledge shaped and determined by a government agenda in-fluenced by the vagaries of Westminster rather than a commitment to new knowledges that are theoretically sophisticated, where the hypotheses are independently determined and where the methods and content of investigation are externally decided.

Government criminologists consulted for this research also confirmed that the Home Office's research agenda was almost exclusively focused on issues of government priority.

> Ninety per cent of research would be done for the government agenda and ten per cent of research would be essentially self-generated. That is, it wouldn't necessarily have any immediate

policy customers. It could be something submitted by an outside university or an idea for research within the Home Office.

Indeed, another government criminologist explicitly stated that criminology made 'no sense' unless it was directly connected to policy and that 'no-one' would be funded to conduct research that was critical of government. This government criminologist suggested that the Cornish and Clarke quotation used to open this chapter was 'naive' as it failed to understand the role of criminology in government.

> I don't think criminology overall makes any sense if it has no connections to policy ... it's absolutely absurd .... There is no way that this government or any government is going to fund people to spend their time attacking the policy of the government of the day.

Hillyard *et al.* (2003) have identified a 500 per cent increase in HORSD's funding for external research in recent years, largely because of New Labour's desire for 'evidence-led policy'. Moreover, they identify, from an analysis of HORSD research outputs during the period 1988–2003, that out of a catalogue of 571 reports 'not one single report deals with crimes which have been committed as part of legitimate business activities' (4), concluding that HORSD research serves to reinforce state-defined notions of criminality while paying lip service to state and corporate crime.

This observation is not surprising, given that the Home Office is legislatively bound to serve the immediate policy needs of the state, or, as the above interviewee describes, is required to produce information for 'policy customers'. Policy customers are a separate and distinct audience to academic scholars. Academics who undertake policy-oriented research often experience tension when confronted with what many perceive as a conflict or a compromise with regard to their academic responsibility. I explore this intersection later in the chapter.

The self-generated research alluded to by the above government criminologist, where there is 'no policy customer', is arguably less than ten per cent of existing outcomes. The HORSD is required to show 'value for money' in the work produced. This requires 'that we should be able to deliver results quickly to satisfy policy demands and that we should be prepared to modify our programme in order to make sure that the most up-to-date customer needs are being satisfied' (Home Office, 1996: 3).

The Home Office commenced a 'Guidance Note Series' for its £250 million crime reduction programme. The purpose of the series was to 'provide guidance on monitoring and evaluating Government-funded crime reduction programmes' (Wiles, 1999). Guidance Note no. 1, published in August 1999, refers to the importance of evaluators conducting cost-benefit assessments of government crime-reduction initiatives. The Home Office aims to 'guide' the evaluation process by providing a 'step-by-step guide to undertaking cost-effectiveness analysis' (Wiles, 1999). Not only does the Home Office propose to guide the evaluation research that it commissions, but its HORSD personnel overtly declare their willingness to abandon certain research areas should they fall outside contemporary political priorities.

> It may even be necessary to curtail research which is no longer of interest to ministers or policy colleagues, either because the research has been so delayed that the results are no longer of any interest or because ministers or officials have changed their priorities (Home Office, 1996: 3).

It is clear that, as British universities experience increasing declines in funding and as the public funds for academic research becomes more competitive (see Monbiot, 2000), organizations such as the Home Office will continue to play an important role in the future funding of criminological research. Moreover, as governments continue to demand effectiveness and accountability in the public sector, there will be increasing pressure on the Home Office to demonstrate the practical value of the research it commissions.

The Director of HORSD at the time of writing, Professor Paul Wiles, has recently reaffirmed the Home Office's commitment to policy-relevant research in what he calls 'criminology for the public good' (Wiles, 2002). In doing so, he acknowledges that the worlds of academic and government criminology must become more closely aligned. For Wiles there has been a lamentable decline in the amount of senior academic engagement with public policy. Moreover, he has identified a greater need for academic criminologists to come to grips with the policy implications of their work.

The Home Office, with its increasing funding of academic criminology, is undoubtedly a powerful site for the production of specific forms of criminological knowledge. As Morgan (2000) points out, 'the Home Office budget now looms so large in the consciousness of university-based criminologists and that all university departments are under increasing pressure to secure external research funding' (75–76). The Home Office has become a site of British criminological hegemony, within a New Labour politics of 'evidence-based research'. As such, its locus of power within the funding and dissemination of criminological scholarship has recently met with opposition from scholars who argue for criminology to be aligned with 'counter hegemonic movements' (see Tombs and Whyte, 2003), and I will discuss this in later chapters.

For some, the time has come for HORSD to be subject to an independent review. Radzinowicz, who for many years worked closely with the Home Office and who supported its place within the criminological landscape, argues that the time has come for the Home Office's work to be critically examined:

> ... since its inception so much has changed in criminological thinking, in the state of crime, and in the directions taken by criminal policy, that the Unit is ripe for a major informative and critical stock-taking of the first fifty years of its existence (Radzinowicz, 1999: 175).

It is likely that the Home Secretary and other politicians concerned will undertake the only critical appraisal of the Home Office with a 'value for money' priority in a neo-liberal political environment.[5] From an evaluative standpoint, what is clear is that HORSD is an important player in the funding of criminological research. As other funds for research become more competitive, criminologists are setting their sights on government and private industry for contract money, which inevitably requires a product with an applied or policy-relevant focus. Even in the United Kingdom, where the total infrastructure for social science research is estimated to be £300 million per year (ESRC, 1999) from both government and non-government sources,[6] there is a recognition by criminologists that funding has become increasingly more competitive as universities create demands for staff to attract external revenue (Morgan, 2000; Hillyard *et al.*, 2003; Walters, 2003).

However, it is clear that HORSD funds and produces a specific kind of criminological knowledge – that which is immediately relevant to government policy and practice – and this is unlikely to change. Moreover, the kind of people currently appointed to HORSD serves to perpetuate its production of administrative and technocratic research – research that furnishes the demands of neo-liberal governing rationalities. As one government criminologist stated, they would not employ graduates with criminology degrees:

> We recruit quite a lot of people and it's very rare that we employ people who have got degrees in criminology because they don't have any skills .... We're employing all sorts of people and the most obvious are those with psychology, economics and physics because they have more skills.

It is clear that the theoretical and critical training offered to criminology students at university is of little vocational benefit to HORSD. While the research director of HORSD is calling for greater alliances between academic criminology and his unit, it is clear that alliances will only ever be formed on Home Office terms. The critical agenda of academic criminology has no place in the policy world of Home Office criminology, and unless universities provide 'rigourous scientific training', based on the models of economics and physics, their students will remain unemployable in HORSD.

The location of an agency such as HORSD within government and its connections with the academic world have provided a model where the state has its own research machinery, capable of drawing on 'independent research' yet within an environment conducive to the machinations of the political process. The Home Office provides 'research at the ready' for the political process. Such a model has been adopted by similar units in other countries, notably the United States and Australia, and I will discuss these in turn.

National Institute of Justice, Washington D.C.

There are several departments across the United States where criminological research units are located; yet none are as influential as the National Institute of Justice (NIJ), a research unit within the United States Department of Justice. The NIJ is currently the largest funding body of academic criminological research among all US government departments. It was created in 1968 by the Omnibus Crime Control and Safe Streets Acts, with the following mandate:

To sponsor special projects, and research and development programs, that will improve and strengthen the criminal justice system and reduce or prevent crime.

To conduct national demonstration projects that employ innovative or promising approaches for improving criminal justice.

To develop new technologies to fight crime and improve criminal justice.

To evaluate the effectiveness of criminal justice programs and identify programs that promise to be successful if continued or repeated.

To recommend actions that can be taken by Federal, State and local governments as well as by private organizations to improve criminal justice.

To carry out research on criminal behavior.

To develop new methods of crime prevention and reduction of crime and delinquency.

A review of the NIJ's publication catalogues since the early 1970s reveals a diverse range of policy-relevant research, on topics such as policing, corrections, courts, drugs and criminal justice administration. In more recent years, between 1994 and 2000, the NIJ provided US$1.597 billion in active awards (National Institute of Justice, 2001).

The NIJ (2000) publication of fiscal awards provides a brief summary of each project funded within the budget year. The overwhelming majority of projects reveal a positivist or administrative criminological focus. There are no readily identifiable theoretical or historically based projects. Likewise, very few research projects appear to explain crime within a social, political or cultural framework. Multi-million-dollar amounts have been awarded to drugs and crime, forensics, weapon detection, technology and development, policing, youth, violence, crime mapping and crime prevention. This is to be expected, given that the NIJ 'Solicitation for Investigator-Initiated Research', published twice-annually, calls for proposals 'to explore any topic of relevance to State or local criminal justice policy or practice' (NIJ, 1997: 1).

Not surprisingly, most successfully funded topics focus on politically salient issues and adopt a variety of quantitative methodologies to address technical or operational criminal justice concerns. For example, the fiscal year 2000 identifies a range of research awards in 11 different categories, including community justice, corrections, courts, crime prevention, drugs and crime, information dissemination and general support, international crime, law enforcement, community policing, schools, sentencing, and technology development. The overwhelming majority of the funding allocation for the year 2000 (for new initiatives and supplementary awards for previously funded projects) went to technology development (computer-chip genetic detectors, forensic DNA databases, anti-drug datafiles, etc.), general crime-prevention initiatives (human development programmes, early intervention initiatives), law enforcement, drugs and crime, and corrections. The NIJ fiscal documentation also identifies that universities across the United States are the largest beneficiaries of NIJ funding (National Institute of Justice Annual Report, 2000).

The most recent NIJ awards (to date) were published on 9 June 2003 and identify a total of US$23.7 million awarded to research projects. Interestingly, the vast majority of this money has been allocated to non-university based research organizations, including police departments, city councils, public safety and planning departments and private companies. Moreover, there are noticeable increments in funding towards the forensic sciences and towards improving laboratory technologies. Indeed, there is a clear move towards funding science and technology, and a move away from examining topics associated with crime causation. Some of these technological developments could also be classified as capital expenditure, and do not even have a noticeable administrative or positivist research element. For example, the largest financial award (US$3.2 million) was granted to the Hennepin County Sheriff's Office for 'Squad Car Unit Identification – SQUID Program' (National Institute of Justice, 2003). This reflects the Bush administration's recent US$1.91 billion investment in science and technology and in technological innovations in fighting crime (United States Government, 2003).

Criminologists across the United States actively seek NIJ funding to conduct research. During the 1998 American Society of Criminology conference in Washington, D.C., one of the best-attended sessions, from a programme of 503, was session No. 55, 'Developing a Research Agenda in a Policy Context', where the sole speaker was the then Director of the National Institute of Justice (see American Society of Criminology, 1998: 71). The director commenced the session by asking members of the audience (some 500 delegates) to raise their hands if they were currently receiving an NIJ grant. About 20 per cent raised their hands. He then asked for those hoping to receive an NIJ grant to raise their hands – almost the entire audience raised their hands.

The former director of the NIJ was interviewed for this book during the Washington conference. His position was as administrative head of an institutional site of power within government criminology, a position that provided an influential role in establishing the criminological research priorities within both government and academia. The interview, therefore, aimed to capture the epistemological and ideological dimensions that shaped government criminology in the United States as well as the internal working practices of the NIJ. The former director suggested that we conduct the interview 'in a quiet corner of the hotel', hoping to avoid interruption, describing himself 'as the most popular person at the conference' – a comment echoed by numerous delegates. While this one encounter may appear an isolated example, it did raise a number of questions. Why should a director of the NIJ be perceived as the most popular person at an international criminology conference with over 2,500 delegates? Why should a conference paper presented by the director of the NIJ be one of the best-attended sessions? It certainly points to the increasing importance that criminological units within government are playing in the funding of academic research. It further highlights what the former director of the NIJ himself was saying at the conference, that 'the academic world and the policy world should be more closely aligned'. This remains a point that continues to be made within academia, and one which has resulted in books being written by academics about 'grantmanship' and 'how to win contracts' (see Davis, 2000). Many academic criminologists interviewed for this book were strongly opposed to this concept:

> The administrative dynamic, which now drives criminology, has made the policy world and academic world an awful lot closer .... There are a significant number of articles published in journals which are rooted in policy reports. I think criminology itself is in trouble because it's following the money research-wise, but also following the money teaching-wise as well, and becoming a criminal justice quasi-discipline.

The popularity of the NIJ among American criminologists also raises questions about who gets funded. What types of criminological research proposals receive government support, and why? These questions were discussed with the former director of the NIJ. He suggested that funding to conduct criminological research in the United States was 'extremely competitive'. While he acknowledged that the NIJ would welcome research proposals on all topics, he concluded that the NIJ:

> ... was unlikely to fund theoretical research. We would be looking for policy implications and we have to show value for what we do. We'd be looking for something groundbreaking, timely, something new or relevant to policy.

He expressed an ongoing commitment to bring the worlds of criminal justice policy and academia closer together, and emphasized that the NIJ had a responsibility to serve the interests and concerns of the government. He also alluded to various tensions with this function, notably the political overtones of the work of the NIJ, arguing: 'There are no absolute safeguards against political interference. It happens, not often, but its something I have to deal with.'

Indeed, the office of director of the NIJ is completely engulfed within the US political process. The director is a presidential appointee, confirmed by the US Senate and, when the incumbent administration's term in office ends, so does the NIJ's directorship. The director interviewed acknowledged that this process had obvious flaws, most notably that his research agenda (which has been favourably received by a large number of American criminologists; see Adler, 1998) will lose continuity. Another government criminologist interviewed for this book argued that almost the entire research agenda of the NIJ is politically determined: 'What the NIJ does by way of research is determined by Congress. I'd say 90 per cent of all our money is allocated to research that Capitol Hill wants done.'

Many US criminologists contacted for this book acknowledged that the NIJ was the most powerful and influential of all criminological research units within the US government. Some criminologists went as far as saying that the NIJ was 'colonizing academic criminology' with its vast resources. Indeed, its research budget continues to expand and is able to fund more projects each year. Yet, as an organization, it is always susceptible to the vagaries of the political process and, as a government department, it is expected to deliver scientifically proven research for pressing criminal justice concerns.

Political realities and pressures are, therefore, features determining the research agenda of the NIJ; as one government criminologist pointed out during President Clinton's term:

> NIJ's agenda has often been influenced by views different from those which support independent, objective research on crime, the justice system and criminal justice policies. We have such value-laden discussions on funding needle-exchange programs, research on fetuses, and, most recently, how to carry out the 2000 census (whether or not to use sampling techniques which might favor the Democrats)

The above quotation provides a clear admission of the NIJ pre-determining a research product that will favour the political position of the current administration. This internal bias towards the existing government's crime-control policies is also reflected in the types of projects that receive NIJ awards. The ramifications of this for criminological scholarship in the United States are serious. As other sources of US funding become more competitive and more limited, academic criminologists are turning to NIJ funding to conduct research. Yet it is clear that the NIJ is a government agency, producing specific forms of information for government use. Theoretical knowledge or knowledge critical of the social order is most unlikely to be supported by the NIJ: if research does not fit within the NIJ's strategic aims, it will be seen as unwanted.

Moreover, recent changes to federal funding for 'all' academic research in the United States, that emphasizes 'earmarking' for specific institutions, has resulted in universities lobbying Congress for funding. Previously, universities in the United States have been allocated research funding based on peer-review assessments of research quality. Now it is intended that peer review be abolished in favour of a system that has individual members of Congress determine the research value of a given university (Weiner, 1999). This new method of allocating funding has been widely condemned by principals of US tertiary institutions, who argue that 'we jeopardize the long-term knowledge base of the country by spending money in a political rather than a scientific way' (R. Walker, quoted in Weiner, 1999: 1). Others have observed that universities will need to maintain close relationships with politicians to ensure resources for future research. Professor R. Park, from the University of Maryland, stated: 'The only factor in getting an earmark is whether you've got the ear of the congressman who sits on the right committee. It can cause a lot of trouble' (Park, quoted in Weiner, 1999).

For comparative purposes, the following section shifts the focus of discussion to the Southern hemisphere and explores the role of government-led criminology through an analysis of the Australian Institute of Criminology.

Australian Institute of Criminology, Canberra

In Australia, there are five leading criminological research units within government: the Australian Institute of Criminology (AIC) in Canberra, the New South Wales Bureau of Crime Statistics in Sydney, the Criminal Justice Commission in Brisbane, the South Australian Office of Crime Statistics in Adelaide, and the National Centre for Crime and Justice Statistics within the Australian Bureau of Statistics in Melbourne. The directors of the first three agencies were interviewed for this book. For now, I focus on the AIC, arguably the agency which has had the greatest influence on the direction and production of criminological research (both academic and governmental) in Australia.

The AIC was established by the Criminology Research Act 1971 (CTh). Its current mission statement reflects the spirit of the inaugural legislation:

To be responsive to the needs of government and the community with respect to policy issues in the fields of justice and the prevention and control and crime;
To be recognised as the national leader in the research and analysis of

criminological issues, and the source of authoritative information at a national level in this field.

The above objectives are consistent with the underlying rationales posited by politicians who first proposed its development. The first official steps towards establishing the AIC occurred at an 'invitation only' Commonwealth Attorney-General's Department seminar in February 1968, entitled 'The Control of Deviant Behaviour in Australia' (Barry, 1968). According to Carson and O'Malley, this seminar, together with its 'pragmatist themes' discussed in Chappell and Wilson (1977), provided 'the core of political proposals which were to culminate in the establishment of a national institute for the study of crime' (Carson and O'Malley, 1989: 342). The focus that the AIC should take was further outlined in the Australian House of Representatives by the then Attorney-General Mr. Bowen on 29 May 1969. He argued:

> There is a need for systematic research to be conducted and sponsored on an Australia-wide basis to help determine the policies that should be adopted to combat the problem of crime …. There is also a need for specialist national training programmes for police, prison and parole officers and others working in the field …. It is proposed that these courses will keep officers informed of modern methods and techniques and enable them to share their experiences and consider their work within a larger frame of reference (*Hansard*, 18 Eliz 11, Vol H of R 63, p. 2458).

While some criminologists in recent years have remonstrated over cutbacks to the AIC and dangers to its autonomy as a research unit, it is clear that from its early beginnings it was an organization designed to serve the immediate policy needs of the federal government. These views have been articulated by academics (Carson and O'Malley, 1989) as well as public servants who worked within the Commonwealth Attorney-General's Department during the 1970s and 1980s. For example, Loof argues that 'The proposals recognised that a governmental institute was needed to represent governmental interests and enable control of research to be exercised to ensure that priorities in research were observed which would bring practical results in areas of greatest need (Loof, 1979: 4). The role of the AIC within Australian criminology has thus been a topic of debate for some time. Many academics have criticized the AIC for funding positivist research (O'Connor, 1980) or research which is likely to 'produce results of relevance to the prevention and control of crime' (Zdenkowski and Brown, 1982).

It is important to understand the underlying principles of government-based institutions in order to establish how such rationales influence or create 'regimes of truth' for criminological scholarship. Regimes that have the potential to colonise what is and what is not legitimate and/or relevant criminological knowledge. In a fashion similar to the director of the NIJ, the director of the AIC is responsible for setting criminological research agendas for government criminologists as well as for those academics seeking government funding. The AIC is responsible for providing policy-relevant research to key 'stakeholders' who include Commonwealth Government ministers and parliamentarians, and Commonwealth departments and agencies. Other stakeholders include State and Territory Governments and agencies, criminal justice practitioners, the criminological research community and community organizations.

A government criminologist pointed out that the AIC provided the strategic vision often lacking in academic research:

> The Australian Institute of Criminology is a Commonwealth statutory authority that is part of the Attorney-General's portfolio. Its role is to provide the material that is of value and use to the minister. Now, a very important component of that is that it has the intellectual breadth as well as the foresight to persuade the minister that they should be interested in more than what might be politically salient on the day. But there is no question, the AIC is not a university department, it's not an independent body researching what it chooses, it has a pretty clear set of stakeholders and its role is to provide the data, the analysis and perhaps an interpretation to help them do their job.

Not all directors of criminological units within Australian government departments share this view. Indeed, the directors of the Criminal Justice Commission and the New South Wales Bureau of Crime Statistics argued that a degree of autonomy from individual politicians and political agendas was important for maintaining quality and a credible research profile. One of the directors stated:

> Each of the directors have had quite different ideas on the way this place should function. Some saw it as an independent authority to produce facts that could influence government policy. Another thought we should be close to government and had us sitting on government committees and taskforces …. My view is that there are real dangers in getting too close to government, real dangers. The seductive appeal of being close to government to do policy

evaluation is easily offset by their desire to have you in the tent. That is, not to broadcast bad news, or if to broadcast it, to broadcast it in the best possible light. Alternatively not to pursue certain questions.

While the AIC has been viewed historically as an arm of government, it has also been praised for employing academics to conduct research, many of whom have been reported to have experienced 'difficulties simply because they have spoken out on controversial criminological issues in a way that has upset people of influence in government' (Sallmann, 1988: 198). Nowadays the AIC is much less 'outspoken'. Its research agenda is confined to its 'core business' as a service provider to the Commonwealth government. As one government criminologist acknowledged, this often takes the form of concise articles of political salience for quick and easy consumption: 'The AIC's main products are our 'Trends and Issues' papers, which are short and crisp, 4,000 word maximum, so because they just fit on three sheets of paper the politicians can read them on the plane'. This statement, while said in a tongue-in-cheek manner, conveys the current strategic emphasis on AIC publications and cannot be easily reconciled with the position of the institute as a beacon of Australian criminology or as an organization providing criminological leadership. As Biles has stated, 'The Australian Institute of Criminology, even though not free of criticism, has become recognised as the major centre for crimi-nological research in Australia and it has gained considerable inter-national recognition (Biles, 1981: 7).

Clearly, the financial downsizing of the institute throughout the 1990s has had a profound impact on the quantity, and arguably the quality, of information published by its researchers. Throughout the 1970s and 1980s, the AIC employed several well-known criminologists in Australia. Academics such as Braithwaite, Harding, Mugford, Biles, Wilson, Chappell, Walker, Hazlehurst and Grabosky were all affiliated with the institute at one time or another and were instrumental in the production of widely quoted and scientifically sophisticated publications for a variety of criminological subjects (Wilson and Nixon, 1988).

Government criminologists described the practical edge to the institute's research in the following way:

Critical in the sense of rigourous. Critical in the sense of being antagonistic, no. Antagonistic is more adversarial, rigorous is more balanced ... more diagnostic and constructive. Just as one studies aircraft accidents so that the future of flight will be safer, just as one studies engineering failures so we can build taller buildings and stronger bridges in the future, I study policy failures so that one can improve policy in the future, so one can avoid the pitfalls that lead to the disasters of the past …. My approach is less evangelical and more analytical.

As a research institute, the AIC is largely focused on administrative criminology. Its statutory role is to serve its stakeholders in ways that are likely to better the effectiveness of existing criminal justice systems in Australia. The AIC also continues to maintain an important place within Australian academic criminology through its administration of the Criminology Research Council (CRC). Outside of the Australian Research Council (ARC), discussed later, the CRC is one of the major funders of academic criminological research in Australia, although the amount of funding available through the CRC is relatively small. For example, during the 2001–02 financial year the CRC allocated AUD $386, 227.88 to eight new projects from a total of 28 submissions (Criminology Research Council, 2002). What sorts of projects will receive CRC funding? One government criminologist suggested the body was:

> … unlikely to fund theoretical work. The Criminology Research Council is funded half by the states and half by the Commonwealth[7] and my thrust on it has been to try and make sure the states get some value for money …. When I first came here what I tried to do was target it a little more, so we put out a couple of advertisements saying next we will receive applications in the topics of young people and violence, repeat victimization and crime against tourism or something like that. So we put up three or four topics and we found that the researchers weren't disciplined enough to stay within those areas. That wasn't terribly successful, so we've hived off some of the money to develop a consultancy programme and we put those out to tender …. The purpose of this is to provide policy material for states …. No, we won't fund 'blue sky research'; universities fund blue sky research. That is, you find a problem up there and go for it, it doesn't have to have an application today, doesn't have to deal with a problem that is right here and now.

This interviewee made it quite clear that theoretical research will not be supported by the CRC. While the eight criteria for CRC funding stipulate that a project must have practical value for the prevention of crime or contribute to improving the effectiveness of the criminal justice system, one criterion is 'the likelihood of the proposed research making a substantial and original contribution to criminological knowledge' (Criminology Research Council, 2002: 79). This criterion would obviously include theoretical and historical research, yet, as the above interviewee indicates, little weighting is given to this criterion when making funding decisions. Indeed, the use of the phrase 'blue sky research' is often seen as trivializing university scholarship that is theoretical (Savage, 2000).

The 2002 annual report of the CRC lists various new research projects funded during the financial year ending 30 June. Most reveal a positivist and/or administrative approach to criminological inquiry, with a commitment to policy relevance.[8]

Moreover, because of a perceived failure of academics to be 'strategic' with their applications, the CRC 'research grants' have been downsized to allow the council to engage consultants to scope projects and carry out audits on topics specifically selected by the CRC. In recent years, these targeted projects have covered topics such as fear of crime, remand facilities in Australia, and the sentencing patterns of violent offenders (Criminology Research Council, 1998). In 2002, the CRC commissioned work on sentencing patterns and the factors that influence decisions to remand offenders into custody, as well as audit and scoping surveys on mental health and criminal justice, high-risk offender profiling, and agricultural crime (Criminology Research Council, 2002: 84).

Similar to comments expressed in England about the Home Office, many academic criminologists interviewed for this book argued that the AIC is known for 'hand picking' its academic consultants to do 'independent' criminological research. A government criminologist commented directly on this issue, but did, however, point out that 'Academics can often deliver the goods provided they can see eye to eye with the thrust of where it's going rather than the detailed content. Whereas the KPMGs and others, they'll give back exactly what they think the client wants.' This government criminologist supported the role of academic criminologists over market research companies, provided they can see 'eye to eye' with the respective client. However, the interviewee also alluded to the unique contributions that academics can provide to criminological research, and I will explore this issue later.

Australian academic criminologists interviewed for this book frequently expressed concern that the CRC was shrinking. They asserted that the AIC continues to provide an important link with the academic world and is supportive of university criminology; however, the extent to which the AIC is supporting academic criminology is often overstated. Its mandate is to support government and its ministers. It is also clear that the AIC is influenced by broader political and economical changes, which demand efficiency and accountability, and that it is operating more clearly than ever before in a policy-relevant and service-provider role for specific government stakeholders. One government criminologist identified the ideological schism confronting academic criminology and the policy world of government criminology:

> There isn't a culture of delivering a product. A lot of academics don't understand where the client or agency is coming from. The agency doesn't want to censure them politically; the agency has a set of issues that it wants explored and analysed and wants it done in a certain way to achieve a certain goal. It doesn't want to be told that a different paradigm might be better or a postmodernist approach is the way to go .... Many academics are often not disciplined enough to give the client what the client wants without going into so much more detail of theory and background. Governments and agencies don't want to give out money to academics to hit them over the head.

These comments allude to ideological and practical differences between the criminological research produced in government and that published by academics. The academic is sometimes viewed as 'undisciplined' and incapable of delivering 'what the client wants', and this may be an important context for understanding the difficulties experienced by academics who undertake contract research with government. The academic criminologist has, in some instances, a professional obligation to be a critic and conscience of society, to produce new knowledges, to question existing state apparatuses (although, as the last chapter argued, a lot of criminological scholarship has followed a narrowly defined and uncritical path), and to publish research in refereed journals and books. Public servants, on the other hand, require concise policy-relevant information and, in order to obtain their needs, often require the researcher to sign detailed and proscriptive contracts to ensure that their product conforms to the style and content sought. The expectations, the audiences and the purpose of research in these two spheres are often quite different. Potential sites for conflict between the academic researcher and the paying client may pivot on professional differences and not, as the above interviewee suggests, on sinister acts by the state to oppress the truth.

For many, the academic world needs to develop a 'culture' of delivering a product. Evidence of this culture and the 'relevance' of a given research proposal are integral factors in the funding of CRC monies and the hiring of consultants to AIC projects. While the AIC has been downsized in recent years, its senior personnel maintain important decision-making roles in the funding of CRC and ARC research. The AIC director is also widely consulted by ministers over national funding strategies to prevent crime, and the AIC continues to provide a clearing-house function and international voice through its conference programme. As with the Home Office and the NIJ, the AIC provides a specific research function for government. And similarly, its research has historically focused on politically salient issues of immediate policy significance, chosen with partiality and closely monitored.

Criminology in Public Policy

Thus far, it has been argued that criminology in government has provided a long history of relevant information for state crime-control policy. A by-product of its scientific and technical roots, criminology has evolved concomitantly with an involvement in public policy. Today, many academic criminologists choose to take part in the production of knowledge for government policy: as advisors to commissions of inquiry, as independent 'experts' or consultants, or as evaluators or reviewers of government policy under contract. In most instances, these intersections with official processes of policy are fee-paying ones, and more often than not involve the production of a written document. Hood (1987) argues that some criminologists, notably those from the critical Left, refuse to participate in what has come to be termed 'jobbing criminology'. Loader defines 'jobbing criminology' as follows:

> The practice of going from criminological job to criminological job either unburdened by intellectual agendas, or else committed only to narrowly construed and preestablished policy goals; research that proceeds with little overt reference to the political and ethical dimensions of the issues at hand. In these respects, jobbing criminology is rarely if ever a position those researchers adhere to. Rather it is an activity, and the extent to which criminologists are required to practice such jobbing will vary across time and space, depending on such matters as how and where criminology is institutionalised, the vicissitudes of research funding and the dull compulsion of the criminological labour market (Loader, 1998: 193; see also Loader and Sparks, 1993).

As mentioned, Hood suggests that many criminologists refuse to engage in jobbing criminology for ideological reasons. He argues that 'Marxists, and other radical thinkers, have no doubts that criminologists who involve themselves, in any way, with evaluating the machinery of crime prevention or criminal justice give credibility to the existing social order' (Hood, 1987: 529).

Yet not all work that eventually changes public policy could be termed 'jobbing' or 'administrative' criminology. Sometimes sophisticated and theoretically driven academic inquiry results in a change to criminal justice policy (see Braithwaite, 1989; Barlow, 1995). This type of academic endeavour seeks to create new knowledges, where the individual researcher and the research is funded in ways that maximize in-dependence and where academic freedom generates the questions for inquiry. In these instances, the criminologist can produce knowledge for multiple audiences rather than for a specific fee-paying client. However, the extent that criminological research will be 'picked up' by government for public policy is often contingent on various factors, including media coverage, market forces, community and agency support, as well as the orientations of individual politicians – factors that are often outside the control and experience of academic researchers (Currie, 1998). As one academic criminologist noted, 'in government and policy terms things are fashionable. For example, family violence is about to go out of fashion …. Why is that? Because the minister is not interested in it.'

Numerous debates have taken place over the past two decades over the role that criminology should play in developing public policy (see Hood, 1974; Dixon, 1995). The non-utilization of criminological research and other forms of social science inquiry for public policy has promoted skepticism among academic researchers (see Patton, 1986). Some argue (see Daly, 1995) that there is little intersection between criminological research and public policy formulation, and that public policy 'is largely driven by media generated stories (including celebrated crime stories) instead of social science research' (Daly, 1995: 6). Indeed, Barak (1988) has argued that academic criminologists must not remain 'spectators' to media generated constructions of crime problems. He argues that criminologists should develop a 'newsmaking criminology', using the mass media to convey a readily and widely consumed knowledge for maximum impact on the processes on policy development (cf. Sim, 2003). Yet this role in influencing public policy has been widely criticized. Chan asks rhetorically, 'What is criminological research all about – producing a defensible and useful knowledge about criminal justice related issues. And this process, I would argue, is never going to keep pace with the six-o'clock news' (Chan, 1995: 28).

However, Chan further argues that the influence of criminological scholarship on public policy is 'pervasive'. Drawing on the works of Weiss (1986) and Majone (1989), Chan argues that criminological research presents 'ideas and arguments' as well as data that are often integrated into public policy. She describes the influence of research on the over-representation of indigenous peoples in the justice system, the repeated cautions to the judiciary and politicians about sentencing tariffs and net-widening, and innovations in juvenile justice such as family group conferencing as examples of criminological research that have been influential in shaping the direction of public policy (Chan, 1995: 27). She suggests, however, that often these forms of knowledge have their impact on the political process via indirect routes, where 'lay people', pressure groups, and community agencies take up information and research results produced by criminologists and mobilize support for change through diverse networks. Several interviewees endorsed the above view, arguing that 'impacting upon the system' was more likely to come about through influencing policy customers and agencies in the field. This 'impact' may not necessarily result in legislative change, but might be witnessed in the delivery of services or the implementation of policy. As one academic criminologist commented:

> I don't think by and large government-funded research informs policy. I think it supports policy. Basically, the research will not have an impact unless it helps to justify the political decisions, but it won't necessarily change the direction of policy. If the government are not committed to a particular direction, research is not going to change their minds ... but you can have an impact through direct contact with policy customers, and you can influence the ways in which they implement the research in the field.

For Hogg (1998), criminological thought has historically been aligned closely with the processes of public policy; yet he concludes, with reference to Garland (1985), that the utility of criminological research for public policy has been regulated by various modes of governance. For Hogg, the production of criminological research, which seeks as its major objective to improve the existing state crime-control apparatus, reduces the utility of criminology to futile debates about the discipline's success or failure. Criminology, he argues, becomes a dynamic genre of knowledge when reconstructed within plural discourses of governance, power and social control: a genre that seeks to question underlying broader assumptions about social order while producing new knowledges for diverse audiences (Hogg, 1998).

Criminology's ongoing interface with public policy continues to provide the catalyst for criminologists to undertake policy-relevant research; it provides the opportunity to 'change the system', to see one's research challenge or improve existing processes of criminal justice. Indeed, some criminology departments are working in partnership with newly developed commercial entities within their universities to produce policy-relevant research. For example, in 2001 the Department of Criminology at the University of Melbourne formalized an alliance with the university's commercial arm, Melbourne Enterprises International, in forming the Melbourne Criminology Research and Evaluation Unit. The aim of this endeavour is for the Department of Criminology to 'strengthen its commitment to remaining 'policy-relevant'. The unit will undertake a range of applied criminological research for government and industry, bringing the quality of independence and intellectual rigour to the problems of the 'real world' (University of Melbourne, 2001: 29).

This point raises questions about the commercialization of universities and the production of criminological knowledge that will be explored in later chapters. It also alludes to a desirable academic aspiration, namely the willingness to influence policy debates. However, as Majone (1989) points out, 'political actors select their ideas and arguments from the supply that happens to be available at a given time' (164). Criminologists undertaking policy-relevant research are subject to the vagaries and machinations of party politics. Tombs (2003) persuasively and authoritatively makes this point. Following her 20-year career at the Scottish Executive (formerly the Scottish Office), Dr Jacqueline Tombs examines 'what counts as evidence in the policy making process'. In other words, how and why are certain forms of knowledge used in the policy making process over and above others? For Tombs the uptake of criminological research into the policy decisions of government, or what she refers to as 'practical logic-in-use', is 'mediated by three main factors – the control of information, the need to render the control invisible, and short term policy making' (Tombs, 2003: 5). In this revealing insight into the internal workings of the production of criminal justice policy, Tombs identifies how government strategically produces what she calls 'generative knowledges', to be available for 'the policymaking machine to draw on as it sees fit'. In doing so, criminological knowledge serves various bureaucratic functions, which include making political bargains, measuring and assessing the effectiveness of the criminal justice system, as well as 'knowledge as non-evidence', where the findings are 'politically unpalatable' and are systematically nuetralized through 'questioning its relevance, its methodology; or its objectivity' (Tombs, 2003: 10). While Tombs uses the category 'formative knowledge' to refer to criminological research that informs and shapes legislation, it is clear from her experience that the ability for commissioned research to influence the system is as much about timing and political appeal as it is about content.

Almost all academics interviewed for this book argued that 'contract or commissioned research' – that is, criminological research for a specific fee-paying client within a designated time period, defined by a legal agreement – has limited impact on changing the system. Several inter-viewees pointed to the possibility of influencing government policy; however, given the overall amount of contract research being undertaken by the academic criminological community, it was felt that only a small amount eventually influenced the political agenda. Often, the results of such work are postponed, dissected and manipulated by the fee-paying client for specific policy directions. As a result, many respondents argued that academics that engage in contract research often overestimate or exaggerate the impact that such research will have on criminal justice policy. One academic criminologist argued that academics should not pursue contract research from the Home Office:

> Universities must be building proper programmes of research. How does policy-relevant research fit into the wider academic agenda? …. We won't go after Home Office money. There are too many problems. Too many problems in the past. Things like delays in getting things published or too short a time span to complete the research. I mean how on earth can you do anything meaningful in such a short space of time. Then there are problems over the terms of reference and how the work is to be done …. No, I've told the Home Office that they have to meet the needs of the university and not the other way around.

As mentioned earlier in the chapter, there is a growing movement of resistance among academic criminologists to undertake government-contracted research. For some, notably those interested in pursuing the crimes of the powerful (see Tombs and Whyte, 2003) government-contracted research serves to suppress critical criminological voices through various direct and indirect ways, which will be discussed further in the next chapter.

The 'needs' of the university and those of government are often in conflict. James Q. Wilson's appeal for a 'realist agenda', back in 1974, argued that criminological research needed to be more attentive to the immediate needs of government by providing the state with pragmatic solutions to pressing crime problems (Wilson, 1974). Indeed, crimi-nology's ongoing search for legitimacy has been characterized by discourses of policy relevance (Radzinowicz, 1961; Robson, 1975). Garland further asserts that criminology's origins and its subsequent evolution into a distinct discipline have been enhanced by a commitment to science and policy relevance: 'the pairing of science and policy relevance has been criminology's major asset in the struggles for research funding and institutional recognition' (Garland, 1985: 2). It is not surprising that this quest for legitimacy has seen criminology absorbed in processes of public policy: the lure of relevance or utility has been necessary for institutional establishments, as well as creating a 'rite of passage' to government resources for research.

It is important to note that criminology's enduring involvement in policy development has necessitated a coexistence with the vagaries of the political process. Criminal justice policy-making is a deeply political and constantly changing process (Rock, 1995). Rock argues that policies are not developed by internal processes of consultation, briefings, and committee meetings. Instead, the process of criminal justice policy-making, premised on 'the politics of populism, moralism and the market' (Rock, 1995: 2), is much less coherent, fragmentary, and much more contracted out. The academic criminologist who enters the world of criminal justice policy-making is inevitably caught up in a complex web of political agendas, power plays, budgets, bureaucratic language, and government objectives (cf Rutherford, 1997). This complex web, spun by the state, serves to sustain its very existence. The complexities of this relationship and the dichotomies of power will be explored later.

This chapter, then, concludes that the postwar years witnessed a substantial growth in criminological research. This growth was fuelled, in part, by the development and expansion of criminology in government. For example, the creation of the Home Research Unit Office in Britain, and the establishment of criminological institutes and university programmes, reflected the state's ambition to address the growing social problems endemic in criminal activity. These government-based criminological centres, for example, the Home Office Research Unit, NIJ and AIC, have been instrumental in the funding and shaping of specific criminological endeavours, and they remain powerful sites in the production of contemporary criminological knowledge. Their focus has been, and remains, clearly orientated towards government policy and practice. To this extent, criminological research has provided sustenance to the political programmes of government. Criminology's ongoing struggle for validity as a discipline or academic specialism has required practical expressions of utility (Garland, 1985). Government-based criminologies are assembled as crucial 'technologies of power' (Miller and Rose, 1990) for the practical ends of those who govern. Government criminology continues to assert an influential position in the funding of research, notably policy-relevant research. The modern-day legacy of criminology's close association with the state's crime-control apparatus is a discipline now tightly constrained by the strategic needs of regulatory authorities in neo-liberal societies.

As Chapter Six explores, the commercialization of criminological research provides an essential mechanism for developing strategic approaches to risk populations identified by governing entities, including the state. Research that measures and assesses specific objectives is increasingly important in 'risk societies' governed by economic rationalism. As a result, administrative and scientific criminological knowledges, which have traditionally appealed to governments, emerge as the dominating genres within current market demands. Historical and theoretical work is further relegated to a diminishing periphery.

The following chapter explores the intrigues surrounding criminological research, the politics of conducting various forms of criminological scholarship in contemporary society, and the kinds of tensions and difficulties experienced by criminologists. If criminological research is a deeply political process, it is important to understand the nature of that process and the form it takes.

Notes

1   As previously discussed, the United Nations asserted a dominant position in the coordination and dissemination of criminological knowledge in the postwar years. The United Nations continued to sponsor conferences on the treatment of offenders and the prevention of juvenile delinquency during the early 1960s, and international criminology conferences in Rome and Paris were held under its auspices in 1962. These were referred to by Andry as 'constituting important milestones in the gradual construction of an international criminological empire' (Andry [1962], quoted in Mannheim, 1972). In the same year, the Far East Institute for the Prevention of Crime and Treatment of Offenders was set up under a treaty with the Japanese Government and the United Nations, to organize training and research in the area of social defence (Mannheim, 1972).

2   The Home Office in England and Wales was established in 1782, with a mandate to preserve civil peace (see Callaghan, 1982). This section will focus solely on the Research, Development and Statistics Directorate.

3   The remaining two projects were funded by NACRO (£14,662) and Urbis Lighting Ltd (£211,750). The latter amount contributed to the establishment of a position at the Institute. The successful Home Office projects were: 'The Introduction, Operation and Service Provision of the Youth Court', 'Remanding and Sentencing of Women Offender's in Magistrates' Courts: Views from the Bench', 'Vulnerability Custody and Incentive Based Regimes for Offenders', 'An Evaluation of Incentives in Prison Regimes', 'Drug Testing in Arrestees', and 'Evaluation of Burglary Prevention Strategies in Cambridge' (see Bottoms, 1996).

4   Research current at Cambridge University's Institute of Criminology in 2002 reflects a commitment to policy-relevant research. Many of the current research

projects are evaluation studies of the policies and practices of existing criminal justice agencies. For example, 'An Evaluation of CCTV in Cambridge Car Parks', 'Cost-Benefit Analysis of Street Lighting and Crime in Dudley, Stoke on Trent and Redbridge', 'Problem Oriented Policing, Evaluation and Best Practice – Exploratory Project with Lincolnshire Police', 'Longitudinal Reconviction Studies of Offenders Supervised by Cambridgeshire, Bedfordshire, Hertfordshire and Northamptonshire Probation Services', 'Evaluating High Intensity Regimes at Thorn Cross and Colchester', 'Pro-social Modelling and Legitimacy: Their Contribution to Effective Probation Practice', and 'Longitudinal Reconviction Studies of Offenders Supervised by Medium Secure Care Study'. These research projects are notably 'applied' in nature, focusing on the improvement of criminal justice policy and practice. Research that is 'critical' comprises a small part of criminological knowledge currently produced by the institute (see Institute of Criminology, 2001).

5   The HORSD is not officially appraised or audited by an independent body. Instead, it is reviewed internally where performance is monitored through: 'the volume and quality of products, and whether these are kept on time and budget; the response from other researchers, academics, pressure groups and others to the publications of HORSD's research reports and regular statistical series; the Research and Statistics Committee (a sub-committee of the Home Office Management Board), which reviews the programme and activities of HORSD and the allocation of priorities and resources; the involvement of customers in planning and carrying out its work programme and evaluating results; and a range of quality control and output measures in the collection and processing of data' (Home Office, 1997).

6   For Example, the ESRC, UK Research Office, European Science Foundation, British Council, European Funding Opportunities for Social Science, Cooperation of Science and Technology, Community Research and Development Information Services.

7   During the 2000–01 financial year the Australian Commonwealth government contributed AUD $281,000 to the CRC and the states and territories provided a total of AUD $142,000 on a pro-population basis (see CRC Annual Report, 2002).

8   Newly funded projects for the financial year ending 30 June 2002 included: 'The Prevalence of Residential Care, Kinship Care and Adoption Experiences in the Victorian Juvenile Justice System', 'Facilitators and Inhibitors of Mandatory Reporting of Suspected Child Abuse and Neglect', 'A Longitudinal Investigation of Psychosocial Risk Factors for Speeding Offences among Young Motor Car Drivers', 'Threats and Intimidation in the Lives of Professionals Employed in the Child Protection Field', 'Investigating the Incidence of Criminal and Antisocial Behaviour by Young People on the Strand in Townsville', 'Youth Justice: Criminal Trajectories', 'Public CCTV in Australia: A Comparative Study of Establishment and Operation', 'Pathways to Prevention: Evaluation of an Early Intervention Crime Prevention Program' and 'Civil Litigation by Citizens against Australian Police between 1994 and 2002' (Criminology Research Council, 2002: 82–83).

Chapter 4

The politics and control of criminological knowledge

> Academic freedom in the field of Criminology is perhaps even more problematic and more important than quite a few other areas of academic endeavour because it's touching the State at a raw nerve .... Almost automatically, if we are studying crime we are messing around with some of the most powerful constructs the State has at its disposal (Carson, quoted in Smellie, 1996).

The previous chapters have argued that a vast amount of the criminological research conducted throughout the twentieth century was been predisposed to scientific analyses of state-defined notions of crime and criminal justice, or, alternatively has aimed to serve the immediate policy needs of government. It has been argued that critical criminological scholarship has provided a marginal knowledge within a discipline constantly seeking legitimacy through an applied logic of relative pragmatism. This book has contended that the contours of criminological knowledge have been governed by the specific needs of the state as well as influential organizations represented by technical experts. To this extent, the broader or 'macro' dimensions of governance (Foucault, 1978) have been explored (and are further analysed in Chapter Five). This chapter aims to examine the micro forms of governance: the 'political' dynamics (in a non-Party sense) or the details of conducting criminological research on a day-to-day basis, which may influence the nature and outcome of criminological knowledge. As Foucault has identified, the 'art of governing' involves not only the protection of principality but also the governing of 'things', the daily events that influence, or are capable of influencing, the economy of the state (Foucault, 1978: 89–91). In doing so, this chapter explores power relations that influence the production of criminological knowledge, with a specific focus on what Foucault (1974) referred to as 'capillary circuits', or power that 'comes from below'.

Research *per se* is a powerful and political process (Weiss, 1975). It is capable of unearthing unwanted information and challenging the decisions of those who govern. As such, the researcher must be aware that they enter a realm of political turmoil when they question the underlying assumptions and philosophies of those in power. Lee argues that research, particularly that involving sensitive topics, is a threatening exercise, capable of trespassing 'into areas which are controversial or involve social conflict' (Lee, 1993: 4, see also Sjoberg, 1967; Callahan and Jennings, 1983). Social research is a risky process, capable of placing the researcher in physical, ethical, legal and psychological danger (Lee-Treweek and Linkogle, 2000).

The production of knowledge and its concomitant nexus with notions of power and governance are not new and date to Aristotle's era in the 4th century BC (see Sinclair, 1979). This nexus has been well established and critiqued by Foucault (1977 and 1978) and will be further explored in the following chapter. For now it is important to note that research is an influential and powerful exercise. However, research can become less influential and less powerful when emptied of its content. When evaluation, in particular, is redefined within neo-liberal concepts of 'strategic outputs', it often loses its potential to scrutinize, audit, or critically assess. Indeed, government officials consulted for this book referred to 'evaluation' as a 'dirty word', preferring to adopt the more politically appealing yet softer terms of 'assess' or 'review'. Criminological research often impinges on topics of sensitivity. It can challenge the existing social order or criticize state policy and practice in ways that directly influence government managers and decision-makers. From the inception of a research topic to the production of its findings, criminological researchers often encounter a range of difficulties. As Hughes argues, the 'finished product' of criminological research, which is often presented as an 'antiseptic and tidy picture', fails to convey the ongoing struggles and tensions involved in 'doing research' (Hughes, 1996: 58).

The struggles involved when conducting criminological research have been raised previously and debated by academic criminologists in Europe. In 1980, the eighth conference of the European Group for the Study of

Deviance and Social Control was held in Leuven, under the title 'State Control of Information in the Field of Deviance and Social Control' (see Brusten and Ponsaers, 1981). It noted that criminological research in Europe was seen by state officials as a means of legitimating penal law and government policy, and that researchers who criticized these positions were unlikely to receive government funding (Schumann, 1981; Behr *et al.*, 1981). Moreover, access to information about the criminal justice system in Europe was heavily regulated by state bureaucracies (Jepsen, 1981) and government contracts were used to legalize state interference while controlling the processes and products of research (see Squires, 1981; Stangl, 1981).

This chapter aims to examine the difficulties that criminologists sometimes endure when conducting research and to chart the ways in which criminological scholarship is influenced, shaped or governed at a micro level. It commences by exploring what is meant by the phrase 'the politics of criminological research', and questions the extent to which there is, or can be, a 'politics-free criminological research'. It then examines the ways in which research is defined and utilized in neo-liberal societies. This chapter also explores the roles of government and commercial contracts in contemporary criminological scholarship as well as the various obstacles (legal and ethical issues, and the difficulties of securing funding, accessing and gathering information, and publishing results) that criminologists must negotiate prior to, during and after the completion of a research project. In doing so, the chapter aims to unearth some of the politics behind the creation of criminological knowledge and the processes by which (to echo Nietzsche and Foucault) 'things come into being'.

What Are the Politics of Criminological Research?

Methodological textbooks in criminology often omit any discussion of the difficulties and tensions of conducting criminological research. Such books share similar patterns by including chapters on sampling, question-naires, bivariate analyses, correlations, control groups, interview techniques, statistical modelling and so on (see Clark, 1977; Johnson, 1981; Mackenzie *et al.*, 1990; Sessar *et al.*, 1991; Coleman and Moynihan, 1996). This literature conveys an impression that criminological research is a technical, scientific exercise. With the exception of some European and British sociologists in the late 1970s and early 1980s (see Cohen and Taylor, 1977; Brusten and Ponsaers, 1981), it has been only since the 1990s that sociologists and criminologists, mostly from Britain, have highlighted the 'political' dimensions of criminological research, and discussed the difficulties facing researchers when investigating topics of sensitivity (Jupp, 1989; Lee, 1993; Hughes, 1996 and 2000; Sapsford, 1996; Brookman *et al.*, 1999; Morgan, 2000).

Jupp (1989) provides the first criminological text on research methods to devote a substantial section to the politics of criminological inquiry. Drawing on the earlier social science work of Barnes (1979), he develops a framework for analysing and uncovering the political dimensions of criminological research. These areas, he argues, include:

> ... problems of getting approval to conduct research in corners of the criminal justice system which, for one reason or another, are closed to outsiders; the ethical dimensions of data by covert means from individuals who have a vested interest in protecting themselves from the prying eyes of criminological researchers; the problems of getting research findings and conclusions into the public domain, particularly where these appear to compromise powerful groups; and the use, or non-use, of research findings by politicians and other decision makers. (Jupp, 1989: 129)

Hughes extends upon this analysis and argues that the term 'political' has two distinct dimensions. He states that 'when political is conceptualised as concerning questions of control, authority, conflict and power alliances and struggles, it becomes obvious that criminological research cannot avoid the epithet of being political' (Hughes, 1996: 60). Here Hughes refers to the day-to-day problems that researchers endure when conducting their work, or what Foucault refers to as 'the governing of things': for example, gaining access to information, securing financial support, seeking ethical clearances, contractual ambiguities, methodological implications, 'hands-on' monitoring by sponsoring agencies, restricting publication and so on. Hughes's second definition relates to 'explicit political ideologies and organised coercive power, most apparent in the modern state' (Hughes, 1996: 60). This includes the setting and funding of specific criminological research agendas by governing authorities, which aim to examine state definitions of crime and social order, as well as broader political ideologies that have influenced the nature of knowledge-producing institutions (discussed in previous chapters and further examined in Chapter Five). This chapter focuses on Hughes's first definition of political: the micro dimensions of criminological research.

It became apparent during the early days of the interview phase of this book that there were various interpretations of and opinions about the politics of criminological research. There were no universally accepted definitions or understandings. For some, the politics of research were interpreted as 'getting into trouble'; for others, they involved any factors that influenced the independent production of criminological scholarship, including unknown factors, such as decision-making processes over funding, often not made public; and, for others, they were the changing political landscapes in late modernity and the effect it has had on universities.

The word 'governance' is further used throughout this chapter to capture the various ways in which the contours and production of criminological knowledge are influenced. For some criminologists working in government, their ongoing concerns related to sustainability and autonomy (providing ministers with useful information without allowing the politicians to dictate what they do). For academic criminologists, the politics of research were varied, and are discussed below. The spectrum is broad, ranging from subtle influences on methodology by external agencies to legal threats and court action. The issues discussed are intended to provide an overview of the ways in which criminological research may be governed as well as exploring how criminologists deal with these hurdles.

(Re)defining Research

New forms of governance and the role of research

Before a research project commences (particularly when it involves a contractual agreement with government) there may be factors influencing the type of knowledge to be produced. The starting point for exploring the various politics of criminological research, therefore, is a discussion of what constitutes research. More importantly, has the meaning of research changed or been redefined in recent years? And, if so, why?

There are many types of social research, such as quantitative, basic, applied, longitudinal, descriptive, comparative, exploratory, casual, observational and so on (see Baker, 1988; Hagan, 1989; Foddy, 1993). Irrespective of the logic and processes involved, the production of research is capable of challenging existing structures and is often seen as a form of power. As Sarantakos (1998: 28) argues, 'research is power that allows those who have access to it to control others; and the options for using that power are many'. These options include influencing the topics to be researched and their methods, the types of information to be gathered, as well as the processes of publication (Jupp, 1989; May, 1993).

Rhodes (1994 and 1997) has written extensively on the restructuring of public sectors in Western democracies and the rise of new public management. He argues that state-owned enterprises have been systematically privatized, and that state services have increasingly been contracted out, creating what he calls 'governing without government'. Driven by neo-liberal economics, new public management endorses a dispersed model of governance premised on the three 'e's: economy, efficiency and effectiveness. This new ethos of management requires a range of accountability mechanisms to ensure that economy, efficiency and effectiveness underpin an organization's *modus operandi*. Accountability, therefore, is an important component of demonstrating the fulfilment of strategic objectives. Research, in its various forms, becomes an essential tool for demonstrating accountability.

It is important to note, as Rhodes (1997) argues, that the neo-liberal 'state' is not a monolith. The restructuring of the public sector has created a complex dynamic between traditionally accepted notions of 'public' and 'private', culminating in changing, ambiguous and diversifying modes of governance. As a result, it is erroneous to talk about the researcher and the 'state' as though the state represents a static and united entity (cf. Foucault, 1978). The corporatization of the public sector has produced intense competition within and across different sectors of modern government. Research in general, and criminological research in particular, may be highly sensitive and controversial for one area of government, and yet advantageous or desirable to another sector, and this is discussed later.

The changes to the public sector premised on new managerialist principles have altered relationships between government and criminological research. These changes were nicely captured by the following government criminologist interviewed for this book:

> In the late seventies the criminological research agenda within government was influenced by outside academics. We responded to research proposals from academics, but now almost everything is determined within government … research officers in government nowadays spend so much time writing research specifications that tell academics and others what research to do and how to do it …. And this shift has come about with new managerialism … so we've seen a shift whereby what gets done now is not research anymore but more information gathering and performance measurement and most of the time criminological research is being used to legitimate decisions that have already been made … and what we've lost is the outside knowledge community's ability to enter the policy debate at all.

Comments such as the above, which were corroborated by several government sources, serve to confirm the suspicions of numerous academic criminologists interviewed for this book: that government contracted research was not in search of a critical appraisal of policy and practice, and was therefore not (in the main) 'influencing policy' but was merely providing a rubber stamp of 'independent' credibility or legitimation to a pre-ordained government decision (this will be further explored throughout this chapter). Moreover, it is important to note that some government criminologists noted that the emerging neo-liberal rationality within the public sector has brought with it a new workforce, one that adheres to and believes in the new managerialism, and one that defines research within the aforementioned criteria of economy, efficiency and effectiveness.

Government accountability and the rise of 'output' research

Performance indicators or outputs are frequently the criteria for determining or measuring success. The distinction between 'output' and 'outcome' becomes important when understanding the nature and content of accountability mechanisms. Crawford identifies it as follows:

> 'Outputs' often refer to internally defined organisational goals over which organisations have considerable control. These may depart significantly from 'outcomes': the effect of an output, or set or outputs, on the wider community. There is a danger that 'outputs' may take precedence over 'outcomes' and that the gulf between the two may grow larger, so that social goals are eclipsed by organisational goals. This can result in a form of 'measure fixation' whereby greater concentration is given to the measure, rather than the service, which the measure is intended to signify (Crawford, 1998: 182).

Researchers contracted to assess or review outputs are often presented with a host of very different questions to researchers who are commissioned to evaluate outcomes. As mentioned in Chapter One, nowadays the level of acceptance, participation or proliferation often determines the success or achievement of a policy or programme. When a business, government sector or community is seen to be embracing a concept, this is presented by government as evidence of the value or merit of that concept, without appraising critically its origins, theoretical underpinnings or application. If the concept is cost-effective, widely embraced, and consistent with an organization's strategic objectives, then an agency may be viewed as successfully achieving its desired outputs. This approach occurs within discourses of crime control. Take, for example, the international growth of community-based crime-prevention initiatives. The French Bonnemaison model[1] of preventing crime, that emerged in the early 1980s, created a domino effect in other countries (with slight variations) such as England and Wales (Tilley, 1993), The Netherlands (Williamse, 1994), Australia (O'Malley and Sutton, 1997), Canada, New Zealand (O'Neill, 1994) and Belgium (Walgrave, 1995). Governments often refer to the success of these policies by describing the growth in community participation, as well as the attainment of strategic outputs (see Hughes, 1998). Yet research that evaluates 'outcomes' continually points to deficiencies in funding, inter-agency collaboration, managerial expertise, cultural exclusion and community empowerment, while suggesting that these initiatives have had limited impacts on the prevention or reduction of crime (see Liddle and Gelsthorpe 1994; Hughes, 1998; Koch, 1998; Hughes *et al.*, 2002; Walters and Bradley, 2002). Community crime prevention has become an avant-garde crime-control policy in neo-liberal Western societies, yet its popularity and widespread acceptance cannot be reconciled (at least empirically) with its mandate to prevent crime and build resources within local communities. The spread of community-based crime-prevention initiatives (like other policies involving the withdrawal of the state) has become commonplace in neo-liberal, post-Keynesian societies (O'Malley, 1994) and must be examined within broader political frameworks (Hughes, 1998).

Government and Commercial Contracts: the Legalization of Interference

The managerialist language of conservative modes of governance, including 'outputs', 'mission statements', 'performance indicators', 'strategic result areas', and the strategic nature of research are producing a defined form of criminological knowledge. Criminologists are often engaged to undertake specific tasks. As mentioned above, when research is conducted for government, it is often defined in terms of reference drafted by the state or regulatory authority. The wording of these contracts stipulates the parameters of the research and articulates the type of product required. Evaluating outcomes is often not required, and detours by researchers into a critique of the social and political consequences of policy may bring strong reactions from governing bodies (discussed later).

Criminologists consulted for this research repeatedly outlined the ways in which government or private contracts were becoming increasingly regulatory in nature. Not only do they contain clauses regarding publication, confidentiality and intellectual property, but they are also, in the opinion of many criminologists, regulating the day-to-day activities of the research. For example, contracts may include legal requirements that the researcher meet monthly with the client to discuss progress, that the researcher notify the client in writing of any changes to the original methodology, that the researcher submit one or two interim reports before the final report, that the principal researcher have all staff approved by the client, and that any changes to the research team be brought to the client's attention in writing. One academic criminologist commented that 'increasingly it's funding bodies that are calling the shots. The Home Office, for example, are setting the parameters and controlling the process'.

This statement reflects an ethical dilemma for academic scholars engaged in contract research. Academics are frequently commissioned by governments to do research, because they bring a stamp of credibility to the process as independent and autonomous experts. State officials, in particular, uphold the value of having a policy or programme 'independently reviewed' outside the corridors of government as a testament to the honest and open processes of accountability and service delivery. Clearly, the integrity of this process is undermined if government officials compromise the researchers' independence by overly regulating the research.

Some authors have argued that the research contract reflects a conscious process of control by the governing authorities (see Brusten, 1981). In this view, the research contract becomes no more than the legalization of interference, and it is always the first formal mechanism used to regulate the research. As Cullingworth pointed out in the 1960s, government contracts often make up this suppression of the truth: 'the freedom of the social researcher – and hence the scientific nature of his work – is largely illusory if he is entirely constrained by terms of reference laid down by a public authority …and by deadlines set by a financial timetable' (Cullingworth, 1969: 13). The commercial contract that establishes the payee as the 'client', and the researcher as the 'service provider', creates a legal arrangement where the client may view the regulation of research as an entitlement.

These commercial arrangements involve signing detailed contracts, conditions that often do not exist when receiving grant money from research committees, trusts or councils (see Downes, 1992; cf. Hughes, 1996). The current president of the Australian and New Zealand Society of Criminology argues that this is an appropriate and acceptable position:

My impression is that meritocracy rules, and that by and large, quality work gets rewarded, while inferior work does not …. The fact that commercial arrangements (as distinct from grants for 'pure' research) may have conditions attached regarding confidentiality or ownership of intellectual property does not constitute interference. Nor is it inappropriate for sources of funding to specify priorities, and to identify the kinds of knowledge that they deem to be useful (Grabosky, 2000: I).

Of course, the determination of 'meritocracy' is not transparent and is often determined by the funding agency on the basis of the 'usefulness' of the research. Many interviewees for this book reported that government contracts have always provided boundaries around the type of knowledge that a researcher could produce. For example, one academic criminologist commented:

> You weren't going to get a large Home Office grant to go out and do research that was highly critical of the system …. If you take money from the state and you don't play the state's game that's when you can get into trouble. Historically in Britain, by and large the people who took the money from the hands of government had a tacit agreement as to the limits and parameters in which they would write. They could be critical but within certain limits and you could never challenge the basic paradigm of the social order.

One government criminologist endorsed this view, noting that the contract served to censor research, not in a coercive way, but through the design of the research question. This interviewee stated: 'The research questions and the research outcomes are all specified in the con-tract …. The entire process is controlled and somewhat censored even before it begins.'

It is arguable that government regulation of research has become more explicit and overt in recent times. This may be a by-product of conservative governing rationalites as well as legislation demanding greater government accountability. For example, governments are increasingly entering into private and commercial transactions with contractors and Australian Commonwealth law has asserted that the Crown is expected to abide by higher standards of conduct than private industry (see Harden, 1992). For example, the Australian High Court, drawing on English Common Law, has ruled that the government and its executive officers are expected to act as a 'moral exemplar' and adhere to 'higher standards of conduct' than is required of the private sector when entering into contractual arrangements (see Australian Law Reports, 1997). Often this requires a clear and consistent articulation of government needs and expectations: the forthright nature of these guidelines and instructions to researchers (discussed below) are viewed by Seddon (1999) as mechanisms that ensure openness across the public sector. He argues that government 'should behave impeccably when contracting with its citizens because it should set an example and should exercise restraint in the exercise of its undoubted power' (Seddon, 1999: 12).

Governments also experience certain contractual liberties not afforded to the private sector, notably with respect to privilege and immunity.[2] Moreover, while there is an expectation that officers of government rigorously oversee contracts in the interests of public expenditure and accountability, it is also expected that agents of the Crown carry out their duties with high ethical and moral standards.

Government criminologists interviewed for this book identified a fine line between ensuring that the state obtains 'value for money'[3] when procuring[4] research and allowing the researcher freedom to engage in independent investigation. There were risks that adopting the latter approach might result in a government not receiving value for money. As one government criminologist stated:

> It would be irresponsible not to closely monitor what goes on; after all we need to be accountable to the minister …. Now that doesn't mean we tell the researcher what to do, although sometimes we have to; it means we make sure the government gets what it wants.

Another government criminologist described how the emergence of contract research brought about greater democratization in the tendering and selection of researchers, arguing that nowadays there exists greater transparency about government research agendas than was previously the case:

> Even if at the end of day the whole process is sorted out over lunch, at least it is a bit more transparent than in the early or mid eighties …. At least in principle there is a democratization of accountability and transparency in the process of awarding contracts.

While many interviewees acknowledged that the processes of government contracting had become more open (dates for submissions, estimated budgets, project objects, reporting deadlines and so on), there still existed clear preferences in terms of individuals and methodologies (discussed below).[5] Indeed, Morgan argues, from his personal experience, that the tendering process is far from transparent, with no 'peer review, or academic representation .... There is, as far as I am aware, no national Home Office notice board through which all research criminologists can discover, well before the date by which bids must be submitted, that certain contracts are to be let. This seems both unfair and inefficient' (Morgan, 2000: 78).

It is clear that contracts with governments and commercial entities are increasingly designed to be business transactions: a fee-paying client (the government or corporate body) purchasing a product (from a criminologist) for a specific purpose (development of state policy or business strategy). As discussed in Chapter Three, the two parties often have very different needs and perceptions of research, different audiences and different structures of accountability.

Some academic criminologists argue that, rather than seeing themselves like builders, who are contracted to provide a specific service, criminologists should see themselves as accountants conducting an audit. As one academic criminologist stated:

> Criminologists working under commercial contract should be viewed like accountants. If an independent accountant is contracted to audit a business and that person reports that the business has lost £45,000 in the last financial year, it would be unthinkable for the business to tell the accountant 'to go away and come back and tell us that we've actually made a profit of 45,000'. I think it's also unacceptable to tell a criminologist to rewrite something or take something out or that a certain answer is not the right one, so go away and come back with a different answer. So I prefer the commercial analogy of contract criminologists as accountants and not builders.

Criminologists sometimes sign contracts with governments and commercial entities without fully understanding all the legal intricacies and implications of the binding agreement. This is also typical of some personnel charged with administering government contracts. From a legal point of view this can create considerable problems; as Seddon (1999: 17) argues, 'Personnel administering government contracts are not properly trained .... Interactions between contract administrators on both sides, even quite casual contacts, can generate significant legal liabilities' (Seddon, 1999: 17).

A common experience identified by interviewees for this book was the way in which government bodies attempted to manipulate a methodology, either throughout the process of contract negotiation or during the early weeks of the research. Several academic criminologists argued that the early stages of contract research often involved tension when various government departments were overseeing or funding the research. The personnel representing the departments often had little legal or research knowledge of the contract they were administering. One academic criminologist summed up the views of several interviewees:

> Committees make up, say, ten people from different government departments and they've all got different agendas, so there's no coherence in the group, they all have different expectations of the research and they may have limited experience of research. Their primary agenda is usually protecting their minister or protecting something and not necessarily to do with the quality of the research, and often this includes trying to determine your methodology.

One way the researcher can safeguard against government interference or regulation is to avoid signing contracts that erode academic freedom. This may, however, jeopardize the winning of a contract. For several criminologists consulted for this book, signing a contract provided a dilemma. A small number stated that they would sign them knowing that they were relinquishing their intellectual property. These criminologists expressed a reluctance to damage good working relations with the government sector: 'If you take a contract to do a particular job you do that to the satisfaction of the client'. This also included not presenting information at conferences if permission to do so was declined by a government agency. The emphasis here was a willingness to abide by government sanctions or regulations. The same academic criminologist went on to say:

> I don't want to alienate key individuals who would be responsible for research funding in the future .... I'm accepting the control .... It's more important for me to be in a position to get contracts and do contract research than speak publicly about the research and risk losing future contracts.

Other interviewees had experienced so many frustrations and difficulties with public- and private-sector contracts that they had decided never again to engage in contract research, preferring to obtain their 'own money' through grants or trusts, or by using their salary. For many criminologists, the signing of a contract immediately compromised the autonomous role of the academic. As one academic criminologist with extensive contract-research experience stated, 'contract research has altered the terms of the trade and it's a way of degrading academic working conditions. You have to meet the expectations of people who are relatively ignorant, who are not as expert by any means compared to one's own team'.

Several interviewees for this book were strongly of the view that criminologists should not sign contracts. Indeed, many argued that there should be active and formal resistance to signing government contracts through criminological associations and societies. As one academic criminologist pointed out:

> A bureaucracy ought never to have, with independent researchers, the ability to control the production of knowledge. So I think what we need to do is constitute ourselves as an independent voice, and I think we should be involved in refusing those agreements [contracts] altogether.

For several criminologists, the government or commercial contract not only attempted to dictate the parameters and direction of the research but also limited its value by setting unrealistic time-frames. As one academic criminologist stated:

> Why would anyone want to do this [contract research]. Proposals go in during the middle of March and then a report three months later in the middle of June comes out. What could be produced of any substance in that short period of time? Nothing! It's not a research time-frame …. But to say you're actually going to have some independent research over a three month period on some quite complicated set of pilot programmes, is ridiculous …. It's not research.

Moreover, others argued that the rationale for sponsoring contract research was embedded in the political agenda of a given governing body. The contract often reflected the political needs of a government department and implicitly excluded from the process any excursions by the researcher into detailed and unwanted 'academic' critique. One academic criminologist described contract research with the following metaphor:

> You've been given a torch, some money, to map and classify something. You've been given this torch and there you are rummaging around in this old garage, and the light shines on something; something old and growing – or maybe a dead hand. So some of the unintended consequences of rather straight positivist criminology research is revealing some of the nasty murk. But that's only in the hands of people who can see and recognize it when it happens …. You can't go into the research not ready to see the dead hand. But if the purpose of the research is to make sure the criminal

justice machine and engine runs more smoothly then you'll either not be looking for the murk or you wont be allowed to go near it if you find it.

The ability to explore and examine 'the murk' – forbidden terrains or those areas likely to unveil criticism of the government – may be prohibited by the gatekeepers of information (discussed below) or by contractual clauses that prevent the researcher delivering any material outside the desired product. From a government point of view, the close monitoring of research to ensure value for money is necessary for accountability. From an academic or independent researcher's perspective, it can be viewed as the policing of knowledge, where the contract acts to legalize control and interference in the research (Squires, 1981): what Cohen and Taylor (1972) refer to as 'the legalisation of state secrecy'. These issues are analysed further in the next chapter.

Ethical and Legal Issues

Government legislation

Topics of criminological inquiry often fail to get off the ground because of processes and laws that inhibit their commencement. Such modes of governance include state legislation that prohibits the investigation of issues deemed detrimental to national security (cf. Shearing and Stenning's (1993) work on policing in South Africa) or the internal workings of universities that regulate the production of 'unethical' research. This is not unique to criminological discourses. Fuller (1988) has written extensively on the ways that state bureaucracies create 'forbidden research terrains' on topics of political and economic sensitivity.

Lee (1993) observes that laws often regulate social science research. He argues that academic departments in the United States and the United Kingdom have required academic researchers to submit research proposals to government-regulated boards prior to the commencement of research, for ethical approval (Akeroyd, 1988; Lee, 1993). Moreover, in the United Kingdom, for example, the Official Secrets Act 1911 was enacted to prevent Civil Servants from disclosing or disseminating 'material gathered during research on or about government agencies (including the police)' (Lee, 1993, 22; cf. Hughes, 1996). This legislation continues to influence research commissioned by the Home Office. All researchers contracted by the Home Office are required to sign a declaration binding them to the provisions of the Official Secrets Act. In addition, Home Office employees express a reluctance to speak about their experiences, citing the

Official Secrets Act. Some government criminologists contacted for this book refused to speak at all about their work. One stated:

> As a former government researcher I am covered by the Official Secrets Act, so that I'm not free to provide any concrete instances. Moreover, the political situation has changed immensely in the last year or two, so that repression is really not the problem here that it used to be – to make a fuss about it now could be counter-productive.

This former government employee alludes to the way in which legislation can serve to silence criticisms of the state, as well as blocking research that attempts to understand the processes and practices of the Home Office.

Feenan (2002) identifies how government is increasingly 'using a raft of legislation to force disclosure or keep secret information to serve its own interests' (762). In this important and well-researched article, Dermot Feenan traces the rise of government legislation and case law in the United Kingdom and United States, which permits research material to be subpoenaed, confiscated and/or seized in cases where contents of the research is deemed capable of uncovering or proving illegal behaviour. These emerging forms of government regulation over the research process have the potential to place the researcher and the researched (as well as funding bodies and universities) in difficult and compromising legal situations *vis à vis* confidentiality, defamation and legal liability, which may result in severe penalties, including imprisonment. Feenan (2002) concludes that the 'researcher who chooses now to research offending behaviour with a clear commitment not to disclose details of offense takes a bold step' (779). He suggests that criminologists should seek the advice and support of ethics boards and committees in universities; however, as the discussion below reveals, this form of internal support for academic criminologists is both unreliable and, in some instances, unavailable.

University ethics committees and corporate management

It is not only state legislation and government officials that monitor and regulate research. University ethics committees are increasingly viewed as responding to broader political and economic developments, raising ethical and legal concerns for those conducting research into illegal behaviours. For example, university ethics committees in some jurisdictions are seeking legal opinions on specific subject areas, notably those that intersect criminal behaviour with public health issues such as drug use and HIV (Fitzgerald and Daroesman, 1995). Moreover, legislative changes to mandatory reporting of issues such as child abuse have brought about ethical dilemmas for academic researchers. There are concerns for both the informants, who may incriminate themselves when providing information on illegal activities, as well as for researchers, who may face charges for offences such as contempt of court, concealment of benefit, and aiding and abetting (Fitzgerald, 1995).[6] The inability of researchers to guarantee confidentiality to participants disclosing criminal activity has generated anxiety within some universities.[7] While the vast amount of litigation brought against academics and their institutions involves medical research, there is a growing trend of nervousness surrounding criminologists who engage in ethnographic studies of drug users and drug traffickers. Ferrel and Hamm (1998), for example, point out the growing struggles with ethics committees in US universities, which have become overly regulative of ethnographic research. Loxley and Hawks (1995) argue that legislation should be passed to exclude universities from civil and criminal liabilities related to their research.

Often the first hurdle that an academic criminologist will encounter is her/his university's ethics committee. Decisions about projects of a 'sensitive' nature are often delayed for lengthy periods or alternatively required to be rewritten. In a growing number of cases, criminologists are finding their research proposals totally rejected by ethics committees. One academic criminologist articulated the reasons for this:

> There is an incredible fear [from ethics committees] that if you talk to criminals you'll receive information and then you'll be somehow complicit in the suppression or the non-revelation of that information, which may lead to conspiracy and misprision of felony. There is concern for the individual researcher but the overriding concern is to protect the good name of the university.

As universities become more competitive within market societies there are increasing expectations for academics to provide quality in all aspects of service delivery. The image, as well as the productivity, of the university is essential for advertising and business endeavour. Research projects likely to impinge on the credibility or reputation of a university are sometimes censured by internal committees. Moreover, universities are becoming more 'business-like', including the adoption of codes of conduct and ethical procedures consistent with the practices of commercial entities. Discourses about business ethics have accelerated in the 1990s as commercial enterprises seek mechanisms of self-regulation to enhance conduct and management as well as profit. The deregulation policies of the 1980s provided fertile ground for widespread corporate misconduct, unethical standards and illicit behaviour (Sampford and Wood, 1993). Corporate enterprises throughout the 1990s have embarked on management models that emphasize ethical standards to strengthen customers' and shareholders' confidence, and as a means of accountability geared towards profit-driven effectiveness. For many commentators (see Braithwaite, 1993; Solomon, 1993), internal forms of self-regulation through adherence to ethical practices also attempt to provide alternatives to state forms of legal regulation. Moreover, as Sampford and Wood (1993) argue, there is a fundamental shift in power from the state as governing or regulating agent to company directors and managers.

The emphasis on ethical rather than regulatory solutions protect private power from 'threatened government limitation' (Sampford and Wood, 1993). University management that is based on corporate principles of efficiency is increasingly becoming wedded to business practices, including the concepts of ethics and self-regulation. For the university, however, there are also state mechanisms of governance, ensuring the delivery of specific outputs. The inculcation of business and management principles within universities coupled with state processes of account-ability (fiscal as well as educational) has intensified both the internal and external regulation of the university environment (discussed further in the next chapter).

Criminological research, like all forms of academic scholarship, is rigorously scrutinized by internal regulations, ensuring quality control. Students as well as staff are now required, in many universities, to submit research proposals for ethical clearance; in some instances, academics are required to sign contracts binding them to the regulations imposed by an ethics committee. Moreover, criminological societies are now writing 'codes of ethical conduct' for all members (see, for example, British Society of Criminology, 1999).

Failure to abide by the regulations of a society's ethical standards can result in formal hearings by one's peers and societal sanction.[8] Academic criminologists interviewed for this book expressed increasing frustrations with the ethical demands of their institutions, which were seen as protracted, coercive and governed by principles of 'pure science' and social science. In some instances, academic criminologists are openly resistant to ethical demands that threaten the viability of specific projects.

> Questions have come up at our ethics committees about the measurement of self-reported criminal offending, where we inter-view people and ask them if they've committed serious offences such as rape. The question asked is: what if the matter ended up before the courts and someone was aware of the fact that your self-report instrument had been given to this defendant and you were subpoenaed to produce the results? My answer to that would be very

clear, you would destroy the evidence, if you hadn't been competent enough to do so already. In my view [your own] research ethics requires you to break the law, destroy the questionnaire and go to gaol.

The above quotation alludes to a moral controversy for many criminologists: the decision-making process that guides one's 'own' sense of right and wrong. In other words, what are 'ethics'? and when is a researcher acting ethically or unethically? For Rawls (1971), there are internalized 'rules of morality', which determine actions. For some, the willingness to step outside the regulations of government contracts or ethics committees may be driven by a utilitarian moral philosophy, which perceives the consequences of actions (or inactions) to be more significant than the actions themselves (see Wallace, 1988). There were some criminologists interviewed for this book who expressed an 'ethical egoism' (Wolfram, 1986) implying that 'whatever action is in your own best interests is moral' (Ross, 1998: 27). For others, ethics were culturally specific and continually changing. Moreover many interviewees (notably those conducting comparative and cross-national research) were frequently frustrated and obstructed by 'mono-cultural' ethics committees that failed to acknowledge the different traditions, customs and expectations of other cultures that were crucial for understanding the implementation of diverse methods.

For some criminologists, the situation required skillful and subtle ways to seek ethical clearance. One academic criminologist described this as the politics of getting an application through an ethics committee. This criminologist explained how important it was to do your 'homework': not just the methodological homework, but ensuring the sympathy of the members of the committee.

I let them know that I'm coming, and I find out what they want .... I do my homework, I ring them individually and discuss what I'm planning to do, so there are no surprises. I would never send off an application without contacting the ethics committee first; it's all part of getting approval.

This lobbying of ethics committee personnel has become an essential process for some US criminologists (see Ferrel and Hamm, 1998), as universities become cautious about sensitive topics likely to jeopardize the good name of an institution.

As an alternative to lobbying ethics committees, some academic criminologists are providing formal advisory mechanisms to aid the processing of research applications for colleagues. For example, the British Society of Criminology has recently established an Ethics Panel to assist members with the 'ethical dimensions of research proposals and to offer a general advisory service where members have queries' (Gelsthorpe, 2000).

The clear message conveyed by academic interviewees for this book is that universities are increasingly becoming concerned about litigation and damage to their 'good name'. As a result, there is a growing conservatism in academic management, whereby ethics are used to prevent freedom of inquiry. The dangers of this are well argued by Whyte and Tombs (2003), particularly concerning research on the 'crimes of the powerful', which are placed immediately in the 'high risk' category by university ethics processes because investigation might result in legal liability, corporate pressure or university scandal.

For Foucault (1985) an intellectual's ethical substance and moral conduct should provide the foundations of what he referred to as the 'will to truth'. University ethics committees that continue to place boundaries around 'risky' or deviant research are defining new and narrowly defined regimes of truth. This form of internal governance in the university environment is clearly driven by neo-liberal political rationalities and serves to unwittingly exclude critical scholarship from the criminological agenda.

Securing Support and Sponsorship

The previous chapter explored the ways in which government organizations have been predisposed to policy or politically relevant research. Benyon argues that traditionally the 'rich and powerful have encouraged hagiography, not critical investigation' (Benyon, cited in Hughes, 1996). As a result, the focus of social science has been on the powerless and not on the elite (cf. Hughes, 1996). Given the vast amount of criminological and other social science scholarship that is government-funded, it was deemed important for this research to explore how criminologists approach the issue of securing funding within environments that favour 'relevant' research.

Government funding for policy evaluation often requires the criminologist to assess the performance of state officers. Lee (1993) argues that this research is always 'sensitive' and the outcomes are therefore threatening. As a result, 'the relationship between the researcher and the researched is likely to become hedged about with mistrust, concealment and dissimulation' (Lee, 1993: 2). Payne et al. (1980) refer to a 'fear of scrutiny' existing within government bodies, where the independent researcher is seen to be in search of 'discreditable information'. Some interviewees for this book emphasized the importance of 'courting' or 'networking' with those personnel who make decisions about funding. Whether such people are members of committees or trusts, or government agencies and private industries, there is an unspoken two-way process of 'courting' that is important for winning a grant or contract.

The first aspect to this is an open and more transparent attempt to promote an individual or department research profile, which often includes sending publications and departmental newsletters to specific organizations as a marketing exercise. Alternative methods include the writing of letters to government bodies, including vignettes of departmental staff and their areas of expertise as a means of promoting awareness, or attending seminars organized by funding bodies to access personally those in charge of the criteria for funding while promoting the skills and strengths of university centres and departments.

A second aspect to this courting, however, is subtler and less direct. Many academic criminologists reported how they attempted to 'get on side' with government personnel, initially through 'seeking them out' at conferences and then by expressing a willingness to act as an unpaid advisor or consultant on an *ad hoc* basis. This was often the first informal step towards developing a network and becoming a 'trusted person'. Gaining the trust of government representatives was seen as essential in order for a criminologist to secure government money for research, particularly if that researcher had not previously worked with a specific government body. As one government criminologist stated, 'if you are going to tender out to someone new or you are going to employ someone who hadn't delivered before, then you're taking a risk as a civil servant'.

Government personnel used the word 'trustworthy' to refer to criminologists who had demonstrated an ability to deliver a product on time, to produce a document free of academic jargon and in a format that ministers could understand. Several government employees stated that the worst thing policy officers or civil servants could do in their job was to embarrass a minister. It was, therefore, important that academic criminologists engaged by the bureaucracy could be trusted not to leak information to the press or publicly discuss preliminary findings. Many academics suggested that 'trustworthy' meant more than mere 'calendar reliability'. Most academics used the term to describe criminologists who had delivered a specific product to government without criticizing the work or personnel of the funding department. To this extent, both parties' definitions intersected at the point of avoiding 'government or minister embarrassment'. One academic criminologist stated:

> The organization of criminological research and the funding of it, the construction of networks of trusted individuals and institutions, is a very invisible and informal process that has evolved over a number of years and has a taken-for-grantedness in various circles …. I can tell who will get funding from the Home Office and who will not; who might be able to get funding from the Economic and Social Science Research Council and who will not. I can tell who will get funded by European organizations, European commissions, European parliaments and who probably won't, and so on. I don't think there's a list on a piece of paper anywhere on someone's desk or filing cabinet that says don't fund X, Y or Z but there's a taken-for-grantedness that certain people, because of what they write, won't get funded. They don't fit into the government agenda.

Indeed, some government personnel supported the views in the above quotation, arguing that there were no 'blacklists' written down and kept in a filing cabinet but there were clear preferences about who should be funded. As one government criminologist stated, 'let's just say that some academics are more preferable to others'.

Brusten and Van Outrive (1981) refer to the 'marking-out' of research projects by government as the 'offensive social control of scientific research' by state bureaucracies, which includes 'stimulating, financing and even organising scientific research in order to achieve better administrative control and legitimation' (11). For Brusten and Van Outrive, the growing number of research units within governments across Europe had served to increase the volume of information supporting a particular government's political programme.

For O'Malley (1992), neo-liberal forms of governance in the late twentieth century have produced private markets of 'prudentialism' (private insurances, individual responsibilities for safety and security, etc.), which rely on actuarial assessments of risk. It can also be argued that these risk-focused technologies (for example, private security firms and insurance companies) produce specific forms of knowledge, in similar ways to state agencies, to meet institutional objectives. Criminologists who were interviewed for this research identified similar processes of proving oneself trustworthy when working for private industry. Many interviewees suggested that this involved a two-way courting process and alluded to the seductive nature of governing agencies, notably in relation to future funding. One academic criminologist commented: 'criminal justice agencies are always holding a carrot out and saying that there is going to be more [research money]'.

A common theme expressed by interviewees was the negative

reputation attributed by government officials to criminologists who developed a public profile. If an academic was in any way seen as 'political', that is, speaking out frequently on television and/or radio, then they were labeled as 'untrustworthy' or 'risky'. One academic criminologist noted:

> I have made three applications to the Home Office for funding. I have made two to the Leverhulme Trust, and I have made two to ESRC, they've all failed …. They don't want me doing it. Why? Because they don't want to problematize the liberalisation of the market …. Governments want to encourage local industry not regulate it and I've spoken out about the problems of liberalisating the market …. I just wont get funded.

Many academics see it as their responsibility to engage in public debate, to speak out against unjust or inconsistent political processes. Yet, the acquittal of this academic role, to be a critic and conscience of society, may be a hazardous undertaking, particularly if an academic is seeking to obtain government funding for research. The acquisition of a public profile through frequent media appearances may confer an invisible branding of distrust on the outspoken academic by decision-making bodies. Even though a governing body may view the media comments as inoffensive, or indeed true, several government criminologists acknowledged that the regularity of academics 'going public' created an image of unreliability in the minds of officials, which acts to the detriment of the researcher's future funding prospects.

Form (1973) refers to a 'politics of distrust' surrounding the funding of social science research and access to information. He argues that interpersonal relationships based on trust are crucial to the funding of research. Lee (1993) endorses this point, stating that 'trust is facilitated because those within the relationship have much information about each other arising from self-disclosure and from observations of past actions' (123).

Many interviewees also suggested that for those criminologists 'on the outside' – that is, not trusted by government authorities – there were ways of securing research money, which included reassuring funding bodies with a 'package' of different people from diverse disciplines. One academic criminologist commented:

> There is something quite pathological about the way research is organized. You get all these senior people lined up, all these names of big senior people as though that is going to ensure some wonderful

> product. What a joke! I've been involved in one study as a chief investigator and I haven't really been involved …. These people get their names on the proposals just to get a grant or whatever, so there's all this kind of packaging as a way of selling it.

The above comments demonstrate the ways in which some criminologists attempt to impress funding bodies with lengthy research proposals that include the names and curriculum vitaes of senior, respected and 'trusted' academics. The proposals often do not reflect the realities of how the research will get done, but are deliberately designed to attract resources. This is not only an emerging response to the increased competitiveness of funded research, but it's also an academic response to university pressures to 'bring in money'. The 'padding out' of research tenders to include various scholars, often from more than one institution, serves to maximize a successful application. In addition, those academics who have had applications for funding repeatedly rejected (for whatever reason) can begin to establish a successful 'grant record' among the safety of a large group. However, as reported by several interviewees, there is often very little genuine commitment to the contract, but rather a degree of 'game playing'. The idea is to be one of the named investigators on a successful contract with a team of six or more others so that the workload is shared around. As a result, the academic criminologist is playing institutional politics with their university. They are raising the required revenue for their university while committing as little time as possible to a research project that is of very little interest to them.

This research has also explored why certain areas of criminological inquiry are funded over others. The previous chapter demonstrated that applied or policy-relevant and administrative research had the greatest utility for governing bodies and was, therefore, preferred to theoretical or historical work. This argument is not always watertight, however. Occasionally, criminologists with outspoken or critical reputations receive large Home Office or NIJ grants. For those criminologists who see themselves in this category, they argue that their expertise may be unique and, therefore, their inclusion in the research gives the government department certain credibility. There are also isolated examples of theoretical projects receiving significant government sponsorship. As one academic criminologist stated:

> … there are individuals who have been funded who you would think would not get funded …. And the reason for this is that there are very few other people in Britain who can get as close to real criminality in certain areas as X. The Home Office has in recent years

attempted to try and get closer to real crime and they've had to use someone like X.

There are also examples of large government grants that have been awarded to theoretical criminological projects. At first glance, this appears to contradict arguments that criminological scholarship is governed by funding arrangements that favour applied or relevant research. However, when analysed within neo-liberal political rationalities, it can be argued that isolated examples of government resources for historical and theoretical research fall within advanced liberal notions of elitism. Rose (1996) points out that neo-liberalism attempts to govern through promoting individual responsibility as well as the advancement of market economies characterized by competition. The perpetuation of the 'elite' serves to maintain power or technologies of rule (Donzelot, 1979) while purporting to represent an 'equal playing-field' (discussed later).

Gathering and Accessing Data

Hughes (1996) points out that gaining access to information while conducting criminological research is an ongoing process of negotiating and renegotiating, one that can often be highly 'procedurized and personalised' (cf. Lee, 1993). Hughes also argues that the 'gatekeepers' of information may be positioned at various levels within a given organization and, therefore, a criminologist must become astute at 'getting in'(accessing a department or agency) and 'getting on' (with those gatekeepers) (cf. Bell and Newby, 1977; Jupp, 1989). The need to develop rapport with those holding essential information is most important. Hobbs provides an amusing description of the lengths that researchers must go to to 'get on' with these gatekeepers. Following his work on police officers in South London, he wrote:

> For the most part I spoke, acted, drank and generally behaved as though I was not doing research. Indeed, I often had to remind myself that I was not in a pub to enjoy myself but to conduct an academic inquiry and repeatedly woke up the following morning with an incredible hangover facing the dilemma of whether to bring it up or write it up (Hobbs, 1988: 6).

Punch (1985) was to observe similar experiences in his ethnographic study of police corruption in Amsterdam. He argued that police officers became adept at masking the truth or providing various cover stories to allegation of corruption. Irrespective of the vast amount of time spent in the field with patrol officers, Maurice Punch was unable to get beneath what he suspected was a charade of superficial lies. Eventually, the success of his project came when he portrayed himself as an ally and not an auditor. This was largely achieved by deleting the word 'corruption' from all research proposals and methodologies. Only when he became 'trusted' would police reveal the reality of corruption and, even then, 'only because some of the officers had had too much to drink' (Punch, 1985, cited in Jupp, 1989: 152).

Accessing information may create obstacles for researchers across various social science disciplines. As mentioned above, state legislation, such as the Official Secrets Act in the United Kingdom, can create barriers to accessing information, notably 'commercially sensitive material'. Legislation can also be used positively to obtain data. For example, Mackenzie (1999) used the Freedom of Information Act (FOI) in the United States to reveal how federal agencies have systematically regulated public access to information. His research focused on the CIA and reveals that this US intelligence service routinely censors and suppresses information from public scrutiny, or alternatively destroys documents considered to be 'damaging' to national security. Many other social scientists in the United States have used the FOI Act to reveal state malpractice and corruption (see Harris, 1980). While acknowledging that accessing confidential government papers in the United States improved under the Clinton administration, Price (1997) argues that fieldwork that relies on the FOI Act remains fraught with difficulties. He reports that the FBI and CIA, for example, may take as long as three to five years to process the simplest FOI requests, that these agencies charge up to US $500 for a basic search, and that it is common that requested information is blacked-out on receipt.

Criminologists interviewed for this book expressed a reluctance to access government documents through FOI legislation. There was a general perception that government officials view such requests as 'threatening' and hence many researchers prefer to build rapport with the appropriate agency in the interests of maintaining an ongoing and positive relationship. Noaks (1999) points out the importance of developing and maintaining good contacts. Her work on the cultures of private police in the United Kingdom details the significance of face-to-face encounters with potential informants as well as sporadic telephone calls, all in the interests of 'cultivating' positive working relationship that would enhance data collection.

Hughes (1996), citing the works of Brewer (1991) and Punch (1993), identifies various informal obstacles that confront criminologists when accessing information. These are institutional barriers that may be quite invisible to the researcher and even unexpected, yet which serve to prevent the researcher from obtaining a close-up view of an organization's internal workings. Brusten (1981) identifies several common reasons presented by state officials for declining access to information. These include suggesting the research would cause disturbance to the daily routines of the government department, which would be of disadvantage to the public, or suggesting there was a shortage of time and that the department could not spare anyone to assist the researchers, or that the agency did not have the resources to fulfil the researcher's request.

These types of responses to requests for information may be legitimate reasons for denying accessing to information or they may be orchestrated techniques to prohibit the gathering of data. Either way, the researcher will often be unable to deduce categorically the 'real' reasons for denied access. Hence several interviewees for this book suggested that criminologists must develop techniques and strategies for negotiating obstacles, if, and when, they appear. These include redesigning the methodology to appear less suspicious to a government agency, establishing an informal arrangement with the government body (for example, a joint media release or public presentation), bringing in known and trusted researchers to be part of the project, establishing informal contacts with relevant government personnel in an attempt to develop rapport, and so on.

Brookman's (1999) analysis of police murder files in England shows that accessing sensitive data owes 'little to the value of the research, and more to serendipity, determination and good negotiation skills' (48). Brookman describes how she formally wrote to senior police commanders, requesting access to police files. Sometimes, this approach resulted in rejection, yet she was able to overcome initial refusals by drawing upon a network of 'trusted' personnel, concluding that 'who you know is a crucial factor in opening up the gateway for research, particularly in sensitive areas as homicide' (Brookman, 1999: 50).

There are occasions when accessing information is simply impossible. Norris (1993) argues that criminologists may be required to engage in what he calls 'overt and covert roles' (cf. Adler, 1985). The overt role is the honest disclosure of what the research intends to achieve; the covert role may consist of the researcher providing an explanation that is 'understandable and acceptable to the researched' (Norris, 1993: 129), not necessarily a dishonest account of one's intentions but a deliberate attempt to 'sell' the research to subjects under review. As described above in the research by Punch (1985), criminologists occasionally do not disclose the real intentions of their research for fear of outright rejection by the official body under review. Hence words such as 'corruption', 'malpractice', 'misadventure' and so on will not be written into proposals or letters requesting access. In this sense, the criminologist may develop a 'cover story' (Noaks, 1999: 150; cf. Jupp, 1989) to pursuade the subjects of the research to grant access to information (see also Calvey, 2000). In other words, they create methods to present the research to the researched in ways that have them believe that the project will benefit their cause. Fountain (1993) argues that such persuasive endeavours to gain access to otherwise 'off-limits' material may provide the criminologists with ethical compromises (cf. Noaks, 1999); yet an up-front account of one's intentions, particularly if they are of a sensitive nature to the organization concerned, is likely to jeopardize the ability to gather any meaningful data. As one academic criminologist commented:

> Ethnographic research about crime can be very very dangerous. You've got to play a part like a stage actor and do things that you wouldn't normally do …. But if you want to really know what goes on in the world of say, organized crime, then you've got to get in on the inside and you don't do that by saying 'hey, I'm going to write a book about all your dodgy deals'; you do it by gaining trust, and that can be very hard work.

As a result, criminological research can be a risky exercise for the researcher. One academic criminologist interviewed for this research explained how ethnographic research on criminals could often lead to suspicion of the researcher. This particular criminologist became subject to daily police surveillance and stated:

> People had this view that because I'd written about crime from an ethnographic perspective that I was actually doing it as well. It's ridiculous. As if people who do work on mental health are nutcases or people who do work on rapists are rapists themselves. But it was so rare at that time and still is, I guess, for academics to do work with criminals. You became suspects particularly if your demeanour and your language fitted a very crude profile.

Kirby and Corzine (1981) refer to the above as 'stigma contagion', where the researcher shares the stigma of the deviant population under review. Alternatively, some writers have suggested that 'occupational stigmatization' (see Troiden, 1987) is a label conferred on researchers who are assumed to have something in common with their criminal subjects. As a result, their careers may be jeopardized (promotion, future funding) by ethnographic work on underworld populations.

A further example of the personal and professional risks associated with researching sensitive areas of criminal justice came from one academic criminologist who was interviewed for this research, and who had co-authored a monograph on police shootings. His research concluded that the police had been negligent and had failed to follow proper procedures when investigating the shootings. His research received media headlines and he spoke publicly about his findings on radio and television. As a result his access to all police personnel was immediately terminated. Police officers whom he had known for years suddenly became hostile or unavailable and his informal requests for information were ignored. Within seven days of his report's release, he was burgled twice, and his co-author's place of work was also burgled. The only items that were stolen were computers, software and documents relating to the research. Moreover, this academic criminologist recalls close police surveillance:

> Both myself and my co-author were subject to ongoing police monitoring, they were using electronic surveillance to track our movements and were very keen to find out the people we'd been talking to .... We were both very active with a local community radio station that broadcasted civil liberty issues and promoted a lot of alternative voices. The police planted a spy at the radio station that worked as a volunteer and it was discovered that his job was to infiltrate our networks and find out as much as he could about our work.

Much of the above fieldwork was covert criminological research. Not only does it raise questions associated with researcher risk but it also raises important issues about informed consent. Gaining the informed consent of the researched is a cornerstone of social science research. As discussed earlier, ethical codes of universities and academic societies actively promote and protect the principle of informed consent. Hughes (1996) argues that there will, however, be occasions when criminological research, particularly that involving 'the powerful and the privileged', must bypass the necessity of obtaining informed consent (Hughes, 1996: 77; cf. Tombs and Whyte, 2003). This form of 'undercover' research seeks to access information that would otherwise be unobtainable by conventional methods. The organization holding the data will have a vested interest in maintaining the good name of their industry. Researchers that attempt to unearth and publish sensitive material are seen as a threat, and agency personnel will either decline access altogether or offer access to standard, uncontroversial material (Lee, 1993). Government departments do not wish to be seen as uncooperative, and in many instances have legislative obligations to fulfil public requests for information. However, researchers will often be denied access to information of any real significance. As one academic criminologist noted:

> You'll get some government departments that couldn't be friendlier. They send you mountains of stuff, glossy booklets, brochures, mountains of paper but it's all totally useless. It's the sort of material you can get off the internet or from a bookshop but it's not the real stuff and the government department knows that, but they don't want anyone saying that they were uncooperative with your research.

Simon and Eitzen (1990: 247) refer to this as a form of political deviance. They claim that the hallmark of any democratic society is the 'reliable flow of information from government'. They argue that government officials who fail to release information of value with the express intent of avoiding external scrutiny often disrupt this flow. For Foucault (1978) this 'conduct of others' conduct' is an insidious form of technocratic power. He argues that governments that claim to prescribe the 'truth' yet prevent or express indifference to it are 'dangerous'. The right to question the truth is subverted by governmental rationalities through mechanisms of power, including policies that require specific processes and practices to be formally adhered to. As a result, Foucault suggests that a critique will be a 'movement by which the subject assumes the right to question truth on its effects of power, and power on its effects of truth – the art of voluntary nonservitude of considered nondocility' (Foucault, cited in Gordon, 2002: xxxix).

The processes of gathering data can also be impeded by official agencies that disagree with methodology or feel threatened by potential outcomes. Cohen and Taylor's (1972) work on long-term imprisonment and its effects on inmates in British prisons has been widely used as an example of how official agencies attempt to delegitimatize research by criticizing methodology. In this case, Cohen and Taylor were denied permission by the Home Office to publish their work-in-progress in the journal *New Society*. The Prison Department of the Home Office objected to the research focusing on specific aspects of incarceration, namely psychological trauma, as well as its 'journalistic' methodology (see Cohen and Taylor, 1972). Cohen and Taylor proceeded to publish their intended article and, as a result, were denied subsequent contact with inmates. Moreover, letters that the researchers wrote to inmates who had participated in their study were returned and the Home Office eventually refused to support the study any further (see Cohen and Taylor, 1972). Bell and Newby (1977) report that for years after publishing their work, Laurie Taylor continued to face barriers at the Home Office. Taylor was banned by the Home Office from entering borstals and remand centres in Britain for the purposes of compiling a BBC documentary on delinquency because, as official sources revealed, 'a book he wrote several years ago about how long-term prisoners coped psychologically with their years inside ... had contravened the Official Secrets Act' (Bell and Newby, 1977: 173).

Reiner (1992) argues that agencies of the criminal justice system may actively seek out the reputation of a researcher in order to establish if they can be trusted (cf. Hughes, 1996).

Gathering and accessing data for criminological research is thus not always a straightforward process. It requires an ability to negotiate protocols, to persevere, to develop rapport with the researched, and to gain trust, while at the same time adhering to the original intentions of the research. Not only is there a commitment to honour the objectives of the research but there is also a responsibility to publish work for public debate.

Publishing Results

Free speech and the importance of publishing criminological research

Hughes (2000) notes that when research is published it enters another political realm, whereby different audiences may feel 'damaged or threatened by the publication of criminological findings' (244).

That said, the main purpose of doing research is to produce results. These may take various forms, including the production of a report for government, publication of a book, or a journal article. Irrespective of the means by which the research has been funded or contracted, academic criminologists have an obligation to make public their work. As Jupp (1989) argues, 'there is an obligation to publish findings and conclusions so that they enter the public domain, not simply in search of personal gratification or to satisfy academic peers but, more fundamentally, because the issues of criminology are of great social and political concern' (156). Here Jupp points to the social and political relevance of criminology – not a policy or government relevance, but one that is capable of advancing public debate, challenging the status quo and uncovering social and political injustices.

In New Zealand, the Education Act (1990) makes special mention of academic freedom (see section 161 (2)) as well as legal obligations for university academics to be 'critic and conscience of society' (section 161 (4)(a)(v)). Here, then, there is a legal obligation and not merely a moral obligation to publish research. The Act states that the purpose of academic freedom should be 'the freedom of academic staff and students, within the law, to question and test received wisdom, to put forward new ideas and state controversial or unpopular opinions' (section 161 (2) (a)).

Other countries without the legislative protections afforded to New Zealand academics have adopted codes of responsibility within the individual charters of universities or academic societies. For example, the Australian and New Zealand Society of Criminology Code of Ethics promotes the dissemination of knowledge and 'the protection and enhancement of intellectual freedom; and the creation of free and independent criminological inquiry' (Australian and New Zealand Society of Criminology, 2000). Similar statements about ethical responsibilities are made by the British Society of Criminology (see Gelsthorpe *et al.*, 1999). The American Society of Criminology also promotes the publication of research. In doing so, it defines unethical conduct as the omission of significant data from published results. Failure to comply with any section of the ASC Code of Ethics may result in sanctions, including 'restrictions or termination of membership' (American Society of Criminology, 1998).

The restructuring of the university sector in Western democracies in recent years has influenced the traditional roles of higher education as well as altering the conditions under which academics work. It is important to recognize that neo-liberal political rationalities in late modernity have been identified as threatening concepts of free speech at an international level. Take, for example, the media – industries that have enjoyed widespread freedom to publish or broadcast items for public debate and consumption. So important is their role that, ever since the US Supreme Court ruling in New York Times Co. versus Sullivan (1964), the media have been permitted legally 'a margin for error in the search for truth'. Yet Sanford (1999), America's foremost expert on constitutional law, argues that First Amendment freedoms in the United States are systematically being eroded by legal challenges that attempt to sue for libel any party that threatens to publish material of a deleterious nature about a multi-national industry. He suggests that, in a market-led society, 'truth' becomes subservient to commercial principles of efficiency and economic gain. Sanford, (1999) argues that the silencing of the media results in the public's understanding of events being generated by governing authorities, for which 'there is no more certain road to the loss of freedom' (10). The silencing of media voices who opposed the Bush Administration's invasions of Afghanistan and Iraq in 2002–03 have further demonstrated the rise of government intolerance to criticism and the suppression of dissent. The following chapter will explore these issues further.

Government techniques of neutralization

For now, it is important to chart some of the difficulties experienced by criminologists when they attempt to publish their work. It is true that not many criminologists are sued. While most withstand some degree of influence or pressure, very few have their contracts or grants rescinded or are taken to court. Avoiding legal conflict arose as a constant theme in the interviews for this book. Some interviewees argued that negotiation or compromise (depending on one's view) was a legitimate and necessary skill when doing research. Avoiding conflict with a funding body or an agency could be achieved by adopting an open and consultative approach to research, which included discussing preliminary observations and phrasing critical findings in a positive light. Many interviewees stated that research funded by government bodies is routinely subject to vetting or approvals prior to release, and this can often involve debate between the researcher and the funding body. The most common experience was the delayed release of research findings. The more unfavourable the findings of a given government agency, the more lengthy the delay there was before publication. Interviewees reported the postponing of release as a deliberate strategy by government to allow time to implement the necessary policy changes identified in a report's recommendations. Therefore, by the time a research report is receiving publicity, all its critical comments about government processes and practices have been addressed. As one academic criminologist stated, 'governments can sit on a report for up to a year; that is very common and it's very frustrating for the researcher ... it's quite a predetermined strategy to avoid bad press'.

Interviewees also reported that not releasing reports was once a common government response to a critical report; yet nowadays there is greater pressure on state departments to be accountable for public expenditure. Sometimes a summary or a portion of a report will be released. The sections released are often those that most favourably reflect the work of a given government department. Hughes (2000) refers to the 'utilization of criminological research by policy-makers' where government officials can 'pick and choose' the sections of a report that most suitably fit the government agenda and 'banish' or 'secretly shelve' the areas that are critical of government or fail to support existing policy directions (245–46). This observation was overwhelmingly supported by interviewees for this research. This process also occurs with government-produced reports, as one government criminologist noted:

The Home Secretary was very, very sharp and he was meticulous when reading reports .... On one occasion he respectfully suggested that we expand or re-work our statistical analysis, because he knew that that particular section would show a slight reduction for certain crimes and would, therefore, support his policies at the time.

Another common occurrence was that criminologists were often required to alter or omit a paragraph or adopt a different terminology. Sometimes such changes can appear subtle and inconsequential and will often be referred to by government officials as 'nit-picky' or 'pedantic'; yet they may significantly change the meaning of what is being said. For example, one academic criminologist was required by a Home Office contract to have all material cleared before publication for a period of 12 months after submitting a report. In a subsequent publication, the Home Office insisted that the article had certain terminology changed.

> The Home Office said: 'We don't say racist victimisation we say racial victimisation', and he went through my article and changed every 'racist' to 'racial'. I resented that bitterly. In a way it's a minor point, but analytically very important because racial pertains to race and racist pertains to racism. Analytically there is a distinction, they mean different things. Having done this piece of work as a consultant, the Home Office felt that the work was owned by them ... and they forced me to adopt that terminology .... It was galling, but how do you get around it, by not showing it to the Home Office and arguing it after the fact .... But at the time I was going for another Home Office consultancy and one of the managers told me that I 'had won the confidence of the office' so I interpret that as meaning that if I hadn't changed the terminology I would not have be given any future work.

The above quotation alludes to a common problem identified by several interviewees, namely, what to do when confronted with a conflict of interest. Several interviewees perceived their own universities to be of little assistance. Many academics decided to deal with contractual issues on their own in preference to seeking internal advice. As one academic criminologist commented:

> The universities in this country are not experienced in dealing with those kinds of problems. You've got people in senior positions of the university from other disciplines, quite often from the science faculty ... the problems I've had with the Home Office would be alien to the senior management of universities, because they wouldn't know what to do. So the people I look to are public relations staff who know journalists.

In some instances, academic criminologists have sought or received support from government officials. In other words, one government department has wished to see a report published, while another has not. Hence, as previously mentioned, the executive of government is not a monolith but often a collection of diverse units, each competing for resources, and each attempting to achieve its own priorities and objectives. One academic criminologist who had received government support to have research published stated:

> There is a misconception of the state as a single entity; one part of the state can take a very different stance from another. In relation to my work, one government department in England was attempting to prevent my book from being published by discrediting my research with all sorts of false accusations. At the same time, however, the Scottish Office and the Scottish legal authorities were incredibly supportive and were telling me to stick to my guns. The Scottish Office had funded the research and they saw the value of the findings and they were prepared to stick their necks out against the people in England, and that sort of support was very important to me at the time, and very important for getting the research published.

The majority of interviewees, however, had not experienced the level of government support referred to in the above quotation. Some mentioned receiving support from junior government officers against the critical objections of their more senior colleagues. However, receiving support from a second government department was rare. The above example highlights the potential avenues that criminologists can, and should, pursue if conflict arises with a governing body.

Some interviewees described the strength of going public by involving the media when pressured to alter findings or when reports were being suppressed. Most interviewees suggested that they would more than likely consent to minor changes or rewrites, but would not permit a report to be 'sat on'. When research was suppressed, most criminologists expressed a commitment to ensure that the report reached the public realm. Braithwaite (1996) argues that academics should go public if a government attempts to suppress a report or to use a contract to prevent academics from publishing: 'I say, "You can try and stop me and you can probably take away the report, but that would be foolish because I will go to the press and get the report out in a much better way"' (quoted in Smellie, 1996).

When academic criminologists 'leak' reports to the press (as several reported to have done when confronted with suppression) or deliberately violate contractual clauses and publish material without government approval, then there is an attempt to discredit the researcher, in what Sanford above refers to as 'shooting the messenger'. Often the government response will be to challenge or renegotiate the methodology rather than question the integrity of the researcher; however, when criminological research conflicts with existing government policy and practice there is a risk that researchers may experience an attempt to discredit their work. As Sim *et al.* (1987) argue, research that is outspoken or critical is often disparaged as unscientific, whereas 'if criminologists were prepared to kiss the state, then their research would be regarded as legitimate and scientific' (11). One academic criminologist described the way in which his research, which was critical of a government department, was neutralized by the department's attempt to discredit his statsitics:

> The government department went into discredit mode .... Saying the statistics in the book were old and didn't reflect the situation as it is today and you can't make these comparisons across time because the way the statistics are gathered ... basically just trying to say that I didn't know what I was talking about.

A good example of discrediting the criminologist's work is found in the case of Associate Professor Kerry Carrington (formerly of the University of Western Sydney), who published *Who Killed Leigh Leigh: A Story of Shame and Mateship in an Australian Town*. This book, released in 1998, examined the police investigation into the rape and murder of a 14-year old girl named Leigh Leigh at a beach party in Newcastle, New South Wales. Dr Carrington traced the events that ultimately led to the conviction of an 18-year-old male, for murder but not for rape. She reports how several males participated in group acts of sexual and physical assault against the victim but were never charged by the police. In her opening chapter, Dr Carrington argues that for the police 'rape doesn't matter', and that the police failed to pursue acts of sexual violation despite overwhelming evidence that such crimes had occurred:

> The police investigation left many questions unresolved. Prosecutions for the rape of the murder victim were never pursued by the investigating police, despite graphic evidence of severe genital injuries and witness evidence of a planned group sexual assault .... The book tells a tale of what can happen when shame and mateship mix with a small-town mentality. It paints a wider portrait

of a culture and a community with a relatively high threshold of tolerance for sexual violence of the kind that occurred at the ill-fated party and of a justice system that considers rape largely irrelevant in cases like this (Carrington, 1998, pp. x–xi).

Dr Carrington's research subsequently became involved in two separate judicial enquiries in New South Wales, and subsequent events are worth describing here in some detail.

Dr Carrington was subpoenaed to court and spent three full days in the witness box. Throughout her three-day cross-examination by six different Queen's Councillors, Dr Carrington's credibility as a researcher and an academic were constantly challenged. Colleagues close to Dr Carrington, who witnessed the events as they unfolded, published their version of them and described how the cross-examination was an 'aggressive inquisition'. In conclusion, Byrne-Armstrong *et al.* (1999) argued that the entire inquiry was an institutional justification for the processes of law, one that aimed to silence and discredit any person who had criticized the conduct of the New South Wales Police Service:

> The hearing became a discursive battleground in which law's power to pronounce final and authoritative judgment on the crime of Leigh Leigh was jealously defended against what was depicted as the unscientific and emotionally based knowledge claims of a feminist criminologist (Bryne-Armstrong *et al.*, 1999: 23–24).

Transcripts of the court case identify the methods used to discredit Dr. Carrington, including the identification of her as a non-lawyer and challenges to her qualifications, all as evidence that she was not entitled to criticize the legal system. The following is a brief excerpt from the court transcript:

> Madam, you are an Associate Professor, aren't you? I don't mean to be facetious but you are an Associate Professor? I'm going to suggest to you straight up-front that what you are doing is hiding behind your academic background because you realise that what you have been saying either personally, or allowing others to publish on your behalf, is absolute rubbish; do you understand that … I suggest to you your real motive in all this is to make your allegations as controversial as possible because you know by creating controversy that will, in effect, sell the book …. This lady has written a book and made countless interviews, without speaking to people qualified to tell her precisely what occurs in a court of law before she wrote the book.

That's what concerns me and should concern an inquiry, because that's how the allegations came about, because of her ignorance (PIC transcripts, 1999, cited in Byrne-Armstrong *et al.*, 1999).

Byrne-Armstrong *et al.* (1999) conclude that the eight lawyers representing the police set about creating an image of Dr Carrington as an ignorant hypocrite as a matter of strategy, someone pushing her own agenda, a sick person, an 'hysterical feminist – which they aimed to use against the image of the corrupt police' (35). As a result, Dr Carrington was scapegoated; her professional reputation was attacked in an attempt to discredit all allegations against the police.[9]

Scraton (2001a) refers to this process as a form of state deviance, whereby knowledge that fails to support existing government policy may be subjected to various techniques of neutralization. Drawing on Sykes and Matza's analysis, Scraton (2001a) argues that state officials, through the use of contracts and the production of administrative criminology, actively disqualify alternative or critical accounts. Moreover, government officials who fail to release reports, challenge statistics or main findings, and threaten to pay final instalments on contracts, are enacting techniques that neutralize or silence the critical voice. He suggests that criminological researchers need to move towards various forms of resistance, which I will discuss later.

More senior criminologists stated that they 'could afford to be brave': namely, they were tenured professors and their livelihoods were not on the line. They argued that they could publish controversial work and did not feel the pressure to conform to government regulations or to seek publishing clearance. More junior academics, on short-term contracts arising out of specific government-funded research projects, were far more vulnerable and had more to lose by not delivering the exact product specified in a commercial arrangement or by not conforming to the regulations or arrangements of government officials. As one academic criminologist stated:

At the time I had a young family, I had responsibilities outside of academia. So you feel vulnerable when your job could be on the line. If the Home Office or whoever says you can't publish something then if your job's on the line you're in a dilemma …. On that occasion I couldn't afford to be out of work so I allowed them to sit on my report and didn't publish anything …. I wouldn't do that now.

The circumstances surrounding one's life can often influence the type of research undertaken and the ways in which a researcher will respond to the various methods of regulation and governance discussed above. As Foucault (1980b) argued, a scholar's work will be influenced 'at the precise points where their own conditions of life and work situate them' (126).

Academic criminology and internal interference

Many interviewees also pointed to censorship of criminological work from within academia, claiming that the publication of chapters and refereed journal articles is often contingent on a network of ideologically sympathetic colleagues: 'It gets read by an editor that you were at the same university as and it gets very very incestuous, and that's at the other end of the scale to people who work for the system'. Moreover, several interviewees suggested that their applications for funding with government research bodies or trusts were often savagely criticised at the refereeing stage by academics with an ideological agenda!

Lynch (1989) has written extensively on the politics of academic publications, arguing that work that challenges dominant liberal assumptions is often rejected by professional journals. This issue was recently debated among criminologists in the United States. Arrigo (1999) suggested that critical scholarship is often rejected for publication in well-known peer-reviewed journals because critical criminologists 'challenge existing political, economic, and social structural dynamics' (10). These comments led to a content analysis of America's leading criminological journals (*Criminology, Justice Quarterly* and *Law and Society Review*). This study concurred with the views of Arrigo (1999), in stating that 'the data suggest that the Editors of *Criminology* should make greater effort to publish critical research' (Wright, 2000a: 2). Moreover, Wright's (2000b) analysis of introductory criminological textbooks published between 1990 and 1999 concluded that contemporary critical/radical perspectives were often 'left out' of such books. Moreover, Tombs and Whyte (2003) can identify no published textbooks in Britain that contain a detailed analysis of state crime and only four that focus on corporate crime (cf. Green and Ward, 2003). They came to similar conclusions about academic journals, stating: 'there remains a dearth of criminological state and corporate crime research being published in mainstream British criminology journals'.

Some interviewees for this research argued that criminological scholarship *per se* could receive a bad reputation by the critical work of one of two outspoken academics. One academic criminologist felt that, 'if someone gets a large government contract then it's important that they do a good job because it can effect all of us'. This comment is linked to what Lee (1993) refers to as the 'chilling effect'. Academics sometimes receive pressure from colleagues not to publish or disseminate information that is not 'politically correct' or damaging to a discipline's reputation.

Other interviewees stated that it was not uncommon for some academics to attempt to usurp the work of others. One academic, who had edited several different journals, reported regular interference from criminologists attempting to prevent the publication of specific works. Often the desire to prevent publication by 'bad mouthing' a given research project or a specific individual was reportedly driven by a motivation to protect one's supply of contract research. This academic criminologist commented: 'You get people ringing you up and saying that X's work is not methodologically sound or that Y's work, if published, could risk everyone's future prospects of getting money from the NIJ ... it's direct interference and it can be very very nasty.'

Furthermore, academic colleagues label some criminologists as 'mavericks', 'media sluts' or 'anti-authoritarians'. These criminologists often 'earn' their reputations by publicly and frequently criticizing the government on radio or television. These phenomena had the effect of alienating or marginalizing the more outspoken criminologists within their own departments or disciplines. Those labelled as mavericks and the like reported that there was a tendency for their work to be dismissed or considered as less significant by peers and/or government officials. One academic criminologist argued that being outspoken and critical was risky; there was always the likelihood that you could become ostracized by members of your own discipline:

> I am regarded as a working-class anti-authoritarian .... People see me as having a good time, drinking with the criminals and criticizing the bosses. They call me a spiv .... I get put in a box and called a maverick ... it's one way of downgrading what I do. What I say makes a lot of people feel uncomfortable so I get these smear campaigns from academics and backhanded comments that I'm some sort of rogue who shouldn't be taken seriously.

Interviewees who reported alienation within their own fields, by their own colleagues, referred to the class make-up of academia, suggesting that the overwhelming majority of criminologists came from middle-class backgrounds not characterized by struggle or oppression. Others concluded that the changing environment of the university sector was placing pressure on outspoken academics to be more conformist.

There were also several examples of more junior academics claiming that they had been 'encouraged' by more senior staff to 'tone-down' their research or not publish it at all in the interests of career development. As one academic criminologist stated:

I got an encouragement not to publish. A suggestion that were I to publish my work it would be damaging to my prospects of getting further work. Certainly it did endanger me getting research funding and endanger my relationships with the criminal justice system … I got so discouraged I tried to get out of academe and had there been more jobs, I'd have been out of it. So happens I didn't get those jobs.

These examples demonstrate what Brusten (1981) refers to as the 'self censorship' of criminological research. He suggests that government and state agencies do not need to regulate or interfere with the processes of independent research, 'as long as criminologists – for whatever reason – practice effective self-censorship in order to evade any conflict problem' (Brusten, 1981: 70). This, of course, extends to the censorship of 'outspoken' colleagues or those deemed to threaten future contracts or grants. The outspoken criminologists often feel vulnerable and wish to protect their future employment prospects. They may be influenced or censored by academic colleagues from their own and other universities. Alternatively, they may be alienated within their field, that is, moved to the periphery and labelled with derogatory terms that attempt to undermine their credibility.

Governing government criminologists

It is also important to note that criminologists working within government are often subject to a range of internal conflicts and tensions from senior public officials. Government criminologists expressed ongoing frustration with not having their names attributed to documents they had written, and several identified that the overwhelming and burdensome nature of their workload prevented them from pursuing a detailed analysis. However, in several instances, criminologists working in government identified deliberate interference with their work. One government criminologist had written a literature review, which concluded that increasing the numbers of police was not going to reduce crime in England and Wales. It summarized all the available research and stated that more police on the streets was not an effective solution to increasing crime. This became very embarrassing for the Home Secretary, who refused to publish the report since it contradicted the public statements of the prime minister. This criminologist stated:

I was told that I was being a tremendous nuisance and causing senior people a lot of worry. It's not very nice to have the Home Secretary angry with you if you're in the Home Office. This sort of tension is not uncommon with government criminology. But honestly I don't see how it can be avoided ... because crime policy is mostly not based on data or empirical facts, it's mostly based on politics. Politicians come in thinking that they know how to deal with crime so they issue their manifestos and promises, then they find that in the Home Office there are people who are publishing things that says that what they've been saying is rubbish.

Moreover, this interviewee emphasized how attempts by government criminologists to re-evaluate crime policy and challenge existing government initiatives were likely to draw criticism or a stony silence:

If you're going to do policy-relevant research in a government department you can either simply produce facts and figures for applied mundane counting exercises on the number of people in prison and how many of them have come from broken homes and so on. But if you are really trying to produce studies that have one re-evaluate policy then you're going to have trouble. Put yourself in the position of a senior administrator in a government department; you don't want some research officer telling you how to run the place, you've already got the minister telling you how to run the place.

Therefore, criminologists within government sometimes experience censorship and regulation. Unlike academics, government employees working in criminal justice research are not granted legislative protections for academic freedom and are often legally required to produce research that satisfies the requirements of a senior manager.

That said, several government criminologists consulted for this book identified that the research aspect of their job had been reduced in recent years. They were now spending most of their time writing responses to ministerial questions or preparing research specifications for tender. Many felt that their skills as researchers were underutilized. As a result, they had become more like administrators than researchers and, therefore, past examples of censorship or control from senior officials had diminished, as they were rarely given the opportunity to produce something provocative or controversial.

Concluding Comment

As discussed at the commencement of this chapter, research is a powerful tool and is capable of challenging those that govern in a way that threatens their power. Irrespective of the content of criminological research, when released it enters a political arena that affects many audiences, including politicians, funders, the researched, other academics, the public, as well as the researchers involved (Hughes, 2000). What has been described above is the mobilization of power as part of the process of the policing of deviant knowledge. Not only does it convey how criminological scholarship may be governed but it also conveys a sense of the personal struggles faced by criminologists – such as illness, termination of employment, and barriers to future funding – which may affect career development.

Irrespective of the seniority or inexperience of the criminologist, or her/his place in academia or government, researching and publishing politically sensitive and institutionally threatening areas of social science are often susceptible to government rebuke and/or challenge (Lee, 1993).

This research shows that the expectations placed on public servants to deliver research consistent with a minister's official position often produces a domino effect on contracted researchers from within academia. Commercial contracts become mechanisms to ensure that a government department 'gets what it wants', and there are various processes, both formal and informal, that are utilized to safeguard against outcomes that may be either threatening or embarrassing.

As Scraton (2001a) has argued, as well as the formal sanctions made available through contracts, there are many informal sanctions used by the regulatory agents to influence the processes of distribution and consumption of research work. These include: making administrative difficulties; making the researchers wait and repeat their demands many times before reacting; requesting that the researcher rewrite sections of the report; delaying the release of research findings; suspecting the researcher of activities that might lead to formal prosecution; alleging 'secret information' in the files of the researcher; failing to pay the final contractual instalments; threatening the researcher's employer, and so on.

While it must be recognized that some criminological research that is critical of government policy and practice does get published, the difficulties and tensions examined in this chapter were widely experienced by those criminologists consulted for this research. Criminologists should be encouraged to negotiate carefully the parameters of their research with funding bodies as well as the conditions of commercial contracts before signing, or seek collegial and association support, and consult with officials prior to the release of research about their organization. That said, many of the political dimensions discussed in this chapter should be foreseen by criminologists as 'part and parcel' of a process with the potential to 'touch those that govern at a raw nerve' (Carson, 1996), to influence the policies and practices of the state crime-control apparatus, and to challenge notions of social and political order.

This chapter has explored the day-to-day politics and governance of criminological knowledge; the following ones contextualize the issues raised above within broader conservative political landscapes.

Notes

1   In 1981 the newly elected socialist government in France established a national commission to review crime. The commission was chaired by a local mayor, named Gilbert Bonnemaison. The findings of the commission (the Bonnemaison Report) recommended the 'need for horizontal solutions to make communities safer from crime and bring people together with different expertise in local partnerships' (Crawford, 1998: 222). The Bonnemaison model, therefore, moved away from the criminal justice system and emphasized 'upstream' crime prevention, involving communities and local agencies.

2   This includes the right to break a contract for an acceptable reason (change of government or a change of policy, although the latter may require damages to be paid), and to make a contract void by introducing an overriding statute (see Seddon, 1999).

3   In 1997 the governments of Australia and New Zealand entered into an Procurement Agreement, the objective of which was to 'create and maintain a single ANZ government procurement market to maximize opportunities for competitive ANZ suppliers and to reduce costs of doing business for government and industry'. This agreement defines value for money as the 'primary determinant in government procurement of goods and services. Application of the value-for-money principle is aimed at achieving the best available outcome for money spent in terms of the procuring agency's needs. The test of the best available value for money requires relevant comparison of the whole of life costs relating directly to the procurement' (see ANZ Procurement Agreement, 1997). The 'whole of life costs' include factors such as performance, price, delivery, and disposal.

4   The definition of government procurement within Australia and New Zealand includes 'purchase, hire, lease, rental, exchange and competitive tendering and contracting (outsourcing) arrangements (see ANZ Government Procurement Agreement, 1997).

5   On 15 December 1999, the Home Office convened, for the first time, a public seminar for all criminology and criminal justice researchers in England at its head office at Queen Anne's Gate, London. This provided an overview of how research proposals should be written for the Home Office, the criteria for selection, reporting requirements and so on.

6   There are four main areas of criminal liability relevant to research into illegal behaviour. First, aiding and abetting, which involves the researcher participating in a criminal act rather than simply observing that act. Second, the concealment of benefit, where researchers may receive a reward (for example,

a salary or career advancement) from failing to disclose information pertaining to criminal activity. Third, contempt of court where researchers are not granted privilege and are required to provide the court with information. Finally, a warrant to search premises which includes a situation where, if 'police form the view that information collected in a research project may provide evidence of the commission of offences, there is nothing to stop an appropriately ranked police officer from obtaining a warrant to search premises. In this case any data collected in a research project can be seized and assurances of confidentiality or anonymity given to study participants may be rendered worthless' (Fitzgerald, 1995: 8).

7   In Australia the Commonwealth Epidemiological Studies (Confidentiality) Act 1981 was passed to assure protection for Vietnam veterans participating in a study of Agent Orange. Research projects officially approved under this Act provide the participants as well as the researchers with legislative assurances of confidentiality, which cannot be revoked by a court of law. Fitzgerald (1995) argues that it is becoming increasingly more difficult for academics researching illicit behaviour to be covered by the Act.

8   For example, The Australian and New Zealand Society of Criminology recently (April 2000) developed a *Code of Ethics* based on the 1999 British Society of Criminology's *Code of Ethics for Researchers in the Field of Criminology*. These codes, together with the American Society of Criminology's *Code of Ethics,* provide mechanisms for complaint against any criminologist who does not comply with the ethical code: a process that involves the respective executive committee members reviewing the complaint and passing judgement. Complaints that are upheld can result in 'sanction' against the criminologist (for example, expulsion from the Society).

9   Dr Kerry Carrington courageously withstood the aggressive attempts to discredit her work. In the end, the allegations against her were not proven, her book remained in public for all to read, her university was not sued and her reputation as a researcher and a scholar was not tarnished. Indeed she continues to be one of Australia's most influential critical criminologists.

Chapter 5

Silencing the critics: the 'War on Terror' and the suppression of dissent

Truth is to be understood as a system of ordered procedures for the production, regulation, distribution, circulation, and operation of statements. Truth is linked in a circular relation with systems of power that produce and sustain it, and to effects of power which it induces and which extend it – a regime of truth. This regime is not merely ideological or superstructural; it was a condition of the formation and development of capitalism .... The problem is not changing people's consciousness – or what's in their heads – but the political, economic, institutional regime of the production of truth .... It's not a matter of emancipating truth from every system of power ... but of detaching the power of truth from the forms of hegemony, social, economic, and cultural, within which it operates at the present time. (Foucault, in Faubion, 2002: 132)

What does a chapter about the 'War on Terror' have to do with the production of criminological knowledge? Here I take this contemporary issue and identify how broader political events may influence both current and future criminological research agendas. The purpose here is to attempt to link the daily workings of criminology (discussed in the previous chapter) with global political events. The US-led War on Terror has already begun to create new laws and new crimes, and as such we will inevitably witness new forms of criminological knowledge that have their origins in contemporary global politics. The new offences created under emerging anti-terrorism legislation will undoubtedly promote a vast amount of criminological scholarship. For example, the NIJ has already commenced funding projects that focus on 'law enforcement and local terrorism', where the grantee is a police executive research forum (see National Institute of Justice, 2003). However, whether this scholarship critically engages with political decision-making or simply serves to administer and fine-tune the state's anti-terrorism apparatus remains to be seen (more than likely, the latter). This chapter also serves to broadly contextualize some of the arguments presented in Chapter Four, notably, the increasing risks associated with 'going public' and the potential ramifications for scholars that adopt a critical position of government officials and powerful political figures during times of growing conservatism.

The previous chapter identified what Foucault referred to as 'capillary power', the day-to-day details of criminological governance. The intentions in this and the following chapter are to explore further the broader political and economic dimensions that influence the production of criminological knowledge. As Foucault (1977a) has so persuasively argued, power/knowledge complexes create and legitimize 'regimes of truth'. These regimes of truth are informed by power relations that operate through various forms of governance.

The argument presented in this chapter is that techniques of neutralization within criminology should also be situated within broader political frameworks. As mentioned, it uses the War on Terror as a case study to show how governmental technologies of power suppress critical knowledge. It examines the suppression of dissent and explores concepts of free speech within governmental regimes of intolerance. As previously discussed, criminological agendas are increasingly shaped and funded by government (in the United States, 90 percent of the NIJ's research programme is determined on Capitol Hill), and this chapter aims to bring into focus some of the discourses and rationales that inform the power/knowledge nexus. This case-study also provides a useful context for understanding the development of new legislation that defines criminality within state-defined notions of terror, risk and dangerousness. In doing so, the emergence of conservatism and governmental regimes of intolerance serve to further promote and shape a vast amount of criminological scholarship that will be predisposed to newly created criminal behaviours.

The War on Terror

The catastrophic events in New York City, Washington D.C. and Pennsylvania on 11 September 2001 sparked, as we all know, an international US-led alliance to seek out and disable networks of terrorist activity – an effort more commonly referred to as the War on Terror. The climate of vengeance that subsequently swept the US administration and its invasions of Afghanistan and Iraq were criticized by various commentators within the United States (see Chomsky, 2001). The months following the tragic events of September 11 also witnessed widespread intolerance for views dissenting from the War on Terror and President Bush's decision to invade Afghanistan. The post-11 September period in the United States represented a fashioning of a single outlook, a time when free speech and criticism were referred to as treason.

It is important to recognize that the examples discussed throughout this chapter occurred within a context of an official rhetoric that was intolerant of criticism. Indeed, President Bush in his many speeches after September 11 referred to his government's position as the 'defender of freedom', which must fight 'evil'. He referred to the United States as the 'home of freedom' and that the time had arrived for all 'freedom-loving people to come together to fight terrorist activity' (Bush, 2001a). He further stated that any nation that opposed his aim to 'smoke out and destroy evil' was implicitly a supporter of terrorism. His position on this was unequivocal: 'either you are with us, or you are with the terrorists' (Bush, 2001b). By implication, anyone who criticized or opposed the War on Terror was not a defender of freedom, but rather someone siding with 'evil', someone on the terrorists' side.

Former US Attorney-General Ashcroft adopted this position. On 6 December 2001, he stated to the Senate Judiciary Committee that civil-liberties critics 'aid terrorists … erode our national unity and diminish our resolve' (Sherwin, 2002). Ashcroft also attacked those who questioned government policy as 'aiding the enemy' and mocked his detractors, saying that their concerns were 'phantoms', whose criticism bring 'comfort to the enemy' (Murphy, 2002). Moreover, John Ashcroft sent a memo to federal agencies urging them to resist most Freedom of Information Act requests made by American citizens in the interests of safeguarding the US government from unwarranted risk (*San Francisco Chronicle*, 2002). It is, therefore, important to bear this political context in mind when reading the following examples.

The voices of dissent have emanated from various sections of American society, including academics, students, broadcasters and journalists, and those seeking to regulate or suppress the 'critical voice' have surfaced from a cross-section of the US public against a backdrop of 'patriotic propaganda', where free speech became subservient to governmental ideals. Individuals who elected to exercise their democratic and constitutional rights to express their opposition to George Bush's war on terror were referred to as 'seditious' and 'traitorous' and subjected to swift and draconian sanction.

'Acts of Sedition': Opposing the War on Terror

Academic institutions are premised on well-founded principles of free speech so that their scholars might act as 'critics and conscience of society'. However, during the post-11 September period academic freedom was curtailed and redefined. There are numerous examples of critical voices within academic institutions bringing about swift and heavy-handed reactions from politicians, employers and governing bodies. For example, on 2 October 2001, the Professional Staff Congress (PSC, the campus professors union) at the City University of New York sponsored a teach-in. The theme was 'Threats of War, Challenges of Peace', and the forum was open to all points of view, including those who supported US military intervention in Afghanistan. When the content of the discussion was subsequently brought to the attention of the university administration, the actions of the staff were condemned. The Chancellor of the university, Matthew Goldstein, denounced the teach-in saying that the academics were making 'lame excuses' for the terrorists. CUNY trustee, Jeffrey Wiesenfeld, stated: 'They're fortunate it's not up to me. I would consider that behaviour seditious at this time' (cited in Jones, 2001). The trustees of the City University debated what form of action should be taken in response to the teach-in. Some of the trustees drafted a resolution, calling for the PSC 'to dissociate itself from the sentiments expressed' at the forum, and to state that the board 'stands in support of the President and Government of the United States in coordination and execution of a plan to root out and destroy terrorist capabilities throughout the world'. The resolution referred to some statements made at the teach-in as 'seditious' and 'un-American' (Associated Press, 2001a).

There is evidence of dismissals of academics for their political and ideological views. For example, Professor Sami Al-Arian at the University of South Florida was questioned by an interviewer on a television news programme about a speech that he had made in 1988 in which he called for 'victory to Islam' and 'death to Israel' (Brink, 2002). Al-Arian responded to the questions by distancing himself from his previous statements. Subsequent to the airing of the interview, the University of South Florida received angry phone-calls and death threats (*New York Times*, 2002). Al-Arian was placed on paid leave; a university spokesperson argued that this was for his own safety (Associated Press, 2001b). Two months later, the university's Board of Trustees decided to dismiss him. They stated that he had failed to make it clear on television that he wasn't representing the University of South Florida. The University claimed that Al-Arian was not being dismissed because of his views but because of the disruption that his presence on campus had on the effective functioning of the university. The actions of the university were publicly supported by Governor Jeb Bush (*New York Times*, 2002).

Another example involved Robert Jensen, Professor of Journalism at the University of Texas, who wrote an article entitled 'U.S. Just as Guilty of Committing Own Violent Acts' (Jensen, 2001). In an attempt to contextualize the events of 11 September within historical acts of terrorism, Jensen identified the role the US government in acts supporting and sponsoring international terrorism. He argued that the terrorist attacks of 11 September 'were reprehensible and indefensible ... but this act was no more despicable [than] the massive acts of terrorism – the deliberate killing of civilians for political purposes – that the U.S. government has committed during my lifetime' (Jensen, 2001a and 2001b; cf. Rothschild, 2001). The president of the University of Texas, Larry Faulkner, responded with a letter, which was published in the *Houston Chronicle* on 19 September 2001 affirming Jensen's right to express his opinions but publicly damning him for them. Faulkner stated that 'Jensen is not only misguided, but has become a fountain of undiluted foolishness on issues of public policy. Students must learn that there is a good deal of foolish opinion in the popular media and they must become skilled at recognizing it and discounting it. I, too, was disgusted by Jensen's article, but I also defend his freedom to state his opinion. The First Amendment is the bedrock of American liberty' (Faulkner, 2001; cf. Jensen, 2001b). This article was followed by a letter-writing campaign to dismiss Jensen (Vincent, 2001).

Free speech on university campuses was also silenced. On 15 December 2001, Janis Heaphy, the publisher and president of a Sacramento newspaper, was invited to give a commencement speech at California State University. In Heaphy's speech she questioned the extent to which Americans were willing to compromise their civil liberties in the name of security. She also commented that it was every individual's right and duty to challenge government policies. Five minutes into Heaphy's speech, graduates and their families began stomping their feet and clapping so that she wasn't able to be heard. After attempting to continue for a short time, Heaphy abandoned her speech and sat down (Rothschild, 2002a;

Lustig, 2002). Local broadcasters referred to her speech as a 'mean-spirited diatribe against the Bush administration' (Salladay, 2001).

In another campus incident, David Westin, the president of ABC News, was speaking to a group of students at the Columbian University Graduate School of Journalism. A student asked him if he believed that the Pentagon was a legitimate target for suicide bombers on 11 September. Westin responded by saying that it was important that he, and other ABC journalists, did not have an opinion on it: 'our job is to determine what is, not what ought to be, and when we get into the job of what ought to be, I think we're not doing a service to the American people'. The remarks were subsequently condemned in a *New York Post* editorial, which reported that Westin wanted ABC journalists 'to be so open-minded that their brains fall out'. Westin issued an apology stating, 'Upon reflection, I realized that my answer did not address the specifics of September 11. Under any interpretation, the attack on the Pentagon was criminal and entirely without justification. I apologize for any harm that my misstatement may have caused (Associated Press, 2001d).'

It was also a time when comments in jest were prohibited. For example, Professor Richard A. Berthold, a historian at the University of New Mexico, commented to his freshman class on 11 September, after hearing about the plane crashes, that 'anyone who would blow up the Pentagon would have my vote'. Thousands of students and alumni complained to the University's administrators about Berthold's comments. Moreover, Republican state legislators and business leaders also requested that he lose his job. Berthold received death threats, resulting in his not returning to the campus for a week. Provost Brian Foster commented about Berthold's statements that: 'there are a lot of things you can't say with impunity, even on a college campus'. In a letter outlining its investigation, the university referred to Berthold's comment as an ethical violation rather than a question of free speech, reprimanded Professor Berthold, and instructed him to undergo an in-depth review that required counselling (Fletcher, 2001). Moreover, John Trainor, a citizen of Albuquerque, filed a lawsuit seeking that the university dismiss Berthold. Trainor's lawsuit claimed that Berthold's comments advocated violence and treason. State Representative, William Fuller, also called for Berthold's resignation. Fuller argued that Berthold could say whatever he wanted to in public, but that he was not covered by the protection of the First Amendment when he was being paid by the state to teach at a public university (Associated Press, 2001c).

There are also numerous examples of university academics being publicly damned for discussing the struggles experienced by peoples living in the Middle East. For example, Asha Samad-Matias, a Professor of

African and Caribbean studies at the City College of New York, pointed out at a teach-in after 11 September how great the suffering of African and Middle Eastern people has been. The *New York Post* described her as 'unpatriotic' (Griswold, 2001). In such instances, academics were not overtly critical of the Bush Administration, but were deemed to be so in an indirect way, sympathizing with the targeted 'enemy of evil'.

In addition to universities, there are numerous examples of teachers and school principals who were censured, suspended or dismissed for criticizing the Bush Administration (Student Press Law Centre, 2001; cf. Rothschild, 2002b). Moreover, the dissenting voices of children at schools were, in some instances, reprimanded by principals who objected to artwork, essays and posters, created as part of the school curriculum, that depicted or described opposition to Bush's Afghanistan invasion. These examples of schoolwork were destroyed, and several students received suspensions and were directed to school counsellors (Rothschild, 2002d; cf. Abelsom and Vaishnav, 2002).

Moreover, after September 11 there are several examples of media personalities being dismissed for dissent as well as journalists distorting events to support the Bush campaign (Rothschild, 2002e and 2002f). Television broadcasters were also prohibited from taking 'certain directions' (*Washington Post*, 2001); and radio programmes and internet sites renowned for their alternative and anti-government commentary were shutdown (Metro Santa Cruz, 2001; Kornblum, 2001). Furthermore, several network executives were requested by White House national security advisor, Condoleeza Rice, to refrain from airing unedited or lengthy videotaped messages issued by Osama Bin Laden in the event that such broadcasts might incite his followers 'to kill Americans' (Fairness and Accuracy in Reporting, 2001; Farhi, 2001; cf. Smith, 2001). In addition, White House officials were reported to have requested that Hollywood directors commit 'themselves to new initiatives in support of the war on terrorism' (Bart, 2001). Finally, there are also numerous other examples of censorship, including artistic exhibitions showing photographs of Afghanistan that were cancelled and replaced with portraits of American patriotism (Stewart and Brownfield, 2001). Radio stations were prohibited from broadcasting anti-war songs such as John Lennon's 'Imagine' and Cat Stevens's 'Peace Train' (Cottin, 2001).

Government Intolerance and the Suppression of Free Speech

The importance of free speech in democratic societies has been well-documented (Castberg 1960; Meiklejohn, 1965; Sunstein, 1993). It stimulates social and political discourse and gives voice to diverse public narratives in a healthy intellectual exchange between government and society. Moreover, as discussed in the previous chapter, the hallmark of any democratic society is the reliable flow of information from government. Therefore, the ideal outcome of free and open discussion is 'political truth', and the dissemination of this 'truth' is important for informed decision-making (Sunstein, 1993).

While proclaiming to be the 'protectors of freedom', the Bush Administration has directly or indirectly subverted freedom and truth in ways reminiscent of the McCarthy era. The post-11 September period was a time when the US government actively sought to mobilize and manipulate public opinion to support its campaign for war in Afghanistan. For example, on 7 October 2001, the day that the United States began bombing Afghanistan, the National Imagery and Mapping Agency signed a contract for exclusive rights to all commercial satellite imagery of Afghanistan and other countries in the region. The National Imagery and Mapping Agency is a 'top-secret Defence Department intelligence agency' and was reported to have paid US$1.91 million for the first 30 days of the contract. Moreover, the US government, in collaboration with the British government, created 'Coalition Information Centres' in Washington DC, London and Islamabad to enable the domination of the news coverage of bombings. The focus of these news centres was to give the US government media domination of the War on Terror (De Young, 2001).

Moreover, in February 2002 it was reported that the Pentagon was planning a public-relations campaign through the establishment of the Office of Strategic Influence. The establishment of the Office was reportedly in response to concerns in the Bush Administration that the United States was losing public support overseas, particularly in Islamic countries. It was to provide 'aggressive campaigns that use not only the foreign media and the internet but also covert operations' to persuade public opinion. Furthermore, the designated head of the new office, Brigadier General Worden, stated that the department should consider using 'black' information campaigns, including misinformation (Hodgson, 2002a). Later in February 2002 it was reported that the Pentagon had decided not to pursue its plan to influence the foreign media. This was reportedly because of the negative reaction to the proposal, both in the United States and overseas (Hodgson, 2002b). As Herman and Chomsky (1994) have so persuasively argued, the power of government to manipulate and orchestrate the media through the dissemination of patriotic propaganda is a far more effective means of controlling public opinion than official policies of censorship.

The flow-on effect of governmental intolerance and patriotic propaganda in the post-11 September period has been a climate reminiscent of McCarthyism, culminating in widespread suppression throughout US society. Indeed, in the style of Joseph McCarthy, the American Council of Trustees and Alumni issued a report, on 11 November 2001, entitled *Defending Civilization: How Our Universities are Failing America and What Can Be Done about It*. The report listed 117 examples, most of which were quotations, by academics and students who had questioned the War on Terror. This included publicly shaming 40 separate college professors and one university president, who were regarded as 'insufficiently patriotic'.

As the examples in this chapter reveal, the critical voice was not only censored but also actively silenced and marginalized as 'seditious'. The offspring of such suppression within a climate of 'patriotic propaganda' is a culture of intolerance and conformity. Images and acts of rebellion are stereotyped and demarcated to a social periphery of exclusion. The critical voice is excluded and marginalized through third-party suppression as well as self-censorship. The suppression of dissent gathers momentum as individual acts are publicly condemned. The sanctions imposed, and the subsequent effects on the dissenter, serve to raise the stakes for future critical commentators. The willingness to 'go public' and express criticism, of, for example, the US government's War on Terror, carries the risk of swift and severe financial and other personal consequences. Therefore, the cornerstone of democratic society is rapidly eroded in such climates of intolerance, which provide political actors and government officials *carte blanche* to pursue strategies unchecked by public, academic and media scrutiny.

The neutralization of critical narrative serves to perpetuate government-endorsed policies. President Bush's mandate for invasions of Afghanistan and Iraq was premised, to a large extent, on notions of freedom and the elimination of oppressive regimes. The irony and hypocrisy in this position has been repeatedly identified (see Scraton, 2001). The leader of the 'free world' has proved to be intolerant of domestic free speech in his overtly stated quest to secure freedom for others.

The Authoritarian Ascendancy

The post-11 September suppression of dissent and the promulgation of patriotism (O'Leary and Platt, 2002) served to fashion a single 'acceptable' outlook in US society: a time when alternative narratives were silenced in favour of a government-led consensus of 'us and them'. The political rhetoric of George W. Bush, which prohibits debate or dissent, is an unequivocal reminder of the power of state actors. Coleman (cited in

Tombs and Whyte, 2003) argues that what is required is an analysis that involves 'bringing the state back in'. Failure to do so would ignore the power and influence of the state in shaping and perpetuating the conservative rationalities and public opinion that influence contemporary society.

This suppression of dissent in the United States, must also be contextualized within analyses of market-led economics and authoritarian ascendancy. For writers such as Christian Parenti, the authoritarian ascendancy or 'lockdown' is characteristic of a political and economic structure that grants hegemony to market capital (see Parenti, 1999). Moreover, the public popularity of repressive law and order regimes is really a reflection of social discontent. Hence, the 'enemies within' become the scapegoats for broader capitalist-led social and economic marginalization. A familiar 'get tough' rhetoric was, in this case, repackaged within a framework of global instability, terrorism and the need to clamp down on internal disorders.

Such recent international trends in state social control, justified as increasing defences against global and domestic insecurities, run the perilous risk of spiralling towards social, cultural and intellectual repression. As Parenti (1999) convincingly argues, the public appeal of tougher law and order is the way in which the impoverished and disenfranchized in society can use it to find an avenue or voice for expressing their more general discontent. The 'imaginary scapegoat', in the form of terrorist threats, gangs and youth crime, serves to deflect public attention away from pressing social problems towards issues of political salience but of individual insignificance.

Embedded in the authoritarian ascendancy is what Schoenwald (2001) refers to as the 'rise of modern American conservatism' and its pervasive influence within political, economic and social structures, including the Republican Party, the media, Wall Street, right-wing think-tanks, the biotechnology industry and the universities. Guided by a moral and economic conservatism, such ideology actively promotes aggressive free-market policies for maximum commercial gain. In recent years when the United States has experienced a number of high-profile corporate collapses and a decline in GDP against a growing trade deficit, Scheoenwald argues that any obstacles that jeopardize the ideology of globalization and free trade, whether it be civil liberties, the Kyoto (environmental) Protocols, or criticisms of the War on Terror, have been actively neutralized. As Klein (2002) argues, free trade in the United States, 'is fast being rebranded, like shopping and baseball, as patriotic duty' (147). Moreover, Schoenwald (2001) suggests that this climate of intolerance has served to silence dissenting voices across a range of professional activities to the peril of free speech and open democratic debate. The manipulation of public opinion by the US Government over the recent invasion of Iraq is well argued by Sheldon Rampton and John Stauber in their controversial book *Weapons of Mass Deception*. This book provides a chilling account of covert government operations (using intelligence and paid P.R. consultants) to fabricate news stories and to orchestrate an emotional state of emergency that would justify a war against Iraq. Eno (2003) refers to this as 'propaganda', arguing that the 'new American approach to social control is much more sophisticated and pervasive ... it's not so much the control of what we think, but the control of what we think about' (p. 29). In other words the knowledge agenda is increasingly controlled and regulated by a growing conservative politics of intolerance and critical criminology is difficult to get onto this agenda.

Within US criminology there are recent examples of book contracts rescinded for 'no longer fitting the market'. Such books have endeavoured to provide a critical account of the Bush Administration's War on Terror, and as a result their publishers have adopted a conservative position and decided to 'hold-off on anything that looks insensitive to the nation's war effort' (Chambliss, 2002, personal correspondence).

The War on Terror has also precipitated a range of laws throughout the United States and other Western nations, which will undoubtedly shape future criminological research agendas. The introduction of such legislation as the US Patriot Act and the UK Crime and Security Act, together with numerous other Acts to address the 'dangerous' and 'anti-social', create the contexts for the production of criminological knowledge. As a result of these kinds of laws, the mentally ill, the young, the 'anti-social', ethnic minorities and asylum seekers are continually objectified through discourses of power as 'the enemy within', who must be measured and managed to limit the risks they pose to society. The introduction of legislation that creates new risk populations will necessitate vast amounts of criminological scholarship to inform government policy (discussed further in the next chapter). The powerless in society will be placed further under the criminological lens as governments seek to review their policies against the 'threats of terror' as well as against the new emerging *classe dangereuse*.

Resistance and Detaching Hegemonic Truth

While the above examples demonstrate that government intolerance of free speech serves to neutralize would-be critics, it should be noted that suppression of dissent is also capable of producing both underground and visible resistance. As Ferguson *et al.* (2002) point out, globalization, war and conservative modes of governance are providing the impetus for social and political protest, or what is more commonly referred to as 'globalized resistance'. As recent anti-war demonstrations reveal, social movements (such as the European Social Forum, consisting of human rights activists, anti-capitalists, anti-globalization groups, unions and so on) have generated immense opposition to the US/UK invasion of Iraq. It is an opposition that continues to spark political rivalry and social unrest (Burke, 2002). For example, there have been some recent publications (notably in the United Kingdom rather than the United States, where the above examples of suppression are drawn) that have given voice to criticism of the Bush Administration, and none do so better than Phil Scraton's (2002) edited collection *Beyond September 11: An Anthology of Dissent*. Scraton's self-titled anthology of dissent provides an unequivocal and comprehensively compiled condemnation of the US-led invasion of Afghanistan. Academics, campaigners, journalists and political commentators provide irrefutable evidence of the contradictions, illegalities, and deceit surrounding the Bush Administration's economically driven and power-motivated War on Terror. Moreover, this collection identifies how the US government's slogan, 'with us or against us', was used not only to condemn the critical voice but was also to marginalize neutral voices as 'enemies of the state'. In other words, to remain silent and not voice a position of support for President Bush was regarded as a complicit act of 'evil'. Such a book currently stands out among the voluminous material currently published on terrorism and the war on terror for its preparedness to criticize governments. Would it have been published had its academic editor been working in the United States and seeking a US-based publisher?

As Foucault (1977c) in the opening quotation to this chapter argues, it is important that criminological scholarship 'detach the power of truth from the forms of hegemony ... within which it operates'. This means adopting a position of resistance that identifies knowledge/power complexes within contemporary forms of governance and critiques the injustice of those governmental regimes that construct notions of truth for material and political gain.

These new modes of conservative governance in contemporary society, which focus on risk management and the free market, have provided new political and economic landscapes for the production of criminological knowledge. As Tombs and Whyte (2003) argue, political economy is important for understanding the silencing and self-regulation of criminological scholarship; 'in other words, current attempts to silence, discredit and marginalize alternative views of the world are both an element in and a symptom of the political re-configuration of university research', and the following chapter will examine this.

Chapter 6

New modes of governance and the commercialization of criminological knowledge

> The move to marketise and contract-out state functions has created a demand for criminological research through consultancy-based work. At the same time, academic criminologists are 'propelled' by resource-starved universities to seek consultancies and research grants to satisfy external demands for productivity, accountability and marketability. Funding agencies in turn demand relevance, value for money and contractual accountability .... These new techniques of governance – marketisation, consumerism, managerialism and accountability – also raise serious questions in relation to intellectual property, political independence, and the future of criminological research (Chan, 2000: 130).

In previous chapters, this book has argued that criminological scholarship has been governed by the policy needs of governments and by medico-legal disciplinary boundaries, which have influenced the production of a pragmatic and state-defined knowledge about crime causation and correction. The previous chapters also began to explore the daily events as well as broader conservative politics that are capable of influencing criminological scholarship. However, it remains important to locate specifically the regulation and governance of criminological research, discussed in the previous chapters, within contemporary modes of conservative governance, and in doing so, to address the following questions. What are the dangers of a 'market-led criminology'? How have new modes of governance in contemporary society influenced the production of criminological knowledge? What is the future of the critical voice in these changing political and economic landscapes?

Throughout the book, concepts of 'governmentality' have been alluded to through the ways in which criminological scholarship is funded and produced. This chapter aims to consolidate these previous discussions by examining the place and purpose of criminological knowledge within post-Keynesian political rationalities and, furthermore, by exploring what it means to be 'critical' under expanding conservative modes of governance.

Governmentality and Criminological Research

New modes of governance

Since the mid-1980s, much academic and political debate has focused on the rise of conservative discourses and economic reform in Western democratic societies. The increasing body of literature on 'neo-corporatism', 'neo-liberalism', 'advanced liberalism', 'new managerialism' and so on examines new modes of governance in late modernity and the influence that such economically driven policies have had on contemporary social life. Influenced by the works of Foucault (1977a, 1978), researchers across a variety of disciplines have examined new methods of rule in what is broadly defined as discourses of governmentality (Smandych, 1999). Within these discourses, we have witnessed flourishing debates about government's accountability, risk society (Simon, 1987; Beck, 1992; Douglas, 1992) and a concomitant nexus with policies of crime control and prevention (O'Malley, 1998).

As Garland (1999) points out, Foucault's work on 'governmentailty' has provoked widespread debate about the role of criminology within discourses of power/knowledge. He argues that the governmentality literature offers 'a framework for analysing how crime is problematized and controlled' (Garland, 1999: 15). In turn, it aids our understandings of criminological discourse, of why certain categories or crimes became the objects of international inquiry, and of what types of knowledge are pursued and produced by researchers in the field of crime control. These questions have been discussed in previous chapters.

Criminological discourses often pivot on modalities of power (O'Malley, 1996; Stenson, 1999). Within contemporary market societies, these modalities of power (such as crime-control industries, private security, state and local regulatory authorities) provide multiple examples of the differing ways in which society is governed. These modes of governance are informed by an ensemble of conservative and 'middle ground' ideologies (for example, neo-liberalism, neo-conservatism, communitarianism and the Third Way), which have become increasingly popular within the United Kingdom (Hood, 1990; Giddens, 1998), the United States (Osborne and Gaebler, 1993), Australia (Castles *et al.*, 1996) and New Zealand (Boston *et al.*, 1996). In this new mode of governance, the 'myth of the sovereign state' is exposed (Garland, 1997). In other words, state sovereignty over the treatment of crime is eroded and dispersed to private industry and the individual (Hughes, 1998).

Moreover, emerging modes of governance foster notions of responsibility. As a result, individuals, families and communities are urged to take greater responsibility for the search for solutions to social and economic ailments (Rose, 1996). In appealing for a more active responsibility in the 'government' of one's own life and that of the family and the community, this emergent mode of governance represents a profound recasting of the relationship between state and citizen (cf. Hughes, 1998). Braithwaite (2000) argues that this relationship is characterized by what he calls the 'new regulatory state', whereby the 'steering process' of policy development is clearly demarcated from the 'rowing process' of implementation (cf. Osborne and Gaebler, 1993) in what is now recognized as a fundamental aspect of 'governing at a distance' (Miller and Rose, 1990). Or, as Rose (2000) has suggested, this advanced form of 'liberal government' is distinguished by the state as 'partner, animator and facilitator for a variety of independent agents and powers, and should exercise only limited powers of its own, steering and regulating rather than rowing and providing' (323–34).

These changing modes of governance are influencing the production of crime-control knowledge. As Simon (1987) argues, new technologies of rule in 'late modernity' are characterized by actuarial forms of governance. These mentalities of rule or governance aim to manage 'risks' within society. The management of risk populations (those 'at risk' of ill health, unemployment, criminal victimization, benefit dependency, and so on) as well as risk industries (at risk of profit loss, share devaluation, and reduced productivity) become the key objectives of regulatory authorities (Simon, 1987; Ericson and Carriere, 1994). The identification of risk groups (through disseminating information and implementing risk-management strategies) becomes wedded to processes of prediction and measurement (Feeley and Simon, 1992). Not surprisingly, 'crime' as a category of risk has created new discourses within criminology and social science, which include references to community, individuals, management, and statistics (Pavlich, 2000a).

Risk management and criminological research

O'Malley (1992) argues that risk management has become a growing industry under conservative political ideologies. Individuals are encouraged by commercialism to secure themselves and their families against an increasing number of risks, in what O'Malley refers to as the 'new prudentialism'.[1] The practice of government has increasingly become one of risk management. The management of risks has occurred simultaneously with the 'hollowing out of the state' (see Rhodes, 1994 and 1997), where the enhancement of personal security and safety, a traditional function of the state, has required the recruitment of the 'community' within a politics of responsibilization and economic reform. Individuals within communities, or 'territories of security' (Rose, 2000), become responsible for the protection and safety of their local environments within modes of governance that promote technologies of prudentialism (cf. O'Malley, 1996).

Rose argues that risk identification, risk assessment and risk management have increasingly become the roles of health professionals, financial advisors, lawyers and other 'experts'. Such professionals have traditionally provided information for the identification and treatment, or solution, to a given problem. Now they must provide strategies 'to monitor and manage risks' (Rose, 1996: 349).

What influence is this changing governing ethos having on criminological researchers? There is a two-fold effect. First, new forms of governance challenge the 'discipline' of criminology. For some academics, criminology must move away from its disciplinary boundaries and be recast within a series of narratives that aid the identification and explanation of new and emerging forms of 'regulatory practice'. As a result, crime does not become the object of study; instead, scholars are organized around a broader focus on regulation or governing rationalities (Braithwaite, 2000). Others researchers such as Hughes (1998) predict that discourses on crime prevention may be supplanted by new disciplines of 'risk management studies' within coming decades. However, while acknowledging that neo-liberalism, for example, is colonizing discourses on crime, Hughes (1998) maintains that 'there will still be the urgent need for a critical social science which is able to relate such new discourses to wider questions of social order, social justice and social control in late modern societies' (156).

The second effect is that the perpetuation of neo-liberalism and 'progressive governance' is affecting the day-to-day practices of criminological research. For example, the researcher has typically decided the essence of the research (including its hypothesis, key questions, methods and written format). However, new modes of governance are continually redefining the parameters of research that is commissioned in order to assess departmental objectives. Thus, the purpose of research takes a new form within the governments of a risk society. For example, the recently established Risk Management Authority (RMA) in Scotland is a policy and administrative unit responsible for assessing and managing crime risks. It fulfils this objective, in part, by contracting experts in criminal justice to provide risk assessments and risk profiles (Mitchell, 2001). Tombs (2003), in her important work on 'what counts as evidence' (discussed earlier), identifies this authority as a 'new penal managerialist structure specifically concerned with risk'. Her ongoing work examines the RMA and asks 'what constituencies of knowledge' were represented to create this Authority and what sources of knowledge will be used by it to acquit its remit? Such authorities provide new sites for the production of private criminological research, where external consultants will be commissioned to generate risk assessments and profiles for Civil Servants to convert into policy.

In this vein, Ericson (1994) has suggested that criminologists are becoming hired 'brokers of knowledge'. Research becomes one way of calculating risk factors as well as measuring outputs. As a result, words such as 'evaluation' either take a new form or are discarded in favour of less intrusive or less critical terms. As Rose (2000) argues, language provides 'a regime of intelligibility' for those that govern. Quoting the works of Poovey (1995), he further asserts that the 'reconstruction of the epistemological field that allows for the production of what counts as knowledge at any given moment, and which accords salience to particular categories' constitutes a 'regime of enunciation' that defines and legitimates what is truth, and what is relevant (Poovey, 2000: 28–29). Language (as discussed in the previous chapter) becomes important for recasting, or redefining, the mechanisms that grant legitimacy to governing rationalities. Therefore, the epistemological horizons of concepts such as 'evaluation' are reformulated according to a framework that grants intelligibility to the rationale of governing authorities. As Scraton (2001b) argues, the word 'evaluation' has become 'a metaphor for self-justificatory and funding-related quantitative results' (p. 3). Or, as O'Malley (2000) argues forcefully, 'social criminologies' and the projects they produce have undergone a 'neo-liberal assault'.

Criminal justice policy and practices have moved away from the long-term and have dispersed social initiatives to a rational-choice model of penality that demands cost-effectiveness and accountability (Garland, 1995b). As discussed earlier, research is not only required to demonstrate the fiscal and managerial responsibility of government policy, but the research itself must demonstrate 'value for money' (cf. Chan, 2000).

O'Malley (2000) argues, for example, that developmental psychology has recently emerged as a discipline identifying 'risk factors', such as 'family isolation, inadequate parenting, single parents, attachment difficulties, low self-esteem, poor social skills, poor cognitive skills and so on' (161). The irony of this, according to O'Malley, is that developmental psychology often identifies and promotes an agenda that reflects the arguments of social criminologies and programmes sponsored by the welfare state. However, increasingly developmental psychology is informing government policies that are not premised on health and welfare but on social responsibility. In the United Kingdom, for example, developmental psychology is integrated into government policy responses to anti-social behaviour. In order to manage 'risk populations' or 'categories' (the latter being the preferred term, because it depersonalizes the individual) must first be measured. As a result, there is a proliferation of government techniques to assess risk (risk in an economic sense, as much as in a social one). Such risk assessments attempt to identify children as young as five years old who may be future candidates for antisocial orders. There have even been suggestions that a risk assessment scale will be used for the unborn in an attempt to identify what could be called 'the deviant fetus'.

Emerging from all this is a repositioning of the research process and a re-evaluation of what counts as knowledge in the contemporary world of policy-making. Research often involves the production of new knowledges and truths about specific policies, which have emerged from within the deepest layers of the political process. Attempts by governing authorities, for example, to reduce research to simply the 'administration of things and events', for fiscal and managerial reasons, is an attempt to disguise the true nature of such work and its ability to produce these new knowledges. Criminological research is capable of unearthing the relationship between politics and policy, which is why servants of the state may seek to control the production, distribution and consumption of emerging new knowledges about their policy-making and practice (Walters and Presdee, 1999). As one academic criminologist interviewed for this research stated:

> Where is the concept of crime rooted, structurally? It's rooted in the power of the state. At the end of the day, the state defines what shall be crime, so once you are into the business of studying crime, you are studying something which lies right at the heart of the state and its relationship with its citizenry. And if you get stroppy in terms of studying that relationship you are, therefore, throwing down the challenge to state power.

Contemporary technologies of governance broaden the responsibility for crime control and personal security. 'Crime' becomes part of the overall risk package and is no longer the sole focus of inquiry. Researchers who challenge concepts of state power and notions of social order often become enmeshed in detailed analyses of modern forms of governance. However, while new modes of governance assert concepts of partnership, empowerment and responsibilization, power remains with those individuals and agencies that have the authority to govern; that is, with those that make decisions, exert influence, control, coerce, profit and so on (Chomsky, 1996). Yet, as Pavlich (2000a) argues, it is a 'post-disciplinary form of power' (139): a more dispersed and diffuse concept of power; one that traverses multiple intellectual and political terrains. As a result, criminological narratives or disciplines become fragmented by a postmodern condition that promotes diversity and uncertainty. In other words, an invisible border demarcates the territory of criminological inquiry. As crime and crime control continue to be recast within the parameters of 'profiling, prevention, managing risks, actuarial calculations, and security' (Pavlich, 2000a: 139), the disciplinary domains of criminology lose meaning.

Moreover, while contemporary modes of governance emphasize devolution and a politics of inclusion that promotes individual choice (and hence participatory power), it is clear these politico-ideological rationalities have expanded (and not contracted) the ways in which individuals are regulated (O'Malley 1998). While the sovereign state may have altered form, the 'new regulatory state' remains committed to governing or maintaining control, yet 'at a distance' (Rhodes, 1997). Therefore, new regulatory regimes have created new forms of power that challenge criminological epistemologies. However, these regimes remain equally susceptible to critical appraisal. As a result, knowledge that challenges the ideologies and power of governing bodies will continue to provoke reaction.

The contractual arrangements between researcher and government, as discussed in Chapter Four, continue to remain an important facet of this knowledge production. The contract provides guidelines on the objects of inquiry and the types of knowledge to be produced. New modes of governance seek information that improves or demonstrates managerial efficiency. Knowledge about crime is thus often an administrative exercise. As one academic criminologist commented:

> Sometimes the criminology bit of the research could be irrelevant to the Home Office and other funders. They just want you to do the research without any frills ... they just want foot soldiers to tell them

how something is being implemented and not any critical assessment of whether these ideas should have been implemented in the first place.

The above quotation identifies the purpose of research for those that govern as the administrative, the politically salient, the uncritical and cost-effective. As mentioned earlier, contemporary political rationalities produce a form of governance that pivots on notions of risk. The measurement and management of 'risk' becomes an essential tool for demonstrating efficiency (Douglas, 1992). As Sullivan (2000) argues, 'the state's first task is not to fight crime but more properly to act as an actuarial agency by assessing the risk of crime, make client-citizens (sometimes also called customers) aware of the current risk trends, and thus empowering citizens to secure themselves (36).

The emergence of actuarialism in a crime-control sense, represented by the scientific management of risk rather than the pursuit of individual and social reform, has as its focus the efficient management of policy (Feeley and Simon, 1992). The production of knowledge within risk society is vital (O'Malley, 1998). The knowledge required to demonstrate efficiency is more likely to be quantitative and focused specifically on a set of measurable objectives. Hence the contracting of criminologists and others to act like the aforementioned 'foot soldiers' has become commonplace. This is an example of what Dean (1999) refers to as 'reflexive government' or the 'governmentalisation of government'. By this, he means governmental agencies being held accountable, efficient and transparent by 'technologies of performance' (Dean, 1999: 193). These technologies include 'the devolution of budgets, the setting of performance indicators, benchmarking, the establishment of quasi-markets in expertise and service provision, the corporatisation and privatisation of formerly public services, and the contracting-out of services' (Dean, 1999: 169).

Chan (2000) argues that technologies of performance have created greater demand for criminological research. As government continues to contract-out and devolve state functions as a method of managerial efficiency, mechanisms of accountability are required to ensure that such devolutionary processes are fiscally and managerially responsible. External consultants provide one way of measuring efficiency. Criminologists are increasingly being engaged as consultants to produce knowledge under contract for government (discussed later). As the opening quotation to this chapter suggests, moreover, this move by academic criminologists to consultancy-based research is also driven by 'resource starved universities', where funding for research is competitive and where governments place pressure on universities to attract financial resources (Chan, 2000).

The academic environment, as well as being a place where much criminological scholarship is produced, is also a locus for critical engagement with existing social and political orders. What effects are the changing modes of governance, discussed above, having on universities? And what are the implications, if any, for criminological research?

University Autonomy and Criminological Research

In 1979, the French philosopher Jean-François Lyotard, published his influential book *La Condition postmoderne*. In this text, he forecasts that universities and the knowledges they produce will experience profound ideological shifts as capitalist societies emphasize the market principles of commercialization and commodification. In the 1984 English translation of Lyotard's work (*The Postmodern Condition*) he writes:

> Knowledge is and will be produced in order to be sold, it is and will be consumed in order to be valorized in new production .... It is not hard to visualize learning circulating along the same line as money, instead of for its educational value or political importance; the pertinent distinction would no longer be between knowledge and ignorance, but rather, as the case with money, between 'payment knowledge' and 'investment knowledge' – in other words, between units of knowledge exchanged in a daily maintenance framework (the reconstitution of the workforce, 'survival') versus funds of knowledge dedicated to optimizing the performance of a project (Lyotard, 1984: 5–6).

Numerous contemporary educationalists and academic scholars have since acknowledged the accuracy of Lyotard's prediction (see Peters and Roberts, 1999; Coady, 2000). The political and economic transformation from social democracy to market liberalism has created international concern and debate within higher education over issues such as university governance, academic freedom, funding, the market-driven curriculum and the commercialization of research (Coaldrake and Stedman, 1998; Kelsey, 1999; Karmel, 2000; Marceau, 2000; Hillyard *et al.*, 2003). While some of these issues have confronted universities for some time, others are new and provide direct challenges to the traditional values of tertiary education.

First, the subordination of universities to external political control has been profoundly accomplished. Most universities have historically relied upon government for financial security and recent cutbacks in funding within the tertiary sector have ignited a need for universities to generate revenue themselves (Clotfelter *et al.*, 1991; Coady, 2000). Second, the inculcation of new-managerialist economic principles has provided new structures of operation and governance. Ministers and senior university management have presented the new business-like culture of universities as a necessary transformation within changing economic landscapes. As a result, individual disciplines within universities are expected to be profit-making units or alternatively can face disestablishment. For many scholars, knowledge has become subservient to market demand (Peters and Roberts, 1999; Kelsey, 2000).

Moreover, individual academics express alienation from the 'processes and products of their labour' (to quote Karl Marx). The commercialization of the university sector has introduced a range of regulations that legally require academics to sign away their copyrights and intellectual property to their employers.

Fergusson *et al.* (2002) identify an alienation within universities, whereby academic labour is simply another form of commodity that produces goods and services for employers. Consider the following contract from the University of Paisley in Scotland, which all new academics are required to sign:

> All findings, discoveries, records, drawings, documents, papers, books, computer software products, or any such material made or acquired by you in the course of your employment, shall be the property of the university, which shall retain copyright and other intellectual rights therein, unless the university intimates in writing that is has decided not to do so (quoted in Ferguson *et al.* 2002: 82–83).

As universities move closer to market models of corporate management, matters such as copyright thus become the property of universities to be used for commercial purposes. Moreover, universities are beginning to commission academics on separate contracts as consultants, to write and deliver teaching materials for newly developed courses, paid for by an external client. For example, the police in New Zealand have recently 'purchased' a Certificate in Contemporary Policing from Victoria University of Wellington, where the course structure and content were signed off by the New Zealand Police after several meetings to review, vet and insist on changes to lecture notes and reading materials. This opens up a new dimension in the governance of criminological knowledge: teaching. Traditionally, the lecture theatre has been a forum where academic criminologists can disseminate uncensored critical knowledge for student learning. Fee-paying clients, who require a specific educational product for their organization, now challenge such forums. As universities become pressed for resources, new avenues for raising revenue are being sought. Therefore, we are witnessing new, emerging forms of governance of criminological knowledge through the regulation of university teaching programmes. Indeed, for those academics not 'bringing in research money' there is the opportunity (given the popularity of criminology) to bring it in through the development of new teaching initiatives that include such tailored programmes (mentioned above) and short courses.

This growing emphasis on market principles and economic reform has received substantial criticism at an international level. Frederic Mayor, Director-General of UNESCO, has publicly condemned the neo-liberal economic influence sweeping universities around the world by stating that 'if we create market universities run purely on market principles, they may be of their age, but they will not be able to transcend it' (Mayor, 1997).

Criminological research and the production of 'private knowledge'

As mentioned above, there is a growing expectation from university managements in many Western countries that academics should bring research money into their institutions.[2] Indeed, government funding formulas are becoming increasingly linked to a university's capacity to demonstrate 'research activity': a phenomenon that is, in part, calculated by an academic institution's level of external grants and contracts (O'Malley, 1997). Or, as Marginson (1997) argues, universities are becoming increasingly entrepreneurial as 'islands of expansionary capitalism' (247).

Criminologists are experiencing pressure to attract external research money: a factor that is influencing the type of knowledge produced. There are also increasing expectations that academics maintain a certain annual level or 'quantity' of recognized publications; often these publications are given a rating as a means of measuring a university's research quality. So there is a growing expectation that academics sustain an acceptable level of 'research activity'. For example, in the United Kingdom, the four higher-education funding bodies (Higher Education Funding Council of England, Scottish Higher Education Funding Council, Higher Education Funding Council of Wales and the Department of Education for Northern Ireland) jointly conduct the four-yearly Research Assessment Exercise (RAE). The purpose of this is to 'produce ratings of research quality which will be used by the higher education funding bodies in the determination of grants for research to the institutions which they fund' (Joint Funding Councils of the United Kingdom, 1996). The RAE is both a mechanism of accountability and a measurement of research activity. It also has been widely criticized by British academics for inhibiting academic inquiry and commodifying academic scholarship. Broadhead and Howard argue:

> The RAE represents a new phase in the 'commodification' of academic research .... The RAE has linked commodification directly to the overall goal of making the intellectual community 'competitive' with Departments adding up their members' currency for declining governing funding .... Individual researchers are coming under increasing pressure not to undertake complex and/or radical work which may not be compressed into the Exercise's four-year cycle .... It is more important than ever to be, and to be seen to be, a 'safe bet' (Broadhead and Howard, 1998: 9).

Within criminology, the RAE has also been strongly criticized for other reasons, including its perpetuation of positivist discourse as well as producing an environment of competition that is deleterious to the production of alternative or critical scholarship. As Scraton argues:

> Academics compete with each other to give keynote papers at prestigious conferences, to have their research published in 'stellar' journals and to win ESRC awards. It is a world of collusion and compromise, of horse-trading and back-scratching, and/or exchanging favors and poaching staff. If you opt out, your central funding dries up; if you opt in, you cannot retain a critical agenda (Scraton, 2001b: 2).

The role and influence of the RAE on the production of criminological research and funding is an important issue, which requires further analysis than I have provided here. There are some UK criminologists who are producing excellent critiques of the RAE and ESRC funding (see Hillard et al., 2003; Tombs and Whyte, 2003) and their works are welcome contributions to this important area.

The increasing commercialization of universities is also an important feature of government policy in Australia. In 1999, the Australian federal government released a discussion paper on higher-education research and research training. This document makes explicit the importance of universities generating income from external sources. Those universities that demonstrate an ability to attract revenue will be rewarded financially by the federal government. The federal minister for Education, Training and Youth Affairs, David Kemp, has written:

Under the proposal's funding arrangements, institutions will be rewarded for their achievements in attracting research related income from all sources (including industry) and for their success in attracting research students through the quality of their research training achievements (Kemp, 1999: 3).

Moreover, Kemp alludes to the changing research culture in Australia within the tertiary sector, one that is competitive and in need of business acumen. He states:

We are living today in the midst of two great research-based technological revolutions: in information technology and in biotechnology. Provided our research is conducted within an entrepreneurial culture and within settings which effectively address issues of intellectual property and encourage investment, there is no reason why our research strengths cannot lead to many new enterprises and to jobs that will accompany them (Kemp, 1999: 3).

Criminologists are also experiencing intense competition when attempting to secure research funding (Israel, 2000). Funding organizations like the Australian Research Council (ARC) and the ESRC in England are becoming increasingly swamped with applications.

Israel (2000) traces the changes in university funding since the late 1980s, and discusses how the ARC, established in 1988, now receives applications from newly formed universities (previously the polytechnics and schools of higher education), making the situation more competitive for academic researchers. Drawing on the analyses of Marginson (1997) and Hill (1993), Israel argues that academics who secure ARC grants bring financial rewards to their universities with increased Commonwealth funding. As a result, 'many universities raised the symbolic significance of ARC grants within the careers of researchers' (Israel, 2000: 5).

For Israel, the commercialization of Australian criminology may bring economic benefits as well as the non-economic benefits of 'improved relations with external bodies, prestige, spillover to basic research and teaching, future consulting, and student recruitment' (Israel, 2000: 7). Yet, he argues, it has also created legal and ethical difficulties.

As mentioned in Chapter One, criminology is experiencing substantial international growth. The expansion of courses, student numbers and journals, and the vast increase in criminological 'experts' or consultants who contribute knowledge to both the public and private sectors, suggests that criminology has asserted its place within competitive markets that demand efficiency and accountability. The increasing amount of criminological research conducted under contract has given rise to what may be termed the production of private, or, in some instances, 'secret' criminological knowledge: that is, knowledge commissioned by a contractor, either governmental or non-governmental, the dissemination of which is determined by the fee-paying agency. Criminologists who act as service providers to paying clients often sign away their entitlements to publish results emanating from the original research. The distribution, and hence consumption, of criminological knowledge becomes regulated by the authorities that have 'purchased' the research. Criminologists who reject contractual clauses that erode their intellectual property rights often risk losing the contract; and those who deliberately violate the contract in order to pursue what they feel is their academic responsibility to publish or to act as 'critic and conscience' of society often experience a range of adverse consequences (discussed in Chapter Four).

Academic criminologists 'for hire' – problems and prospects

For many criminologists, university managements or external political pressures do not necessarily drive their reasons for undertaking contact research. Why do many criminologists engage in fee-paying research under contract to a client? First, there is a belief by those criminologists who sign contracts or accept consultancies that they will have access to information that would otherwise be unattainable (cf. Hughes, 2000). As one academic criminologist commented, 'I think you can find out lots of interesting things doing contractual work. And you often get access to documents and lots of interesting people who would otherwise be very difficult to get hold of.' Second, there is a view that contractual research, notably with a government agency, will have an impact on processes and practices of criminal justice. Interestingly, criminologists interviewed for this research, including those who undertook vast amounts of contract research, considered that contract research had a minimal affect on government decision-making, even when the findings were consistent with the status quo.

> Only very few have an impact on policy and they tend to be done by well-known and senior criminologists in Britain. I can think of one or two people, who have definitely changed things. But overall most contract research, like most policy work within government, doesn't go anywhere. And there is a hell of a lot of policy work done by analysts that never sees the light of day.

Moreover, there were suggestions that problems exist for academic career development by continually doing contract research, notably, the

149

difficulty in converting reports for government into a format suitable for academic publication:

> If you're fully involved in contract research you're working to deadlines all the time and you haven't always got the reflective time to contextualize the contract report within the academic literature, or the research that is going on elsewhere. You haven't got the time to produce a format that goes into an academic or refereed journal.

That said, it is clear that many academic criminologists involved in contract research do manage to publish their work in refereed journals. Both the *British Journal of Criminology* and the *Australian and New Zealand Journal of Criminology* have witnessed a substantial growth of 'administrative criminology' in published articles. Pratt and Priestley (1999) refer to this as a reflection of 'the increased need to chase external funding' (324).

Many interviewees argued that younger or more junior academics are increasingly exploited by university departments that emphasize 'money-led research'. They are expected, in some instances, to be involved in contract and consulting research to the detriment of their academic development.

> Departments that do a lot of contract research tend to use people with no forethought to their career. They just want them to do the work, but don't actually help them build a career. So there are social implications of money-led research. It is no longer an apprenticeship for younger researchers. They are fodder. They get the job done, but the department or the university doesn't really care about them.

Here it is possible to argue that there is not only underdevelopment of academic careers, as university promotion committees grant only peripheral significance to contract research reports in contrast to refereed outputs, but also, more importantly, an inability for those concerned to contribute knowledge to ongoing public debate. The criminological work conducted under contract is often not debated in academic forums, nor often, if the paying client so desires, in any forums at all.

Furthermore, private consultancies provide opportunities for academics to 'make money', and hence we are witnessing 'a criminology for profit'. Many criminologists are entering a growing industry, or market, where their knowledge and expertise has considerable commercial value. There is growing evidence of criminologists leaving academia and opening their own consultancy businesses or alternatively operating their own private research companies while maintaining their academic posts. The primary motivation for engaging in these commercial arrangements is not the production of new knowledges or an attempt to influence policy and practice, but to make money.

In the United Kingdom there is a growing amount of private work undertaken by academic criminologists for security firms. Several interviewees viewed this as 'dangerous', in both an ideological and ethical sense. One academic criminologist stated:

> Working with Group 4 and other security firms is beyond the pale. I see that as really dangerous. Security firms are there to make money; you can mess with ideology but you can't mess with capitalism. I can talk to people at the Home Office and maybe I can strike some form of negotiation up with them, and it is possible to change ideology and government thinking. But I know that's not going to happen if I start talking to the Managing-Director of Securicor because their motivation is profit .... I don't think we [academics] should do that sort of work at all; I think they should employ market research-firms. We shouldn't be giving a stamp of respectability to their accounts .... But why are academics doing work for security firms, insurance companies and other businesses – because it's possible to make money, and, with the right contacts, a lot of money.

These commercial transactions involve new types of clients. Traditionally, criminologists have entered contractual agreements or received grant funding from government organizations. However, criminologists are seeking and finding new fee-paying clients within corporate markets. Private-sector companies (such as insurance agencies and security firms) are seeking criminological expertize within a growing risk society (cf. Tombs and Whyte, 2003). The discourses of 'risk society' and the growing debates around governmentality (see O'Malley, 1998) provide important frameworks for understanding the contexts in which the emergence of 'private' criminological research is taking place. Moreover, some scholars suggest that the rise of contract and consultancy research may see the end of critical criminological work. As Chan argues:

> The proliferation of contract research and the rise of criminologists in the private sector must be subject to close scrutiny, because, more than anything else, there is a distinct danger that the acceleration of these trends will spell the end of critical – reflexive – criminology (Chan, 2000: 132).

For Scraton (2001b), the 'lucrative contracts' offered by government for administrative research involving crime audits, victim surveys and crime prevention have seduced campaign organizations and critical academics. These voices, which have previously provided 'knowledges of resistance' to the politics of the New Right, are now attracted by the financial incentives of government consultancies, resulting in a growing dilution of alternative perspectives in the United Kingdom.

Critique and Post-disciplinary Criminologies

If, as Chan suggests, broader political and economic change threatens 'spell the end' of critical criminological scholarship, it is important to examine what impact new modes of governance are having on notions of critique. Criminologists have, in recent years, begun to question the extent to which criminology is being 'lured by relevance' at the expense of critical scholarship (Cohen, 1994; Hogg, 1996; van Swaanigen, 1999; Tombs and Whyte, 2003). Moreover, Barak (2001) suggests that the word 'critical' in the title of a book is likely to reduce its audience and its sales. In his review essay on Ian Taylor's *Crime in Context*, which won the American Society of Criminology's 2000 Hindelang Award, Barak asks:

> At the turn of the 21st century, what does it mean and what does it say about the field of criminology when a book receives its discipline's most prestigious award, presented by the largest organization of criminologists in the world, and relatively few of its members bother to read it?

This quotation provokes several questions worthy of further discussion. For example, it raises issues about definitions of 'critical', and about the place of critical criminology in broader criminological discourse as well as within changing neo-liberal landscapes. First, it is important to assess whether neo-liberal political rationalities have (re)defined what it means to be critical. If so, how? And what does this mean for future critical discourses on crime?

During the rise of radical criminologies in the 1970s, there was a consensus regarding the use of such terminology as 'critical criminology'. It was a radical agenda, which rejected crime as an ontological category, preferring to locate socially constructed behaviours as problematic within broader analyses of power, class and capitalism (Taylor *et al.*, 1973). Nowadays, some argue that the distinction is less apparent, with critical and administrative criminology becoming increasingly blurred within changing epistemologies (see Pavlich, 1998a; Rock, 1994). Today, critical or radical criminology is subject to various meanings and interpretations. For some, it is an old fashioned concept with little practical expression (hence the reluctance to read Taylor's book). For others, it involves political and economic analyses of crime deemed essential to identifying the 'truth' about crime causation and crime control (cf. Berry, 1997).

Throughout the 1990s, notably in North America, numerous scholars wrestled over the meaning and future direction of critical criminology (see Thomas and O'Maolchatha, 1989; Maclean and Milovanovic, 1991; DeKeseredy and Schwartz, 1996; Schwartz, 1997). Critical criminology emerged from these debates as an umbrella term for a range of left-of-centre perspectives. For some, the various hybrid forms of critical scholarship comprize a 'fuzzy' and unconnected set of splintered knowledges (Schwartz, 1997). However, Pepinsky (1997) suggests that fragmentation and lack of intellectual cohesion within modern critical genres typifies the strength of critical scholarship. He argues that emergent intellectual currents claiming a critical status (anarchist, deconstructionist, post-modernist, aboriginal, human rights and so on) represent a broadening (and thus strengthening) of critical scholarship from its narrowly defined status in the 1960s. Others (see O'Reilly-Fleming, 1996) call for a post-critical criminology, suggesting that existing theories (notably Left-realism) have fragmented integrative discourse and alienated or dismissed other alternative or Left theoretical perspectives as uncritical and unhelpful.

In an attempt to unravel what it means to be critical, Caringella-MacDonald (1997) traces the origins of modern critical criminology to the Frankfurt school of social theory, and identifies the writings of Marcuse, Adorno, and Habermas as influential in developing a form of critique that 'stood adamantly against structures of inequality, authority and power, as well against the ideological hegemony that sustains this nature of status quo' (p. 4). Having articulated a specific genesis of modern criminological critique as that which examines 'dominance structures' and 'postures against systems of inequality and oppression', Caringella-MacDonald opts for the umbrella approach, with a five-dimensional categorization of critical scholarship: Left realism, feminism, postmodernism, peace-making, and abolitionism.

The above writers provide a melting pot of opinions and definitions about critical criminological scholarship, which is seen to carry both weaknesses and strengths. The development of critical criminology and its notions of 'critique' have recently been examined in depth by Pavlich (2000a and 2000b). His comprehensive analysis of critique and radical discourses on crime provides an innovative framework for contextualizing the production and legitimation of new knowledges, and I will return to his contributions shortly.

Emerging from interviews and discussions with academic and government criminologists is a distinction between 'critical criminology' and 'critical criminological scholarship'. Many criminologists identified 'critical criminology' as relating to theoretical genres within academia, where as 'critical criminological scholarship' was a much broader category, relating to all forms of research that 'criticized' existing policy and practice.

One academic criminologist interviewed for this research defined radical or critical criminological scholarship as follows:

> Radical is where you cause the practitioners and the politicians to draw breath and say 'hey, you've raised something really important and we've missed that; it's really fundamental to our thinking'. Radical is proposing ideas that confront the status quo ... but traditional objective quantitative research can also be extremely radical because it actually demonstrates things that the organization wasn't aware of.

This same academic went on to condemn the sociological origins of critical genres within criminology, arguing that what is required is a greater emphasis on developmental psychology:

> I think psychology, as a discipline, has to become far more main-stream within criminology. In fact it has to become the backbone of criminology, because it's the only coherent social science with a solid empirical foundation. Sociology in this country is a ratbag discipline ... it's a failed discipline, intellectually incoherent, it's not dealing with fundamental issues ... it will increasingly be seen as the joke it is.

The above view (from an academic criminologist who disclosed earning almost double his/her university salary annually from private con-sultancy work) reflects the integration of criminological scholarship with new modes of governance, which emphasize risk assessment and 'useful' knowledge. Disciplines such as psychology provide positivist analyses to governing regimes requiring statistical and scientific analyses. As dis-cussed in Chapter Four, the Home Office seeks to employ psychology, economics and physics graduates in preference to criminology graduates because they have the skills and knowledge base most useful for con-temporary government-produced criminology. As a result of this development, critical research is increasingly seen as that which challenges existing policy and practice through scientific analyses of measurement. Therefore, 'critique' is limited to the realm of positive science.

While most interviewees suggested that critical or radical criminological research 'in an academic sense' implied political ideologies of the Left, many argued that being critical could be demonstrated through challenging a government policy or programme.

> I am probably a relatively conventional criminologist in terms of my training and approach but I would still see myself as critical. Research by definition is critical. It's something new, it's measuring policy against practice, and it's measuring the rhetoric against what is actually happening. So yes, criticizing policy and practice is a form of critique .... I don't buy that at all [that 'critical' criminological scholarship comprises only Left ideologies] ... I wouldn't accept for a minute that I'm not a critical criminologist because I'm looking at improving specific policies and that involves saying critical things.

In this view, the blurring of the epistemological boundaries referred to by Rock (1994) and Pavlich (1998) is confirmed. That is, critical criminological research has become, in some instances, subsumed within administrative criminology. Pavlich (2000b) argues, drawing on the works of Pepinsky (1980) and Cohen (1998), that radical and administrative criminologies have 'partially sustained' each other. In other words, the fulcrum upon which radical discourses have turned has comprized 'traces of administrative concepts in formulating their radical images at any given moment' (Pavlich, 2000b: 118). As a result, administrative criminologies have provided the impetus for alternative narratives.

Several interviewees disagreed with the views presented in the above quotations. For example, one academic criminologist, when asked whether administrative criminological research can be critical, stated:

> I don't believe so, not in any real sense. It can be critical in that it can say that the young offenders programme hasn't produced good results .... If that's critical then it's a very very low level of criticism and it's a very safe kind of criminology .... But in terms of challenging basic concepts, and being prepared to put the state and citizen relationship on the line, administrative criminology just doesn't do that.

The above quotation alludes to what Pavlich (2000b) refers to as 'judgmental criticism': a form of critique emanating from the works of Kant and Marx that 'defines criticism as authoritative judgment' (28). Critical judgement, in a Kantian sense, involves reflexive and socio-historical analyses of truth, of systems, of political structures and of attempts to isolate and challenge the reasons by which given objects or 'truths' are granted legitimacy. This, like other forms of critique, requires intellectual engagement and disputation: to wrestle with concepts, to trace lines of argument, 'to speak the truth to power' (Said, 1994) and to challenge accepted truths and narratives. Interestingly, this element of 'intellectual struggle' was identified by many interviewees as a characteristic of the radical or critical movement of the 1960s. However, nowadays it is seen to be vanishing within contemporary criminological discourses. Several interviewees echoed the following:

> Many of the criminology conferences that I go to seem very fearful of real debate. For example, the British conference last year in Belfast was astonishing to me and to others for the adoption of an American format of a conference in which there was actually a lot of pressure to prevent discussion … you were meant to sit there and listen to papers of extremely uneven quality and show your appreciation. And if you tried to challenge papers, this evoked very little response except a kind of disapproval. It's not a field where there is very much intellectual struggle going on.

O'Malley (1996) has argued that post-social political and economic conditions have disposed of the 'distinction between administrative and academic criminology' (35), whereby the latter has become enmeshed in the former. As a result, neo-liberal environments, for example, have 'pushed' academics into commercial arrangements and brought about distinct and favoured forms of criminological knowledge. These tend to be outcome measures of short-term projects and not research that focuses on broader and longer-term social issues. Hogg argues that there are several negative effects of the increased production of market-led criminology: 'There is thus the omnipresent fear of either being intellectually and politically sidelined or, in courting policy relevance, of surrendering criminology's critical edge and perhaps even worse becoming one of the new zoo keepers of deviance' (Hogg, 1996: 45).

Pavlich (2000b) examines in detail a range of searching questions about radical discourses on crime. Among these he includes an analysis of what exactly is the 'critical edge' that criminology is purported to be losing. He argues that modern critical genres in criminology are premised on notions of legal judgement. These judgmental practices (that is, a critique that judges specific conditions and events against established and accepted criteria established through disciplinary epistemologies), which were once encouraged under welfare and/or 'modern' political ideologies, are losing meaning under postmodern conditions. For Pavlich, the ontological status of 'crime' is diluted by governmental technologies that encapsulate 'crime' and 'deviance' within broader parameters of risk, security, and personal safety. He argues that criminological 'critique', which has to date been defined within disciplinary boundaries, must be re-examined within a post-disciplinary framework that articulates a grammar, or 'logos', and which deconstructs existing governmental regimes through the use of diverse narratives (including fiction and ethnography) rather than relying on positivism and scientific absolutes (Pavlich, 2000a and 2000b).

Pavlich traces the etymology of the term 'crime' from its Latin and French origins and identifies that it was not historically related to a fixed reality but was broadly used to describe 'accusation', 'cries of distress', 'crisis' and 'critic'. Therefore, Pavlich suggests that criminologists 'recover a lost facet of this etymology by re-conceiving crimen as accusation' (Pavlich, 2000a: 144): a grammar of critique that adopts accusation as the organizing referent and has the potential to place the criminologist (and not just those who govern) in the position of accuser, which involves calling 'someone to account for their actions' (Ayoto, 1990, cited in Pavlich, 2000a). As a result, criminological critique as accusation is given new horizons by shifting the analytical emphasis away from accepted realities and the causes of crime to the rationales of new regulatory regimes and their determination of what is to be labelled and governed as 'risk', 'deviant', 'harmful' and so on (Pavlich, 2000a and 2000b).

Contemporary forms of governance have created a post-disciplinary power/knowledge nexus. As a result, criminological discourses from the Left and administrative discourses from the Centre-Right have, in many instances, formed an unexpected and unintended coalition. 'Critical' criminological scholarship is now often viewed as anachronistic or, alternatively, as a 'catch-all' term for all forms of research that raise questions or challenge assumptions. All criminologists can, therefore, legitimately lay claim to a critical status. This is clearly problematic if critique becomes softened or watered-down. As previous chapters have demonstrated, a vast amount of funding for criminological research is directed to those positivist/administrative projects that seek answers to crime causation or aim to improve existing apparatuses of crime control. This research often serves the priorities of contemporary governing technologies: to assess and manage risk, to improve practice, to calculate policy failure, to measure cost-effectiveness. Critical criminological scholarship is often viewed as research that addresses these areas. Interestingly, governments sometimes challenge the 'critical' components of administrative criminological research, which, in an academic sense, is often viewed as conservative. Hence, governing rationalities are often viewing the more conservative academic criminology as critical scholarship.

Radical criminological genres have thus lost their purchase on critical discourses as the terrain or object of critique has evolved into more complex and diverse institutions. Pavlich (2000b) suggests that radical criminologies be revitalized within a governmental grammar of 'how not to be governed in a particular way' (166; cf. Foucault, 1977b and 1978). Rather than accepting the technical lure of a crime-solving ethos, criminologists should develop a critique that attempts to question the rationales of governing regimes and the power/knowledge arrangements that assert what should and should not be governed.

Concluding Comment

This chapter concludes that new modes of governance in contemporary society, which focus on risk management and a politics of responsibilization, have provided new political and economic landscapes for the production of criminological knowledge. Academic environments are changing under new-managerialist philosophies, which require servicing a market demand.

Emerging from these demands of the market is a 'criminology for profit': a privatization of knowledge where the academic role of 'critic and conscience of society' is replaced by that of service provider to a fee-paying client and by commercial arrangements with legally binding agreements, which often determine the parameters and outputs of both teaching and research. Consistent with broader political and economic trends, criminologists are becoming entrepreneurial, as both public- and private-sector interests seek their expertise. Moreover, new governing rationalities require specific forms of criminological knowledge, which address a range of management questions about broader issues of risk and regulation.

Finally, we are witnessing a variety of post-social criminologies that provide short-term and actuarial solutions to pressing problems. Furthermore, notions of 'critique' have become either wedded to or subordinate to the politics of existing governing rationalities. As a result, post-disciplinary criminologies must begin to re-examine critical scholarship within frameworks that focus on the politics and rationales of new modes of governance, and I will discuss this further in the next chapter.

Notes

1 The old, or original, prudentialism emanates from nineteenth-century trade associations, which urged responsible working men to be 'prudent' and safeguard against misfortune by subscribing to insurance schemes (see Defert, 1991).

2 The requirement to 'bring in money' is often made explicit during recruitment. For example, a newly created position in criminology at RMIT University in Melbourne, Australia, stipulates that the new appointee will be required to engage in consultancy work and client-focused short-course teaching for the express purpose of increasing departmental and faculty income. The job description listed nine 'specific accountabilities'. Two of these include 'to initiate and contribute to Departmental consultancy activities in order to assist in achieving Department income targets' and 'to initiate and actively contribute to short courses and other income earning activities in order to assist achieving Departmental and Faculty income targets' (see RMIT University, 2000). More recently, some universities are hiring specialized support staff to assist academics to maximize commercial opportunities. For example, The UK's Nottingham Trent University recently advertised a position for 'Consultants in Research Grant Capture' to support academics 'in making successful applications for research grants and contracts' (*Times Higher*, 2003: 57).

Chapter 7

Reflections and new horizons

Looking Back and Moving Forward

Criminology's origins and development reveal that it has been an intellectual enterprise largely dominated by scientific empiricism to explain the causes of state-defined crime for the purposes of developing a more efficient crime-control apparatus. Theoretical and historical contributions, which question definitions of crime and social order, have comprised marginalized knowledges within this larger body of criminological work.

Criminological research has, therefore, been dominated by a spirit or legacy of pragmatism, which has promoted a scientific and administrative criminology to aid the immediate policy needs of government. 'Crime', as defined by law (and not 'deviance' or 'social harm') has preoccupied the criminological agenda and, as a result, the legal frameworks and political structures of governing bodies have shaped criminological research.

The contexts for the development of postwar power/knowledge complexes of criminological research were not academic concerns about crime and social order but such things as international political concerns for social defence and social reconstruction. As discussed earlier, the United Nations reaffirmed 'crime' as an ontological category and provides important insights into how crime at an international level was problematized, and how governmental rationalities within the United

Nations categorized and prioritized 'delinquent behaviour' and 'crime prevention' as key areas for global concern. As a result, the directions of criminological research, notably in the postwar years, were influenced by debates occurring at an international level: debates motivated by the economic and social rebuilding of the United Nations' member states.

The pragmatic and state-oriented foundations of criminology are important for understanding the development and orientations of government-based and government-funded criminological centres and institutes, as well as for contextualising the increasing amount of contemporary government-funded consultancies. For example, the creation of the Home Office Research Unit in Britain and the establishment of criminological institutes and university programmes reflected the state's ambition to address the growing social problems endemic in criminal activity. Government-based criminological centres have been instrumental in the funding and shaping of specific criminological endeavours, and they remain powerful sites in the production of present-day criminological knowledge. Their focus has been, and remains, clearly orientated towards government policy and practice, where commissioned research is selected with partiality and is closely monitored.

The modern-day legacy of criminology's close association with the state's crime-control apparatus is a discipline now often constrained by the strategic needs of regulatory authorities in neo-liberal societies. Criminology's ongoing claim as an academic specialism is repeatedly asserted in the realm of positivism, with arguments resting on scientific empiricism and practical relevance. Moreover, criminology's historical and contemporary 'relevance' to government policy and practice has produced growing sites of governance for criminological researchers under changing political conditions. These genealogical analyses contextualize the production of criminological knowledge within historical epistemologies. This book argues that contemporary criminological scholarship is governed by its own historical and technocratic limitations as well as by existing governing rationalities, which have recast the parameters of crime and criminological research within notions of risk management and responsiblization.

These new modes of governance, focusing on risk management and a politics of responsibilization, have provided new political and economic landscapes for the production of criminological knowledge. Academic environments are changing under new-managerialist philosophies that require the meeting of market demand. The commercialization of criminological research provides an essential mechanism for developing strategic approaches to risk populations. Research that measures and assesses specific objectives are increasingly important in risk societies governed by economic rationalism. As a result, administrative and scientific criminological knowledges, which have traditionally appealed to governments, emerge as the dominating genres within current market demands.

As discussed in the previous chapter, emerging from these market demands is a privatization of knowledge, where the role of the academic as 'critic and conscience of society' is subsumed, or in some instances replaced, by that of service provider to a fee-paying client and by commercial arrangements with legally binding agreements that often determine the parameters and production of research. Consistent with broader political and economic trends, criminologists are becoming entrepreneurial, as both the public sector and private sector interests seek their expertise. Moreover, new governing rationalities require specific forms of criminological knowledge that address a range of management questions about broader issues of risk and regulation.

The advent of 'mission statements', 'strategic plans', 'output audits', and of language such as 'efficiency' and 'accountability' is driven by economic rationalist policies, which are changing the dynamics of academic institutions. New forms of governance within universities, such as management boards and trustees, are structures that aim to make the university more financially accountable and efficient. These developments have promoted intense competition within universities to access resources. Funding sources, both internal and external to the university, have become hotly contested as governments calculate budgets on 'research activity'. The increased competition for grants has resulted in criminological researchers seeking funds through commercial sources. In some instances, academics are strongly urged or directed to apply for commercially based research funds. The emergence of consultancies and other forms of private work place the researcher in a relationship of service provider to a client, where there is a responsibility to deliver a product by a nominated date. The nature and content of that product and the ways it is disseminated often rests with the client. Hence, such financial transactions often involve criminological researchers relinquishing intellectual property and copyright as well as allowing the client to determine the ways in which the research is released and reported. While academic researchers may attempt to avert conflict with a fee-paying client through establishing protocols and processes of negotiation, unless the research delivers what the regulatory authority requires for its internal needs, the researcher is likely to experience the tensions and difficulties explored throughout this book.

It should be remembered that research is an expression of power and is capable of challenging those that govern. Irrespective of the content of criminological research, when released it enters a political arena that reaches many audiences. Many of the political dimensions discussed throughout this book should be foreseen by criminologists and recognized as part and parcel of a process that has the potential to confront governing authorities and influence the policies and practices of the state crime-control apparatus. Therefore, engaging in various forms of conflict becomes inevitable. The criminologist is often confronted with a series of moral, ethical and legal dilemmas, which determine the eventual fate of her/his work. The pathways that individual criminologists will choose, whether they be conforming or compromising to the demands of governing authorities, or actively pursuing a stance of resistance and conflict, are likely to produce multiple consequences: for future funding, for future access to information and personnel, for individual and institutional reputations, as well as for the types of knowledges that inform political and public debate about crime and social order. Some criminologists at present are resisting the demands of their institutions and opting for a 'contract-free' research environment. But such a stance is becoming increasingly difficult in the competitive and market-driven tertiary sectors, where there is increased pressure for funding.

Intellectual Independence and Collective Concern

Criminologists who experience difficulties and conflict when conducting research often express a sense of isolation and marginalization within their institutions as well as within their discipline. Academic criminologists often therefore seek support from journalists and public officials rather than their universities or academic colleagues. There is a noticeable lack of institutional support for criminologists. Indeed, academic researchers are sometimes frowned upon by senior university management for comments and research deemed likely to compromise the commercial interests of the institution. What is needed is a reaffirmation and, in some instances, a declaration of academic freedom that upholds the principles of acting as 'critic and conscience of society' and asserts intellectual independence. The unique characteristics of a university include its intellectual autonomy, its critical engagement, its production of new knowledges and its ability to challenge and develop minds. Such features provide tertiary institutions with a degree of exclusivity that sets them apart from commercial research companies. Paradoxically, it is this exclusivity that regulatory authorities often seek when approaching academics to conduct research (cf. Peters and Roberts, 1999; McCalman, 2000). It gives the end product a cachet that enables governing entities to implement plans, develop strategies and create policies with a recognized credibility. To compromise or erode well-founded principles of academic freedom and the role of the academic as critic and conscience of society for short-term commercial gain is actually to set in motion the potential demise of the most marketable quality that universities have to offer.

Moreover, criminological associations and societies must begin to provide collegial support and advice to their members. Now that some criminological societies are becoming legally incorporated with charters on conduct as well as indemnity insurances to cover professional liabilities, they must also begin to establish formal networks of professional concern that endeavour to promote the production of all criminological knowledges as well as providing much needed support, both legal and professional, to criminologists that experience difficulties when conducting and publishing research. Criminological associations can glean important lessons from discourses on social movements and collective action (see Burgmann, 1993; Tarrow, 1994) about ways of upholding integrated collegiality for collective objectives. As Jasper (1997) points out, the mobilization of resources and personnel towards a collective goal is an effective form of social and political protest. Within academic environments, Peters and Roberts (1999) argue that processes of collective action can defend university ideals such as 'fostering public debate and enhancing democratic citizenship' (205), which are challenged by models of marketization. Drawing on the works of Freire (1985), they assert that scholarship that is 'investigative, curious, probing, questioning, dialogical, and critical' must be promoted by alliances of collective concern. Among their long list of possible actions, they advocate:

> ... alliances on a national and international scale ... marches, occupations, letters and visits to MPs, strikes of various kinds, refusing to complete seemingly pointless bureaucratic tasks demanded in the new environment of performance indicators. Making the most of new technologies to gain support from colleagues overseas (Peters and Roberts, 1999: 205).

The above recommendations are made in the spirit of Michel Foucault, who urged that critical voices should be expressed through diverse narratives (see Rabinow, 1997; Faubion, 2002). Or as Chomsky (1996) argues, the task is to seek out audiences or communities of 'collective concern' to identify injustice. As Stan Cohen cogently demonstrates in his excellent book *States of Denial* (2001), there exists what he calls an 'intellectual denial' where 'well-functioning minds become closed, and the gaze is averted from the uglier parts of their ideological blueprints and experiments. Or they allow themselves – for tangible rewards or an eagerness to please the powerful – to be duped into pseudo-stupidity. These shameful records of collusion go way back.' (280). If academic criminologists are to become nothing more than mere information gatherers for government, and are not prepared to critique the role of the state, or challenge new modes of conservative governance, or address questions relating to the sociology of law in fear of losing contracts, then the academic criminologist is reduced to a co-conspirator in the policing of knowledge.

There is much to be gained through establishing networks of collective concern, which advocate the promotion of multiple criminological narratives, academic freedom and the dissemination of new knowledges about crime and social order. Such networks, while they may themselves become new modes of governance, should at least actively promote assistance to criminological researchers. As a result, criminologists should be able to enter the political realms of research with the institutional backing of their universities as well as their discipline in ways that assert the value of ideas and the value of independent scholarship.

The Value of Critique

This book has examined the ways in which critical criminological scholarship has been influenced by new modes of conservative governance. The lure of relevance and commercialization of crimi-nological research dilutes critical scholarship. A 'critical position' about crime, deviance or criminal justice policy and practice is likely to evoke reaction from governing authorities that have become sensitive to, and threatened by, criticism. The increasing amount of 'jobbing criminology' or 'criminology for profit', through consultancies and short-term contract research, fails to provide a critique of power and social order, and thereby reduces the value of criminology to discussions about relevance and usefulness.

Criminological discourses from the Left and administrative discourses from the Centre-Right have, in many instances, become united under the same banner. As a result, criminologies that transcend traditional disciplinary boundaries must begin to re-examine critical scholarship within frameworks focusing on the politics and rationales of new modes of governance. Pavlich argues that what is needed is a criminological critique that relinquishes disciplinary loyalties and promotes a 'politics of truth', which involves dismantling *a priori* governmental assumptions about crime. He argues:

Now, when subjects contest the governmental truths and techniques that help create their identities, they embrace degrees of insubordination and desubjectification. The general aim, as Foucault puts it, is this: 'Maybe the target nowadays is not to discover what we are, but to refuse what we are (1982: 216)' .... Hence, the critic who refuses particular dimensions of governmental subjection engages in a politics of truth, and seeks to resist particular incarnations of being in given contexts (Pavlich, 2000b: 103).

Hence, Pavlich (2000b) suggests that what is needed is an 'art of governmental critique' that asserts as its *modus operandi* 'how not to be governed in a particular way' (166). He argues for a new language or grammar of critique that allows the criminologist to explore existing regulatory authorities within expanded horizons not confined to restrictive and compartmentalized analyses. Existing methods of critique are often rendered impotent by their own disciplinary labels. As a result, the parameters of criminology must move outwards and scrutinize new terrains in governance, in regulatory practices, in risk and so on. Such analyses have the capability to provide new and proactive ways of interpreting what is meant by 'harmful', 'deviant' and 'criminal'.

Importantly, these horizons for future criminological scholarship provide possible routes beyond existing pathways, as they attempt to destabilize the structures and processes that inform contemporary political ideologies.

Phil Scraton (2001a) argues that what is needed is the expansion of 'knowledges of resistance'. Such knowledges, he argues, cannot be generated under contract, where they are often silenced or neutralized. They require criminologists to stand outside the often lucrative and profitable domains of commercial criminology and actively assert a position of resistance. Elsewhere I have called for a 'criminology of resistance' (see Walters, 2003), a position that promotes critique, that challenges concepts of power and social order, that wrestles with notions of truth and adheres to intellectual autonomy and independence. I am not advocating that all academic criminologists adopt a complete boycott of all contract research. The resistance should be to the increasing colonization of contract research, which in many instances continues to assert a priority among academics and within their criminological research agendas. Moreover, academic criminologists should never sign away their intellectual property and copyright to a governing body that prevents their free speech or places controls over teaching and publication. In addition, academics should refuse to participate in contract research where the methods, questions, content and conclusions of the research are framed, determined and even altered by government. To do so devalues the role of academic scholarship and the importance of critique in contemporary democratic societies.

Contemporary markets and the value of knowledge

Is it merely romantic Left idealism to speak of the value of intellectual autonomy and the need for critical scholarship? Can such values, and the shape and directions of criminological knowledge, be maintained within current and future market economies. Indeed, in contemporary global markets, criminological knowledge, like all forms of knowledge, is seen as an essential part of economic growth. The rise of the services sector in recent years has placed significant commercial value on non-tangible company assets, such as ideas, education, experience and intellectual networks (Miles and Boden 2000). This growth has seen a shift away from acquiring and converting raw materials and goods-based production to a sharp rise in computing, telecommunications and other high-skill, knowledge-based technologies (Neef, 1998). Global commercial environments are continually seeking added-value or competitive advantages through the development and promotion of knowledge economies. These economies, whether individual, organizational or national, are underpinned by a new economic theory that is driven by a cost-reduction productivity (Drucker, 1998). Hence, information and knowledge for new and growing service sectors have become the keys to economic growth for contemporary business (Boisot, 1998). Included among these sectors are areas that require criminological expertise and knowledge, for example, crime prevention, security, insurance and risk and evaluation.

Discourses on knowledge economies also identify intellectual capital as the most profitable investment and most valuable asset of corporate entities (Edvinsson and Malone, 1997). Intellectual capital, comprising human capital (knowledge, competence and individual experience), structural capital (information systems and databases) and customer capital (customer relationships and networks), has emerged as 'the engine of the new economy' (Roos *et al.*, 1997: 8). The intersection of intellectual capital with economics has produced a definition of knowledge based on 'a capacity to act' (Sveiby, 1997: 37). In other words, knowledge has become a key and practical ingredient for corporate practices. Abell and Oxbrow (2001) define knowledge as 'The combination of explicit data and information to which is added tacit expert opinion, skills and experience to result in a valuable asset which can be used to make key decisions. The essential factor in adding meaning to information.' (267).

As a result, corporate environments utilize the knowledge/power nexus for commercial gain. Hence, knowledge must be measured and managed in order to realize a company's true value (Edvinsson and Malone, 1997). As mentioned earlier, such economic rationales have underpinned changes to the public sector and university management in recent years. This has occurred in the restructuring and relabelling within institutions as well as the ways in which knowledge is managed and valued. Various modes of governance recognize that knowledge is a valuable commodity. Marginson (2000) argues that knowledge economies and managerial principles based on neo-liberalism have created new modes of governance conducive to applied and practical forms of research. He argues:

> Research in a money economy must become research that happens in recognisable chunks that are capable of sale and calculation, like pieces of meat. In research administration and funding, the project format becomes dominant, and this has implications for the character of the research. Projects require precise objectives that are forecast and limited in advance. This in turn lends the research process more readily to all kinds of utilitarian purposes, including the structured competitions for research funding itself. By the same token, speculative and open-ended research programs become hard to sustain. They are rarely funded. Funding – its amount, its method of allocation, the terms and conditions attached to it – becomes the overwhelming driver of research activity …. Research management depends on a system that is common and across the university. Money becomes the common language of this system and the common index of measurement of value in research (193–4).

The commodification of knowledge and the inculcation of models of corporate management within universities present new challenges for institutions founded on teaching and research and not on profit. Criminological research finds itself drawn into this new managerial vortex where its value is increasingly being measured by application, relevance and its ability to attract external funding. This is consistent with university emphases on business principles of 'customer capital', which include networks and clients capable of generating income. This is an institutional response to recent government cutbacks in tertiary funding – cutbacks that are often accompanied, paradoxically, by political rhetoric about the importance of a knowledge society.

Therefore, scholars that produce research are entering unchartered waters where an emphasis is placed on the commercial value of their knowledge. If knowledge is the key to innovative and productive global markets, then universities, corporate research firms, and government research units are seen as 'brokers' of ideas for commercial growth and prosperity. Clearly, universities have bought into this position and actively promote their contributions to these new market opportunities. However, the 'knowledge for sale' ethos does not re-route intellectual endeavours beyond existing modes of governance but instead places them firmly within the control of conservative political rationalities. As a result, the producers of knowledge become key players in their own ongoing and entrenched governance. The growing production of relevant and applied criminological knowledge, for example, serves to perpetuate governing rationalities premised on actuarialism, risk and management. It is not difficult to conceive of intellectual work that deconstructs, critiques and theorizes as a kind of 'aknowledge' or 'the new deviant knowledge' within market societies. As knowledge continues to be defined and recast within concepts of commercial value, those forms of knowledge outside the parameters of market utility will continue to be marginalized. To avoid this, universities should promote their distinctive features, where the creation of new and critical knowledge is seen as having value within the commercial world.

Final Thought

This book should be read as a way forward, and its purpose is to open debate and provoke further scholarship on the ways in which criminological knowledge is produced and consumed. It reveals that historical, political and economic developments have governed the processes and practices of criminological research. It aims, therefore, to inform and assist criminologists in the production of their work. 'Crime' is a socially and politically constructed category. What is harmful, and what is not? What is deviant, what is not? What should be defined as crime, and what should not be defined as crime? What works in the criminal justice system, and what does not? These are questions that involve challenging the existing social and political order. Such questioning, which I've referred to throughout this book as deviant knowledge, inevitably provokes reaction from governing authorities, because it criticizes or jeopardizes ideological agendas, discourses and realms of power. Such knowledges are increasingly unwanted or rendered irrelevant or useless by governments within neo-liberal political landscapes, as they do not fit the risk-management and measurement model of contemporary governing rationalities.

This book also points out that there are challenges facing criminologists in emerging market economies, but suggests that such markets may provide opportunities for critical criminological scholarship as well as new ways of thinking about how individual scholars, disciplines and universities can challenge neo-liberal regulatory regimes. The broadening of the criminological gaze to include areas of regulatory practices and governance may provide additional intellectual capital in market economies that place a premium upon knowledge and ideas. The challenge is to uphold and assert the value of independent and critical knowledge as fundamental principles of a democratic society and not to be drawn into the 'service-provider ethos', which governs and regulates the production of criminological knowledge for specific needs in ways that devalue criminological scholarship.

Finally, reflexivity, as Foucault so persuasively argued, is a useful and insightful process. Academic criminologists and students alike often cast a wry smile when discussing the earlier works of Lombroso. The writings of the early positivists are often viewed as innovative yet simplistic and scientifically flawed. How will future criminologists reflect on the current period of criminological scholarship? Will the rising numbers of crimi-nology students, the expansion of university courses and criminology departments, the vast amounts of income generated by contract research, and the increase in market-driven and relevant criminological research be upheld as the measures of success? Or will contemporary criminological knowledge be judged on its commitment to diverse and critical scholar-ship, which struggled for academic freedom and intellectual autonomy?

Appendices

A. List of Interviewees

Semi-structured interviews (most of which were tape-recorded) were conducted with the following between 1998 and 2003.

Dr Ben Bowling. Lecturer, Institute of Criminology, University of Cambridge, England (at the time of interview). Former Research and Policy Analyst, Home Office Research and Planning Unit. Interviewed in Cambridge on 26 November 1998.

Professor John Braithwaite. Research School of Social Sciences, Australian National University, Canberra, Australia. Interviewed in Canberra on 15 July 1998.

Dr David Brereton. Director of Research, Queensland Criminal Justice Commission, Australia (at the time of interview). Interviewed in Brisbane on 7 July 1998.

Professor David Brown. Faculty of Law, University of New South Wales, Australia. Interviewed in Sydney on 13 July 1998.

Professor Pat Carlen. Visiting Professor, Department of Criminology, University of Keele, England. Interviewed in Edinburgh on 29 November 2002.

Associate Professor Kerry Carrington. School of Critical Social Science, University of Western Sydney (at the time of interview). Interviewed in Sydney on 28 February 2001.

Professor W.G. Carson. Honorary Distinguished Professorial Fellow, Department of Criminology, University of Melbourne, Australia. Vice-Chancellor, University of Auckland, New Zealand (at the time of interview). Interviewed in Auckland on 9 February 1998.

Professor Ron Clarke. Dean, School of Criminal Justice, Rutgers University, New Jersey. Former Director of Research at the Home Office Research Unit, England. Interviewed in Newark, New Jersey on 20 November 1998.

Professor Kathleen Daly. Associate Professor, Griffith University, Brisbane, Australia. Interviewed in Wellington on 28 October 1998.

Professor David Downes. Professor of Social Administration, London School of Economics. Interviewed in London on 4 December 2002.

Professor Mark Finnane. Dean, Faculty of Humanities, Griffith University, Brisbane, Australia. Interviewed in Brisbane on 7 July 1998.

Professor Arie Freiberg. Chairperson, Criminology Department, University of Melbourne, Australia. Interviewed in Melbourne on 20 July 1998.

Dr Lorraine Gelsthorpe. Senior Lecturer, Institute of Criminology, University of Cambridge, England. Interviewed in Cambridge on 25 November 1998.

Dr Peter Grabosky. Director of Research, Australian Institute of Criminology, Canberra, Australia (at the time of interview). Interviewed in Surfers Paradise on 10 July 1998.

Dr Adam Graycar. Director, Australian Institute of Criminology, Canberra, Australia. Interviewed in Wellington on 7 April 1998.

Professor Penny Green. Professor of Law, Westminster University, London. Interviewed in London on 4 December 2002.

Professor Chris Hale. University of Kent, Canterbury, England. Interviewed in Canterbury, England on 7 December 1998.

Professor Dick Hobbs. Department of Sociology and Social Policy, University of Durham, England. Interviewed in Durham on 30 November 1998.

Professor Ross Homel. School of Justice Administration, Griffith University, Brisbane, Australia. Interviewed in Brisbane on 7 July 1998.

Professor Gill McIvor. Professor of Social Work at the University of Stirling, Scotland, and Director of the Social Work Research Centre. Interviewed in Stirling on 14 October 2002.

Dr Pat Mayhew. Senior Policy and Research Advisor, Home Office Planning and Research Unit, England. Interviewed in London on 24 November 1998.

Professor Allison Morris. Director, Institute of Criminology, Victoria University of Wellington, New Zealand (at the time of interview). Interviewed in Wellington on 29 May 1998.

Professor Pat O'Malley. Deputy Dean, Faculty of Law and Management, La Trobe University, Melbourne, Australia (at the time of interview). Interviewed in Melbourne on 16 July 1998.

Professor Sir Leon Radzinowicz. Founding Director of the Institute of Criminology at the University of Cambridge, England. Interviewed in Philadelphia on 18 November 1998.

Professor Robert Reiner. Professor of Criminology, Department of Law, London School of Economics. Interviewed in London on 3 December 2002.

Professor Paul Rock. Professor of Social Institutions, Department of Sociology, London School of Economics. Interviewed in London on 3 December 2002.

Dr Fiona Spencer. Researcher, Scottish Executive (formerly the Scottish Home Office). Interviewed in Edinburgh on 3 February 2003.

Professor Ian Taylor. Department of Sociology and Social Policy, University of Durham, England (at the time of interview). Interviewed in Washington, D.C., on 12 November 1998.

Dr Richard Titus. Research Manager, National Institute of Justice, Washington, D.C. Interviewed in Wellington on 17 September 1999.

Dr Jacqueline Tombs. Criminological Researcher, with the former Scottish Office, 1976–97. Currently an independent consultant. Interviewed in Edinburgh on 22 November 2002.

Dr Jeremy Travis. Director, National Institute of Justice, Washington, D.C. (at the time of interview). Interviewed in Washington, D.C., on 13 November 1998.

Dr Don Weatherburn. Director, New South Wales Bureau of Crime Statistics, Sydney, Australia. Interviewed in Sydney on 14 July 1998.

Professor Paul Wiles. Director, Home Office Research and Statistics Directorate. Interviewed in London on 16 January 2003.

Professor Jock Young. Department of Criminology and Sociology, Middlesex University, Enfield, England. Interviewed in London on 23 November 1998.

Dr Peter Young. Faculty of Law, University of Edinburgh, Scotland (at the time of interview). Interviewed in Edinburgh on 30 November 1998.

Professor Warren Young. Faculty of Law, Victoria University of Wellington (at the time of interview). Former Director, Institute of Criminology, Victoria University of Wellington. Interviewed in Wellington on 17 December 1998.

B. List of Other Persons Contacted

In addition to those semi-structured interviews listed in Appendix A, there have been numerous discussions (some quite lengthy), written correspondence, and email communications with a variety of individuals. They include:

Professor Gregg Barak. Department Sociology, Anthropology and Criminology, Eastern Michigan University, United States.

Professor Manfred Brusten. Faculty of Social Sciences, University of Wuppertal, Germany.

Professor Bill Chambliss. Department of Sociology, George Washington University, United States.

Dr Marilyn Corsianos. Department of Sociology, Central Michigan University, United States.

Professor Adam Crawford. School of Law, Leeds University, England.

Associate Professor Chris Cunneen. School of Law, University of Sydney, Australia.

Dr Willem de Lint. Lecturer in Criminology, Department of Sociology, Windsor University, Canada.

Professor David Dixon. Faculty of Law, University of New South Wales, Australia.

Dr Paul Ekblom. Research and Statistics, Home Office, England.

Professor Jeff Ferrell. Department of Criminal Justice, Northern Arizona University. United States.

Professor Mark Findlay. School of Law, University of Sydney, Australia.

Ms Marian Fitzgerald. Crime and Criminal Justice Unit, Research Statistics, Home Office, England.

Mr Peter Goris. Criminology Department, Catholic University of Leuven, Belgium.

Professor Mark Hamm. Department of Criminology, Indiana State University. United States.

Professor Stuart Henry. Department of Sociology, Valparaiso University, United States.

Dr Gordon Hughes. Senior Lecturer in Criminology and Social Policy at the Open University, England.

Professor Tony Jefferson. Criminology Department, Keele University, England.

Dr Murray Lee. Lecturer in Critical Social Sciences, University of Western Sydney, Australia.

Professor Dag Leonardsen. Department of Sociology, Lillehammer College, Norway.

Professor Mike Levi. Department of Criminology, Cardiff University, Wales.

Mr Martin Lodge, formerly of the Home Office, England.

Dr Gail Mason. Senior Lecturer in Law, University of Sydney, Australia.

Professor John Muncie. Professor in Criminology and Social Policy, Open University, England.

Professor Tim Newburn. Goldsmiths College, University of London, England.

Mr Darren Palmer. Lecturer in Police Studies, Deakin University, Australia.

Professor George Pavlich. Department of Sociology, University of Alberta, Canada.

Mr Mike Presdee. Reader in the Department of Sociology and Social Policy, Sunderland University, England.

Associate Professor Rick Sarre. School of International Business, University of South Australia, Adelaide.

Professor Phil Scraton. Centre for the Study of Crime and Social Justice, Edge Hill University College, Liverpool.

Professor Joe Sim. Professor of Criminology, John Moores University, Liverpool.

Professor Rene Van Swaanigen, Criminal Law and Criminology, Erasmus University of Rotterdam, the Netherlands.

Ms Christy Visher, National Institute of Justice, United States Department of Justice, Washington, D.C.

C. Research Methodology

The 36 semi-structured interviews for this book were conducted between 1998 and 2003 in Australia, New Zealand, the United States, England and Scotland. The average time for each interview was 1 hour and 20 minutes (the shortest interview was 45 minutes and longest was 2 hours and 25 minutes). The majority of interviewees were academic staff working in criminology, sociology, and law departments. They were, in the main, senior and tenured university personnel. They were selected for a range of reasons, including their having experience with contract research, having worked in both academia and government research units, having coordinated a university research unit or department, and/or having previously published work about the 'difficulties' of conducting criminological research.[1]

There was also a deliberate attempt to speak with more junior academic staff to ascertain whether different problems or issues exist for staff without tenure or those working under short-term contracts. In addition, the research interviewed a select number of government criminologists/researchers, at both the senior and middle-management level. The experiences of criminologists within government are often unheard and this book aims to capture some of the dynamics and difficulties that confront government criminologists.

In addition to the semi-structured interviews, there were numerous informal discussions held with academics and government researchers. I have found that presenting conference papers and seminars of 'work in progress' has provided a useful method for generating discussion and follow-up correspondence with a variety of personnel, who either had 'a story to tell' or who contributed to the theoretical dimensions of the book. These discussions were enormously helpful for developing ideas. The views of more than 50 international scholars and government officials have, therefore, been integrated into the overall picture presented here. Not all the names of those contributing to informal discussions were known or could be recalled, as many comments were exchanged quite briefly, and hence the list of individuals in Appendix B is not exhaustive. While I have not closely monitored the time spent gathering information from informal discussions, it is estimated that hundreds of hours have been spent listening to the views of scholars from around the world, who have openly shared their thoughts and experiences about the 'politics' of conducting criminological research. The internet also provided an invaluable mechanism for confirming ideas or obtaining additional insights.

The formal interviews aimed to elicit individuals' experiences of criminological research; they included discussions of the various developments and genealogies within the study of crime and deviance, the emergence of research institutions and criminological centres, tensions and struggles with funding bodies, the increases and decreases in grants and contracts and the regulations surrounding these sources of funding, as well as charting the changes within universities over time. Moreover, the interviews aimed to capture a series of case-studies of the ways criminological research is often policed or governed and the impact that such regulation has on research. The interviews also gave rise to a number of themes relating to new and increased forms of governance over the production of criminological knowledge. There was also a deliberate attempt to speak with those people who fund or approve research projects in an attempt to understand why and how decisions are made as well to as understand the issues that confront criminologists working inside government.

The interviewees for this book provided their informed consent for quotations to be used throughout this text. However, in accordance with codes of ethical practice expressed by criminological societies in the United Kingdom, the United States, Australia and New Zealand (notably where the research was carried out) every effort has been made to render the participants anonymous.

In trying to access and sift through the volume of opinion, I deployed a variety of interview and research techniques. While most of my interviews were semi-structured – adhering to a standard set of questions, as well as formulating new questions as and when required, to generate information in specific areas of an interviewee's expertise – they often combined with other well-known interviewing techniques. For example, I would often conduct a focused interviewing style (see Chadwick *et al.*, 1984), a method which introduces scenarios or hypothetical situations in an attempt to elicit specific information about professional conduct, or ethical principles, as well as to bring to life previous experiences.

There were also several occasions when I adopted a receptive interview style (Kleining, 1988), allowing the interviewee to discuss issues at length without interruption, preferring to adopt the role of 'active listener'. I would often couple the receptive technique with the use of narrative interviews (see Schutz, 1979), which involve less questioning and more narration, where the interviewee recounts or reconstructs a history of events describing specific themes. Schutz (1979) argues that this approach is less of a question and answer format and more of a 'story-telling' approach. The researcher remains passive and allows the interviewee to recall, without prompting, how certain events unfolded. Some respondents wrestled with the chronology or factual content of certain events; and often their verbal accounts differed from their written work, the latter having been published decades earlier.[2]

In conjunction with interviews I also endeavoured to capture issues through the use of case-studies informing the development of themes discussed in Chapters Four to Five. As readers will be aware, case-study research is 'an empirical inquiry that investigates a contemporary phenomenon within its real-life context when the boundaries between phenomenon and context are not clearly evident, and in which multiple sources of evidence are used' (Yin, 1991: 23). In other words, case-studies aim to 'bring to life' research questions as well as themes identified through data collection (Bouma, 2000). It became clear early on in the research that this area of study involved a number of contradictory, and often vitriolically expressed, opinions.

The use of case-studies aids the capturing of a process of events; they provide a sequence and structure that is often omitted in surveys or interviews. They also provided a useful means by which to chart ideas and develop themes for analysis. Some of the case-studies have been included in Chapter Four; however, the majority have not been written up into the book, largely because they comprised 'working notes', but nevertheless they have informed the theoretical dimensions and categories of the book.

In addition to an examination of literature across various disciplines and topics, this book has also conducted an extensive documentary analysis of official information from several sources. A critical documentary analysis identifies the connections between official sources of knowledge and the exercise of power by governing authorities (Jupp and Norris, 1993). The documents analysed included records of parliamentary debates in Australia and the United Kingdom, the League of Nations and the United Nations, and reports to the US Congress. This review was most helpful for charting the development of the centres and research bodies discussed in Chapter Three, as well as identifying those events that have shaped criminological research in Britain, the United States and Australia.

Notes

1   The names and positions of interviewees are not identified in quotations throughout the book. In order to maintain anonymity, I refer to interviewees as either 'academic' or 'government' criminologist.

2   Contemporary researchers refer to the above as 'false memory syndrome' (Garry and Loftus, 1994) or as the 'misinformation effect' (Garry *et al.*, 1996): a position which argues that memory is not ordered and precise but often built on by circumstances outside our own experience, where events may be created or altered in subtle ways that distort the original facts (Garry *et al.*, 1996). In those cases where interviewees were unable to record specific events vividly they were subsequently able to furnish the research with published work or written comments.

References

Abell, A. and Oxbrow, N. (2001) *Competing with Knowledge: The Information Professional in the Knowledge Management Age*, London: TFPL.

Abelsom, J. and Vaishnav, A. (2002) 'School Silences Speaker on Mideast', *Boston Globe* (5 April).

Adler, F. (1996) 'Presidential Address': www.asc41.com

Adler, P. (1985) *Wheeling and Dealing: An Ethnography of an Upper-Level Drug Dealing and Smuggling Community*, New York: Columbia University Press.

Akeroyd, A. (1988) 'Ethnography, Personal Data and Computers: The Implications of Data Protection Legalisation for Qualitative Social Research', in R. Burgess (ed.) *Studies in Qualitative Methodology* (annual), volume one, *Conducting Qualitative Research*, Greenwich, Connecticut: Jai Press.

American Society of Criminology (1998a) *American Society of Criminology Code of Ethics*: www.asc41.com/ethics9

American Society of Criminology (1998b) *Crime, Justice and Public Policy: Examining Our Past and Envisioning Our Future*, ASC's 50th Annual Meeting, (11–14 November 1998), Washington, D.C.

Ancel, M. (1962) 'Social Defence', *Law Quarterly Review*, 78, 497–503.

Ancel, M. (1965) *Social Defence: A Modern Approach to Criminal Problems*. London: Routledge and Kegan Paul.

Aristotle (1979) *The Politics*, translated with an Introduction by T.A. Sinclair, Harmondsworth: Penguin.

Arrigo, B. (1999) 'Critical Criminology's Discontent: The Perils of Publishing and the Call to Action', *Critical Criminologist*, 10(1),10–13.

Associated Press (2001a) 'University Trustees Echo Condemnation of "Un-American Forum"' (8 October 2001): www.freedomforum.org

Associated Press (2001b) 'Colleges Provide Chilly Climate for Free Speech since Attacks' (15 October): www.freedomforum.org

Associated Press (2001c) 'Speak up at Your Own Risk' (26 September): www.freedomforum.org

Associated Press (2001d) 'Networks Cautious in Covering War' (2 November): www.freedomforum.org

Australia and New Zealand Government Procurement Agreement (revised 1997): www.ctc.gov.au/publications/purchasing/international/gpa.htm

Australian and New Zealand Society of Criminology (2000) *Australian and New Zealand Society of Criminology Code of Ethics*: www.uwa.edu.au/anzsoc/crim

Australian Law Reports (1997) *Hughes Aircraft Systems International V Airservices Australia*, 146, ALR 1.

Australian Procurement and Construction Council (1997) 'National Action on Small to Medium Enterprises in Government Procurement', meeting of procurement and construction ministers, Perth, 1997: www.apcc.gov.au/aus_pro.html

Ayoto, J. (1990) *Dictionary of Word Origins*, New York: Arcade.

Bachman, R. and Schutt, R. (2001) *The Practice of Research in Criminology and Criminal Justice*, Thousand Oaks, California: Pine Forge Press.

Baker, T. (1988) *Doing Social Research*, New York: McGraw-Hill.

Barak, G. (1988) 'Newsmaking Criminology: Reflections on the Media Intellectuals and Crime', *Justice Quarterly*, 5(4), 565–87.

Barak, G. (ed.) (1994) *Varieties of Criminology: Readings from a Dynamic Discipline*, Westport, Connecticut: Praeger.

Barak, G. (2001) 'Review Essay', *Critical Criminology: An International Journal*, 10(2), 137–45.

Barlow, H. (ed.) (1995) *Crime and Public Policy: Putting Theory to Work*, Boulder, Colorado: Westview Press.

Barnes, J. (1979) *Who Should Know What? Social Science, Privacy and Ethics*, Harmondsworth: Penguin.

Barry, J. (1968) 'The President's Foreword', *Australian and New Zealand Journal of Criminology*, 1, 1–2.

Bart, P. (2001) 'White House Enlists Hollywood for War Effort', *Variety* (18 October).

Bauman, Z. (1998) *Globalization: The Human Consequences*, Cambridge: Polity Press.

Baynes, N. (ed.) (1942) *The Speeches of Adolph Hitler, April 1922–August 1939*, volume one, London: Oxford University Press.

Bebbington, B. (1968) 'Home Office Police Research and Planning Branch', *British Journal of Criminology*, 8(1), 55–59.

Beccaria, C. (1963 [1764]) *On Crimes and Punishment* [*Dei delitti e delle pene*], Indianapolis, Indiana: Bobbs-Merrill.

Beck, U. (1992) *Risk Society: Towards a New Modernity*, London: Sage.

Behr, C., Gipser, D., Klein-Schonnefeld, S., Naffine, K. and Zillmer, H. (1981) 'The Use of Scientific Discoveries for the Maintenance and Extension of State Control – on the Effect of Legitimation and the Utilization of Research', in M. Brusten and P. Ponsaers (eds) *State Control on Information in the Field of Deviance and Social Control*, Working Papers in European Criminology, no. 2, Leuven: European Group for the Study of Deviance and Social Control.

Beirne, P (1993) *Inventing Criminology: The Rise of 'Homo Criminalis'*, Albany: State University of New York Press.

Bell, C. and Newby, H. (eds) (1977) *Doing Sociological Research*, London: Allen and Unwin.

Bentham, J. (1879) *An Introduction to the Principles of Morals and Legislation*, Oxford: Clarendon Press.

Berkeley, G. (1932) *Italy in the Making*, Cambridge: Cambridge University Press.

Berry, B. (1997) 'The Future (and Past and Present) of Critical Theory in Criminology', *The Criminologist*, special issue, 1 (Winter).

Biles, D. (1981) 'The Current Status of Australian Criminological Research', in D. Biles (ed.) *Review of Australian Criminological Research*, Canberra: Australian Institute of Criminology.

Boisot, M. (1998) *Knowledge Assets: Securing Competitive Advantages in the Information Economy*, Oxford: Oxford University Press.

Bonger, W. (1916) *Criminality and Economic Conditions.* London: Heinemann.

Boston Herald (2001) 'High School Speech by Peace Prof Raises Ire', editorial (20 November).

Boston, J., Martin, J., Pallot, J. and Walsh, P. (1996) *Public Management: The New Zealand Model*, Auckland: Oxford University Press.

Bosworth, R. (1979) *Italy, the Least of the Great Powers: Italian Foreign Policy before the First World War*, Cambridge: Cambridge University Press.

Bottoms, A. (1996) 'Report by the Director of the Institute of Criminology to the General Board's Review Committee on the Current and Future Work of the Institute', unpublished.

Bouma, G. (2000) *The Research Process*, fourth edition, South Melbourne: Oxford University Press.

Braithwaite, J. (1989) *Crime, Shame and Reintergration*, Cambridge: Cambridge University Press.

Braithewaite, J. (1989) 'The State of Criminology: Theoretical Decay or Renaissance?', *Australian and New Zealand Journal of Sociology*, 22, 129–35.

Brereton, D. (1997) 'Research for Policy', paper presented to the Second National Outlook Symposium on Violent Crime, Property Crime and Public Policy, Canberra (March), unpublished.

Brink, G. (2002) 'Professors' Group Enters al-Arian Fray', *St Petersburg Times* (7 February 2002): www.sptimes.com

Broadhead, L. and Howard, S. (1998) '"The Art of Punishing": The Research Assessment Exercise and the Ritualisation of Power in Higher Education', *Education Policy Analysis*, 6/8, 1–14.

Brookman, F. (1999) 'Accessing and Analysing Police Murder Files', in F. Brookman, L. Noaks and E. Wincup (eds) (1999) *Qualitative Research in Criminology*, Aldershot: Ashgate.

Brookman, F., Noaks, L. and Wincup, E. (eds) (1999) *Qualitative Research in Criminology*, Aldershot: Ashgate.

Brusten, M. (1981) 'Social Control of Criminology and Criminologists', in M. Brusten and P. Ponsaers (eds) *State Control of Information in the Field of Deviance and Social Control*, Working Papers in European Criminology, no. 2, Leuven: European Group for the Study of Deviance and Social Control.

Brusten, M. and Van Outrive, L. (1981) 'The Relationship between State Institutions and the Social Sciences in the Field of Deviance and Social Control', in M. Brusten and P. Ponsaers (eds) *State Control of Information in the Field of Deviance and Social Control*, Working Papers in European Criminology, no. 2, Leuven: European Group for the Study of Deviance and Social Control.

Bulmer, M. (1982) *The Uses of Social Research*, London: Allen and Unwin.

Burke, J. (2001) 'Antiwar Protest Draws 400,000', *Observer* (10 November).

Burgmann, V. (1993) *Power and Protest: Movements for Change in Australian Society*, St Leonards: Allen and Unwin.

Bush, G. (2001a) 'International Campaign against Terror Grows', presidential address (25 September): www.whitehouse.gov

Bush, G. (2001b) 'Address to a Joint Session of Congress and the American People' (20 September): www.whitehouse.gov

Butler, Lord (1974) 'The Foundation of the Institute of Criminology in Cambridge', in R. Hood (ed.) *Crime, Criminology and Public Policy: Essays in Honour of Sir Leon Radzinowicz*, London: Heinmann.

Byrne-Armstrong, H., Carmody, M., Hodge, B., Hogg, R. and Lee, M. (1999) 'The Risk of Naming Violence: An Unpleasant Encounter between Legal Culture and Feminist Criminology', *Australian Feminist Law Journal*, 13, 13–37.

Callaghan, J. (1983) 'Cumber and Variableness', in *The Home Office: Perspectives on Policy and Administration*, London: Royal Institute of Public Administration.

Callahan, D. and Jennings, B. (eds) (1983) *Ethics, the Social Sciences and Policy Analysis*, New York: Plenium Press.

Calvey, D. (2000) 'Getting on the Door and Staying There: A Covert Participant Observational Study of Bouncers', in G. Lee-Treweek and S. Linkogle (eds) *Danger in the Field: Risk and Ethics in Social Research*, London: Routledge.

Carbin, J (2001) 'Boondocks Speaks: An Interview with Aaron McGruder', *City Paper*, Philadelphia (5 November): www.alternet.org

Caringella-MacDonald, S. (1997) 'Taking Back the Critical: Reflections on the Division of Critical Criminology in Light of Left Realism, Feminism, Postmodernism and Anarchism', *Critical Criminologist Newsletter*, special issue, 2 (Winter).

Carlen, P. (1998) 'Criminology Ltd: The Search for a Paradigm', in P. Walton and J. Young (eds) *The New Criminology Revisited*, London: Macmillan Press.

Carmignani, G. (1831) *Teoria delle leggi sulla sicurezza sociale*, Pisa.

Carrington, K. (1998) *Who Killed Leigh Leigh? A Story of Shame and Mateship in an Australian Town*, Sydney: Random House.

Carroll, M. (1938) *Key to League of Nations Documents Placed on Public Sale 1934–1936; Fourth Supplement to Key to League of Nations Documents 1920–1929*, New York: Columbia University Press.

Carson, W.G. and Ditton, J. (1979) 'The Tyranny of the Present: Post-War British Criminology, the Rediscovery of the Past, and the "Dinosaur Theory" of History', unpublished.

Carson, W.G. (1983) 'The Challenge of White Collar Crime', inaugural lecture (28 September), LaTrobe University: LaTrobe University Press.

Carson, K. and O'Malley, P. (1989) 'The Institutional Foundations of Contemporary Australian Criminology' *Australian and New Zealand Journal of Sociology*, 25(3), 333–55.

Castberg, F. (1960) *Freedom of Speech in the West*, Oslo: Oslo University Press.

Castles, F., Gerritsen, R. and Vowles, J. (1996) *The Great Experiment: Labour Parties and Public Policy Transformations in Australia and New Zealand*, Auckland: Auckland University Press.

Chadwick, B., Bahr, H. and Albrecht, S. (1984) *Social Science Research Methods*, Englewood Cliffs, New Jersey: Prentice-Hall.

Chambliss, W. (1975) 'Toward a Political Economy of Crime', *Theory and Society*, 2, 149–70.

Chan, J. (1994) 'Crime Prevention and the Lure of Relevance: A Response to Adam Sutton', *Australian and New Zealand Journal of Criminology*, 27(1), 25–29.

Chan, J. (2000) 'Globalisation, Reflexivity and The Practice of Criminology', *Australian and New Zealand Journal of Criminology*, 33(2), 118–35.

Chappell, D. and Wilson, P. (1977) *The Australian Criminal Justice System*, second edition, Sydney: Butterworth.

Chomsky, N. (1996) *Power and Prospects: Reflections on Human Nature and the Social Order*, St Leonards: Allen and Unwin.

Chomsky, N. (2001) *September 11*, Crows Nest: Allen and Unwin.

Clark, R. (1977) *Fundamentals of Criminal Justice Research*, Lexington, Massachusetts: Lexington Books.

Clarke, P. (1996) 'The Keynesian Consensus and Its Enemies. The Argument over Macroeconomic Policy in Britain since the Second World War', in D. Marquand and A. Seldon (eds) *The Ideas That Shaped Post-War Britain*, London: Fontana.

Clarke, R. (1977) 'Penal Policy-Making and Research in the Home Office', in N. Walker (ed.) *Penal Policy-Making in England*, Cambridge: Institute of Criminology, University of Cambridge.

Clarke, R. and Cornish, D. (eds) (1983) *Crime Control in Britain: A Review of Policy Research*, Albany: State University of New York Press.

Clarke, R. (1980) 'Situational Crime Prevention: Theory and Practice', *British Journal of Criminology*, 20(2), 136–47.

Clotfelter, C., Ehrenberg, R., Getz, M. and Siegfried, J. (1991) *Economic Challenges in Higher Education*, Chicago: University of Chicago Press.

Coady, C. and Sampford, C. (eds) (1993) *Business Ethics and the Law*, Sydney: Federation Press.

Coady, T. (ed.) (2000) *Why Universities Matter*, St Leonards: Allen and Unwin.

Coaldrake, P. and Stedman, L. (1998) *On the Brink: Australian Universities Confronting Their Futures*, Brisbane: Queensland University Press.

Cohen, S. (1981) 'Footprints in the Sand: Criminology and the Sociology of Deviance', in M. Fitzgerald, M. McLennan and J. Pawson (eds) *Crime and Society: Readings in Theory and History*, London: Routledge and Kegan Paul.

Cohen, S. (1988) *Against Criminology*, New Brunswick, New Jersey: Transaction Books.

Cohen, S. (1994) 'Postscript: If Nothing Works, What is Our Work?', *Australian and New Zealand Journal of Criminology*, 27(1), 104–07.

Cohen, S. (1998) 'Intellectual Scepticism and Political Commitment: The Case of Radical Criminology', in P. Walton and J. Young (eds) *The New Criminology Revisited*, London: Macmillan.

Cohen, S. (2001) *States of Denial: Knowing about Atrocities and Suffering*, Cambridge: Polity Press.

Cohen, S. and Taylor, L. (1972) *Psychological Survival: The Experience of Long-Term Imprisonment*, New York: Vintage.

Cohen, S. and Taylor, L. (1977) 'Talking about Prison Blues', in C. Bell and H. Newby (eds) *Doing Sociological Research*, London: Allen and Unwin.

Cole, G. (1956) *The Post-War Condition of Britain*, London: Routledge and Kegan Paul.

Coleman, C. and Moynihan, J. (1996) *Understanding Crime Data: Haunted by the Dark Figure*, Buckingham: Open University Press.

Commission Internationale Pénale et Pénitentiaire (1951), *Douzième Congrès pénal et pénitentiaire*, in French and English, Berne: Commission Internationale Pénale et Pénitentiaire.

Commonwealth Epidemiological Studies (Confidentiality) Act 1981, Canberra: Federal Printing Office.

Cornish, D. and Clarke, R. (1986) *The Reasoning Criminal: Rational Choice Perspectives on Offending*. New York: Springer.

Cottin, H. (2001) 'Biased Media Backs War Drive', International Action Center (26 September): www.iac.org

Crawford, A. (1994) 'The Partnership Approach: Corporatism at the Local Level?', *Social and Legal Studies*, 3(4), 497–519.

Crawford, A. (1997) *The Local Governance of Crime: Appeals to Community and Partnerships*, Oxford: Clarendon Press.

Crawford, A. (1998) *Crime Prevention and Community Safety: Politics, Policies and Practices*, Harlow, Essex: Addison-Wesley Longman.

Criminology Research Council (1998) *Criminology Research Council: Annual Report*, Canberra: Government Printing Office.

Criminology Research Council (2000) *Criminology Research Council: Annual Report*. Canberra: Government Printing Office.

Croft, J. (1982) 'The Research and Planning Unit', *Home Office Research Bulletin*, 13.

Currie, E. (1998) 'Crime and Market Society: Lessons from the United States', in J. Walton and J. Young (eds) *The New Criminology Revisited*, London: Macmillan.

Dahl, R. (1970) *Modern Political Analysis*, second edition, Englewood Cliffs, New Jersey: Prentice-Hall.

Daly, K. (1995) 'Celebrated Crime Cases and the Public's Imagination: From Bad Press to Bad Policy', in D. Dixon (ed.), *Australian and New Zealand Journal of Criminology* special supplementary issue, *Crime, Criminology and Public Policy*, Sydney: Butterworth.

Daly, K. and Maher, L. (eds) (1998) *Criminology at the Crossroads: Feminist Readings in Crime and Justice*, Oxford: Oxford University Press.

Dantzker, M. (1998) *Criminology and Criminal Justice: Comparing, Contrasting, and Intertwining Disciplines*, Boston: Butterworth-Heinemann.

Davis, M. (2000) *Grantmanship for Criminal Justice and Criminology*, Thousand Oaks, California: Sage.

Dean, M. (1999) *Governmentality: Power and Rule in Modern Society*, London: Sage.

De Young, K. (2001) 'U.S., Britain Step up War for Public Opinion', *Washington Post* (1 November).

Defert, D. (1991) '"Popular Life" and Insurance Technology', in G. Burchell, C. Gordon and P. Miller (eds) *The Foucault Effect: Studies in Governmentality*, Hemel Hempstead: Harvester Wheatsheaf.

Dekeseredy, W. and Schwartz, M. (1996) *Contemporary Criminology*, Belmont: Wadsworth Press.

Derrida, J. (1994) *Specters of Marx: The State of the Debt, the Work of Mourning and the New International*, London: Routledge.

Dixon, D. (ed.) (1995) *Australian and New Zealand Journal of Criminology*, special supplementary issue, *Crime, Criminology and Public Policy*, Sydney: Butterworth.

Donzelot, J. (1979) 'The Poverty of Political Culture', *Ideology and Consciousness*, 5, 71–86.

Douglas, M. (1992) *Risk and Blame*, London: Routledge.

Downes, D. (1988) 'The Sociology of Crime and Social Control in Britain, 1960–1987', in P. Rock, *A History of British Criminology*, Oxford: Clarendon Press.

Downes, D. (ed.) (1992) *Unravelling Criminal Justice: Eleven British Studies*, London: Macmillan.

Downes, D. and Rock, P. (1982) *Understanding Deviance: A Guide to the Sociology of Crime and Law Breaking*, Oxford: Clarendon Press.

Drucker, P. (1998) 'From Capitalism to Knowledge Society', in D. Neef (ed.) *The Knowledge Economy*, Boston: Butterworth-Heinemann.

Durkheim, E. (1964 [1895]) *Rules of Sociological Method*, New York: Free Press.

Edvinsson, L. and Malone, M. (1997) *Intellectual Capital: Realizing Your Company's True Value by Finding Its Hidden Brainpower*, New York: HarperCollins.

Eichengreen, B. and Kenen, P. (1994) 'Managing the World Economy under the Bretton Woods System: An Overview', in P. Kenen (ed.) *Managing the World Economy: Fifty Years after Bretton Woods*, Washington, D.C.: Institute for International Economics.

Eno, B. (2003) 'Lessons in how to lie about Iraq'. *The Observer*, Sunday 17 August 2003: 29.

Ericson, R. (1994) 'The Division of Expert Knowledge in Policing and Security', *British Journal of Sociology*, 45, 149–75.

Ericson, R. (1996) 'Making Criminology', *Current Issues in Criminal Justice*, special issue, *The Future of Criminology*, 8(1), 14–25.

Ericson, R. and Carriere, K. (1994) 'The Fragmentation of Criminology', in D. Nelken (ed.) *The Futures of Criminology*, London: Sage.

Erikson, K.T. (1962) 'Notes on the Sociology of Deviance', *Social Problems*, 9.

ESRC (1999) 'The Research Resources Board's Strategy for Underpinning Social Science Research': www.esrc.ac.uk/rrbstrat.htm

Esyenck, H. (1970) *Crime and Personality*, London: Paladin.

Evensen, A. (1973) *Social Defence in Norway*,Oslo: Ministry of Justice.

Fairness and Accuracy in Reporting (2001), 'Networks Accept Government Guidance' (12 October): www.fair.org

Farhi, P. (2001) 'The Networks: Giving Aid to the Enemy?' *Washington Post* (12 October).

Fattah, E. (1997) *Criminology: Past, Present and Future: A Critical Overview*, London: Macmillan.

Faubion, J. (2000) (ed.) *Power: Essential Works of Foucault 1954–1984*, third edition, London: Penguin.

Feeley, M. and Simon, J. (1992) 'The New Penology: Notes on the Emerging Strategy of Corrections and Its Implications', *Criminology*, 30, 449–74.

Feeley, M. and Simon, J. (1994) 'Actuarial Justice: The Emerging New Criminal Law', in D. Nelken (ed.) *The Futures of Criminology*, London: Sage.

Feenan, D. (2002) 'Legal Issues in Acquiring Information about Illegal Behaviour through Criminological Research', *British Journal of Criminology*, 42, 762–81.

Ferguson, I., Lavalette, M. and Mooney, G. (2002) *Rethinking Welfare: A Critical Perspective*, London: Sage.

Ferrell, G. (1994) 'Confronting the Agenda of Authority: Critical Criminology, Anarchism and Urban Graffiti', in G. Barak (ed.) *Varieties of Criminology: Readings from a Dynamic Discipline*, Westport, Connecticut: Praeger.

Ferrell, J. and Hamm, M. (eds) (1998) *Ethnography at the Edge: Crime, Deviance and Field Research*, Boston: Northeastern University Press.

Ferri, E. (1895) *Criminal Sociology*, London: Fisher Unwin.

Ferri, E. (1996 [1901]) 'The Positive School of Criminology: Three Lectures by Enrico Ferri', in J. Muncie, E. McLaughlin and M. Langan (eds) *Criminological Perspectives: A Reader*, London: Sage.

Fitzgerald, J. and Daroesman, S. (1995) 'Ethical and Legal Issues When Conducting Research into Illegal Behaviours', proceedings of a forum (8 August), University of Melbourne, unpublished.

Fletcher, M. (2001) 'Dissenters Find Colleges Less Tolerant of Discord Following Attacks', *Washington Post* (30 October).

Foddy, W. (1993*) Constructing Questions for Interviews and Questionnaires: Theory and Practice in Social Research*, Melbourne: Cambridge University Press.

Form, W. (1973) 'Field Problems in Comparative Research: The Politics of Distrust', in M. Armer and A. Grimshaw (eds) *Comparative Social Research: Methodological Problems and Strategies*, New York: Wiley.

Foucault, M. (1977a) *Discipline and Punish*, London: Allen Lane.

Foucault, M. (1977b) 'Nietzsche, Genealogy, History', in D. Bouchard (ed.) *Language, Counter-Memory, and Practice*, Ithaca, New York: Cornell University Press.

Foucault, M. (1977c) 'Truth and Power', in A. Fontana and P. Pasquino (eds) *Microfisica del potere: interventi politici*, Turin: Einaudi; reprinted in J. Faubion (ed.) (2002) *Power: Essential Works of Foucault 1954-1984*, London: Penguin.

Foucault, M. (1980a), 'Two Lectures', in C. Gordon (ed.), *Power/Knowledge: Selected Interviews and Other Writings 1972–1977*, by Foucault, New York: Pantheon.

Foucault, M. (1980b) 'Truth and Power' (interview), C. Gordon (ed.), *Power/Knowledge: Selected Interviews and Other Writings 1972–1977*, by Foucault, New York: Pantheon.

Foucault, M. (1985) *The History of Sexuality*, volume two, *The Uses of Pleasure*, New York: Pantheon.

Foucault, M. (1991 [1978]) 'Governmentality', in G. Burchell, C. Gordon and P. Miller (eds) *The Foucault Effect: Studies in Governmentality*, Chicago: University of Chicago Press.

Foucault, M. (2001 [1980]) 'Questions of Method', in J. Faubion (ed.) *Power: Essential Works of Foucault 1954–1984*, London: Penguin.

Fountain, J. (1993) 'Dealing with Data', in D. Hobbs and T. May (eds) *Interpreting the Field: Accounts of Ethnography*, Oxford: Clarendon Press.

Frate, A., Zvekic, U. and van Dijk, J. (eds) (1995) *Understanding Crime: Experiences of Crime and Crime Control*, United Nations Publication Series, no. 49, Rome: United Nations Interregional Crime and Justice Research Institute.

Freire, P. (1985) *The Politics of Education*, London: Macmillan.

Fuller, L. (1988) 'Fieldwork in Forbidden Terrain: The US State and the Case of Cuba', *American Sociologist*, 33, 99–120.

Galliher, J. and McCartney, J. (1973) 'The Influence of Funding Agencies on Juvenile Delinquency Research', *Social Problems*, 27, 298–308.

Garland, D. (1985) 'Politics and Policy in Criminological Discourse: A Study of Tendentious Reasoning and Rhetoric', *International Journal of the Sociology of Law*, 13, 1–13.

Garland, D. (1988) 'British Criminology before 1935', *British Journal of Criminology*, 28(2), 1–17.

Garland, D. (1994) 'Of Crimes and Criminals: The Development of Criminology in Britain', in M. Maguire, R. Morgan and R. Reiner (eds) *The Oxford Handbook of Criminology*, Oxford: Clarendon Press.

Garland, D. (1995a) 'F.H. McClintock, Criminologist at Edinburgh University (United Kingdom): Obituary', *British Journal of Criminology*, 35(1), 134–37.

Garland, D. (1995b) 'Penal Modernism and Postmodernism', in S. Cohen and D. Blomberg (eds) *Punishment and Social Control*, Aldine: New York.

Garland, D. (1997) 'Of Crimes and Criminals: The Development of Criminology in Britain', in M. Maguire, R. Morgan and R. Reiner (eds) *The Oxford Handbook of Criminology*, second edition, Oxford: Clarendon Press.

Garland, D. (1999) 'Governmentality and the Problem of Crime', in R. Smandych, (ed.) *Governable Places: Readings on Governmentality and Crime Control*. Aldershot: Ashgate.

Garofalo, R. (1882) *Cio che dovrebbe essere un guidizio penale*.

Garry, M. and Loftus, E. (1994) 'Memory: A River Runs through It', *Consciousness and Cognition*, 3, 438–51.

Garry, M., Manning, C. and Loftus, E. (1996) 'Imagination Inflation: Imagining a Childhood Event Inflates Confidence That It Occurred', *Psychonomic Bulletin and Review*, 3(2), 208–14.

Gatrell, V. (1990) 'Crime, Authority and the Policeman State', in F. Thompson, (ed.) *The Cambridge Social History of Britain 1750–1950*, volume three, Cambridge: Cambridge University Press.

Gelsthorpe, L. (2000) 'BSc Ethics Panel', *British Society of Criminology, Newsletter*, 37 (May).

Gelsthorpe. L. and Morris, A. (eds) (1990) *Feminist Perspectives in Criminology*. Milton Keynes: Open University Press.

Gelsthorpe, L. and Morris, A. (1994) 'Juvenile Justice 1945–1992', in M. Maguire, R. Morgan and R. Reiner (eds) *The Oxford Handbook of Criminology*, Oxford: Clarendon Press.

Gelsthorpe, L., Tarling, R. and Wall, D. (1999) *British Society of Criminology Code of Ethics for Researchers in the Field of Criminology*: www.lbro.ac.uk/ss/bsc/council/codeeth

Giddens, A. (1998) *The Third Way: The Renewal of Social Democracy*, Cambridge: Polity Press.

Gladstone, J., Ericson, R. and Shearing, C. (eds) (1991) *Criminology: A Reader's Guide*, Toronto: Centre of Criminology, University of Toronto.

Gordon, C. (2002) 'Introduction', in J. Faubion (ed.) *Power, Essential Works of Foucault 1954–1984*, London: Penguin.

Grana, C. (1964) *Bohemian versus Bourgeois*, New York: Basic Books.

Grabosky, P. (2000) 'Diversity in Criminology', president's message, *Australian and New Zealand Journal of Criminology*, 33(1), i–ii.

Green, P. and Ward, T. (2003) *State Crime and Human Rights*, London: Pluto Press.

Grenville, J. (1994) *The Collins History of the World in the Twentieth Century*, London: Harper-Collins.

Griswold, D. (2001) 'At NYC Meeting on U.S. Terror at Home and Abroad: Ramsey Clark Warns of Plutocracy', *New York Post* (19 December).

Grounds, A. (1996) 'Research and Statistics Directorate: One Day Conference Friday 13th September 1996', in A. Bottoms 'Report by the Director of the [University of Cambridge] Institute of Criminology to the General Board's Future Work of the Institute' (December), unpublished.

Hagan, F. (1989) *Research Methods in Criminal Justice and Criminology*, second edition, New York: Macmillan.

Hall, J. (1947) *Principles of Criminal Law*, Indianapolis, Indiana: Bobbs-Merrill.

Harden, I. (1992) *The Contracting State*, Milton Keynes: Open University Press.

Harris, B. (1980) 'The FBI Files on the APA and SPSSI' *American Psychologist*, 35, 1141–44.

Hawkins, G. (1971) *Report of a Seminar on Social Defence: Proceedings of the Institute of Criminology, No. 2*, Sydney: Faculty of Law, University of Sydney.

Herman, E. and Chomsky, N. (1994) *Manufacturing Consent: The Political Economy of the Mass Media*, London: Vintage.

Hill, S. (1993) *The Window behind the Filing Cabinet: The Contribution of Social Science Research to Understanding the Purposes and Processes of Research Funding*, Woolongong: University of Woolongong, Centre for Research Policy.

Hillyard, P. and Sim, J. (1997) 'The Political Economy of Socio-Legal Research', *Social-Legal Studies*, 6(5), 45–75.

Hillyard, P., Sim, J., Tombs, S. and Whyte, D. (2003) 'Leaving a Stain upon the Silence: Critical Criminology and the Politics of Dissent', paper presented at the European Group for the Study of Deviance and Social Control, Chester (22–24 April), unpublished.

Hinde, R. (1951) *The British Penal System*, London: Duckworth.

Hirschi, T. (1969) *Causes of Delinquency*, Berkeley: University of California Press.

Hobbs, D. (1988) *Doing the Business: Entrepreneurship, the Working Class and Detectives in the East End of London*, Oxford: Oxford University Press.

Hodgson, J. (2002a) 'Pentagon Steps up Propaganda Efforts, *Guardian* (19 February).

Hodgson, J. (2002b) 'Pentagon Makes 'War on Terror' U-Turn', *Guardian* (26 February).

Hoffman, J. (1988) *State, Power and Democracy*, Brighton: Wheatsheaf Books.

Hogg, R. (1996) 'Criminological Failure and the Governmental Effect', *Current Issues in Criminal Justice*, 8(1),43–59.

Hogg, R. (1998) 'Crime, Criminology and Government', in P. Walton and J. Young (eds) *The New Criminology Revisited*, London: Macmillan.

Hogg, R. and Brown, D. (1998) *Rethinking Law and Order*, Sydney: Pluto Press.

Home Office (1996) 'Home Office Research: The Way Ahead: A Discussion Paper for the Seminar on 13 September 1996', RSDAC, 96(1), unpublished.

Home Office (1997) *Home Office Annual Report*, London: HMSO.

Home Office (1998) *Home Office Annual Report*, London: HMSO.

Home Office (2002) *Home Office Annual Report: The Government's Expenditure Plans 2002–03 and Main Estimates 2002–03 for the Home Office*: www.homeoffice.gov.uk/annrep/2002/2002_report.pdf

Hood, C. (1990) 'De-Sir Humphreyfying the Westminster Model of Bureaucracy: A New Style of Governance?', *Governance*, 3, 205–14.

Hood, R. (ed.) (1974) *Crime, Criminology and Public Policy: Essays in Honour of Sir Leon Radzinowicz*, London: Heinmann.

Hood, R. (1987) 'Some Reflections on the Role of Criminology in Public Policy', *Criminal Law Review* (August), 527–38.

Hood, R. (1997) 'Professor Sir Leon Radzinowicz, LL.D, FBA: a Tribute to Mark His 90th Birthday', *British Journal of Criminology*, 37(1), i–iv.

House of Commons (1947) *House of Commons, Parliamentary Debates: Official Report*, volume 449: HMSO.

House of Commons (1948–49) *House of Commons, Parliamentary Debates: Official Report*, volume 468: HMSO.

Howard, J. (1973 [1777]) *Prisons and Lazorettes*, volume one, *The State of Prisons in England*, Montclair, New Jersey: Patterson Smith.

Hudson, B. (2000) 'Critical Reflection as Research Methodology', in V. Jupp, P. Davies and P. Francis (eds) *Doing Criminological Research*, London: Sage.

Hughes, G. (1996) 'The Politics of Criminological Research', in R. Sapsford (ed.) *Researching Crime and Criminal Justice*, London: Sage.

Hughes, G. (1998) *Understanding Crime Prevention: Social Control, Risk and Late Modernity*, Buckingham: Open University Press.

Hughes, G. (2000) 'Understanding the Politics of Criminological Research', in V. Jupp, P. Davies and P. Francis (eds) *Doing Criminological Research*, London: Sage.

Hughes, G., McLaughlin, E. and Muncie, J. (eds) (2002) *Crime Prevention and Community Safety: New Directions*, London: Sage.

Institute of Criminology, University of Cambridge (2001) 'Current Research': www.law.cam.ac.uk/crim/rschnow.htm

Israel, M. (2000) 'The Commercialisation of Australian University-Based Criminology', *Australian and New Zealand Journal of Criminology*, 33(1), 1–20.

Jasper, J. (1997) *The Art of Moral Protest: Culture, Biography, and Creativity in Social Movements*, Chicago: University of Chicago Press.

Jeffrey, C.R. (1972) 'The Historical Development of Criminology', in H. Mannheim (ed.) *Pioneers in Criminology*, second edition, Montclair, New Jersey: Patterson Smith.

Jensen, R. (2001a) 'U.S. Just as Guilty of Committing Own Violent Acts', *Houston Chronicle* (14 September).

Jensen, R. (2001b) 'Against Dissent: Why Free Speech is Important as the U.S. Drops Cluster Bombs on Afghanistan', a talk to the University of Texas Teach-In (1 November): www.zmag.org

Jepsen, J. (1981) 'Control of Criminologists: State and Science and the State of Science in the State of Denmark', in M. Brusten and P. Ponsaers (eds) *State Control on Information in the Field of Deviance and Social Control*, Working Papers in European Criminology, no. 2, Leuven: European Group for the Study of Deviance and Social Control.

Jewkes, Y. and Letherby, G. (eds) (2002) *Criminology: A Reader*, London: Sage.

Johnson, E. (1981) *Research Methods in Criminology and Criminal Justice*, Englewood Cliffs, New Jersey: Prentice-Hall.

Johnson, E. (ed.) (1983), *International Handbook of Contemporary Developments in Criminology*, volumes 1–2, Westport, Connecticut: Greenwood Press.

Joint Funding Councils of the United Kingdom (1996) 'Research Assessment Exercise': www.niss.ac.uk

Jones, D. (1986) *History of Criminology: A Philosophical Perspective*, Westport, Connecticut: Greenwood Press.

Jones, S. (2001a) 'Academics Critical of War Face Harassment in US' (22 October): www.wsws.org

Jones, S. (2001b) 'CUNY Vows Crackdown on Anti–US Hatefest', *New York Post* (4 October).

Jones, S. (2001c) 'New Attacks on Academic Free Speech in US' (22 November): www.wsws.org

Jupp, V. (1989) *Methods of Criminological Research*, London: Allen and Unwin.

Jupp, V. (1996) 'Contours of Criminology', in R. Sapsford (ed.) *Researching Crime and Criminal Justice*, London: Sage.

Jupp, V. and Norris, C. (1993) 'Traditions in Documentary Analysis', in M. Hammersley (ed.) *Social Research: Philosophy, Politics and Practice*, London: Sage.

Karmel, P. (2000) 'Funding Universities', in T. Coady (ed.) *Why Universities Matter*, St Leonards: Allen and Unwin.

Kelsey, J. (1999) 'Academic Freedom Needed More Than Ever', in R. Crozier (ed.) *Troubled Times: Academic Freedom in New Zealand*, Palmerston North: Dunmore Press.

Kelsey, J. (2000) 'Academic Freedom: Needed Now More Than Ever', in R. Crozier (ed.) *Troubled Times: Academic Freedom in New Zealand*, Palmerston North: Dunmore Press.

Kemp, D. (1999) *New Knowledge, New Opportunities: A Discussion Paper on Higher Education Research and Research Training*, Canberra: Commonwealth of Australia.

Kemp, D. (2001) 'Backing Australia's Ability Keeps Australia's Researchers at the Leading Edge of Innovation', media release (29 January): www.detya.gov.au/ministers/kemp/jan01

Kenen, P. (1994) *Managing the World Economy: Fifty Years after Bretton Woods*. Washington, D.C.: Institute for International Economics.

Kirby, R. and Corzine, J. (1981) 'The Contagion of Stigma', *Qualitative Sociology*, 4, 3–20.

Klein, N. (2002) 'Signs of the Times', in P. Scraton (ed.) *Beyond September 11: An Anthology of Dissent*, London: Pluto Press.

Kleining, G. (1988) *The Receptive Interview*, Bielefeld: University of Bielefeld.

Koch, B. (1998) *The Politics of Crime Prevention*, Aldershot: Ashgate.

Kornblum, J. (2001) 'Radical' Radio Shows Forced from the Net', *USA Today* (16 October).

Kretschmer, E. (1921) *Körperbau und Charakter*, Berlin: Springer; English translation in J. Sprott (1964) *Physique and Character*, New York: Cooper Square.

Lapis, T. (1981) 'The Political Economy of the Development of Italian Criminology', in M. Brusten and P. Ponsaers (eds) *State Control on Information in the Field of Deviance and Crime Control,* Working Papers in European Criminology, no. 2, Leuven: European Group for the Study of Deviance and Crime Control.

Laster, K. (1994) 'The Lure of Relevance', *Australian and New Zealand Journal of Criminology,* 27(1), 3–4.

Lea, J. and Young, J. (1984) *What is to be Done about Law and Order?,* Harmondsworth: Penguin.

League of Nations (1933) *Gradual Unification of Criminal Laws and Co-operation of States in the Prevention of and Suppression of Crime,* Geneva: League of Nations.

League of Nations (1934) *Penal and Penitentiary Questions: Report of the Secretary-General to the Assembly 6 September 1934,* Geneva: League of Nations.

League of Nations (1938) *Essential Facts about the League of Nations,* Geneva: League of Nations.

Lee, R. (1993), *Doing Research on Sensitive Topics,* London: Sage.

Lee-Treweek, G. and Linkogle, S. (eds) (2000) *Danger in the Field: Risk and Ethics in Social Research,* London: Routledge.

Liddle, M. and Gelsthorpe, L. (1994) *Crime Prevention and Inter-Agency Co-operation,* Crime Prevention Unit Series, paper no. 53, Home Office Police Department, Police Research Group, London: HMSO.

Loader, I. (1998) 'Criminology and the Public Sphere: Arguments for Utopian Realism', in P. Walton and J. Young (eds) *The New Criminology Revisited,* Basingstoke: Macmillan.

Loader, I. and Sparks, R. (1993) 'Ask the Experts', *Times Higher Educational Supplement* (16 April).

Lodge, T. (1974) 'The Founding of the Home Office Research Unit', in R. Hood (ed.), *Crime, Criminology and Public Policy: Essays in Honour of Sir Leon Radzinowicz,* London: Heinemann.

Lombroso, C. (1876) *L'uomo delinquente,* Milan: Hoepli.

Loof, P. (1979) *Establishment of the Australian Institute of Criminology and the Criminology Research Council,* Canberra: Attorney-General's Department.

Lopez-Rey, M. (1974) 'United Nations Social Defence Policy and the Problem of Crime', in R. Hood (ed.) *Crime, Criminology and Public Policy: Essays in Honour of Sir Leon Radzinowicz,* London: Heinemann.

Loxley, W. and D. Hawks (1995) 'Legal Protection for Illicit Drug Use Research', in J. Fitzgerald, J. and S. Daroesman (eds) *Ethical and Legal Issues When Conducting Research into Illegal Behaviours,* proceedings of a forum (8 August), Melbourne: University of Melbourne.

Lustig, J. (2002) 'Free Speech: Casualty of War?', *San Francisco Chronicle* (9 January); also on the Academic Freedom website: www.academicfreedomnow

Lyotard, F. (1984) *The Postmodern Condition: A Report on Knowledge,* translated by Geoff Bennington and Brian Massumi, Manchester: Manchester University Presss.

McCalman, J. (2000) 'Blurred Visions', in T. Coady (ed.) *Why Universities Matter,* St Leonards: Allen and Unwin.

McGregor, O. (1981) *Social History and Law Reform*, London: Stevens.

Mackenzie, A. (1999) *Secrets: The CIA's War at Home*, Princeton, New Jersey: University of Princeton Press.

Mackenzie, D., Baunach, P. and Roberg, R. (eds) (1990) *Measuring Crime: Large-Scale, Long-Range Efforts*, Albany: State University of New York Press.

Maclean, B. and Milovanovic, D. (eds) (1991) *New Directions in Critical Criminology*, Vancouver: Collective Press.

Maddison, J. (1971) 'The Case for a Ministry of Social Defence in New South Wales', in G. Hawkins (ed.) *Proceedings of the Institute of Criminology, No. 2: Social Defence*, Sydney: University of Sydney.

Maguire, M., Morgan, R. and Reiner, R. (1997) 'Introduction', in their (eds) *The Oxford Handbook of Criminology*, second edition, Oxford: Clarendon Press.

Maguire, M., Morgan, R. and Reiner, R. (2002) 'Introduction', in their (eds) *The Oxford Handbook of Criminology*, third edition, Oxford: Clarendon Press.

Mair, G. and Nee, C. (1990) *Electronic Monitoring: The Trials and Their Results*. London: HMSO.

Majone, G. (1989) *Evidence, Argument, and Persuasion in the Policy Process*, New Haven, Connecticut: Yale University Press.

Malpas, J. (1996) 'Speaking the Truth', *Economy and Society*, 25(2), 156–77.

Mannheim, H. (1946) *Criminal Justice and Social Reconstruction*, London: Routledge and Kegan Paul.

Mannheim, H. (1960) (ed.) *Pioneers in Criminology*, London: Stevens.

Mannheim, H. (1962) 'The United Nations Asia and Far East Institute for the Prevention of Crime and the Treatment of Offenders', *British Journal of Criminology*, 3(2), 181–82.

Mannheim, H. (1972) 'Introduction', in H. Mannhein (ed.) *Pioneers in Criminology*, second edition, Montclair, New Jersey: Patterson Smith.

Mannheim, H. and Wilkins, T. (1955) 'Prediction Methods in Relation to Borstal Training', in *Home Office Studies in the Causes of Delinquency and Treatment of Offenders*, London: HMSO.

Marceau, J. (2000) 'Australian Universities: A Contestable Future', in T. Coady, (ed.) *Why Universities Matter*, St Leonards: Allen and Unwin.

Marginson, S. (1997) *Markets in Education*, Sydney: Allen and Unwin.

Marginson, S. (2000) 'Research as a Managed Economy: The Costs', in T. Coady (ed.) *Why Universities Matter*, St Leonards: Allen and Unwin.

Martin, J. (1988) 'The Development of Criminology in Britain 1948–60', in P. Rock (ed.) *A History of British Criminology*, Oxford: Clarendon Press.

Mayor, F. (1997) 'The Recommendation on the Status of Higher Education Teaching Personnel' (11 November): UNESCO General Conference.

Meiklejohn, A. (1965) *Political Freedom: The Constitutional Powers of the People*, New York: Oxford University Press.

Merton, R. (1957) *Social Theory and Social Structure*, New York: Free Press.

Metro Santa Cruz (2001) 'Uncivil Liberty' (26 October): www.metrocactive.com

Miles, I. and Boden, M. (eds) (2000) *Service and Knowledge-Based Economy*, London: Continuum.

Miller, P. and Rose, N. (1990) 'Governing Economic Life', *Economy and Society*, 19, 1–31.

Milovanovic, D. (1994) 'Law, Ideology and Subjectivity: A Semiotic Perspective on Crime and Punishment', in G. Barak (ed.) *Varieties of Criminology: Readings from a Dynamic Discipline*, Westport, Connecticut: Praeger.

Mitchell, D. (2001) 'Lifelong Controls Proposed for Serious Offenders in Scotland', *Guardian* (12 June).

Monbiot, G. (2000) *Captive State: The Corporate Takeover of Britain*, London: Macmillan.

Morgan, R. (2000) 'The Politics of Criminological Research', in R. King and E. Wincup (eds) *Doing Research on Crime and Justice*, Oxford: Oxford University Press.

Morris, A. (1975) 'The American Society of Criminology: A History, 1941–1974', *Criminology* (August), 123–67.

Morris, T. (1988) 'British Criminology: 1935–1948', in P. Rock (ed.), *A History of British Criminology*, Oxford: Clarendon Press.

Morris, T. (1989) *Crime and Criminal Justice in Britain since 1945*, Oxford: Blackwell.

Mueller, G. (1983) 'The United Nations and Criminology', in E. Johnson (ed.) *International Handbook of Contemporary Developments in Criminology: General Issues and the Americas*, Westport, Connecticut: Greenwood Press.

Muncie, J. (1984) *The Trouble with Kids Today: Youth and Crime in Post-War Britain*, London: Hutchinson.

Muncie, J. (1998) 'Reassessing Competing Paradigms in Criminological Theory', in P. Walton and J. Young (eds) *The New Criminology Revisited*, London: Macmillan.

Muncie, J., McLaughlin, E. and Langan, M. (1996) 'Criminological Perspectives: An Introduction', in their (eds) *Criminological Perspectives*, London: Sage.

Murphy, L. (2002) 'ACLU Appalled by Ashcroft Statement on Dissent: Calls Free Speech Main Engine of Justice' (10 December): www.aclu.org

Naffine, N. (1997) *Feminism and Criminology*, Sydney: Allen and Unwin.

National Institute of Justice (1996) *The NIJ Publications Catalogue 1985–1995* (fifth edition), Washington D.C.: US Department of Justice.

National Institute of Justice (1997) *Solicitation for Investigator-Initiated Research*, Washington D.C.: US Department of Justice.

National Institute of Justice (1998) *NIJ Research Portfolio 1998*, Washington D.C.: US Department of Justice.

National Institute of Justice (2001) 'Fiscal Year 2001: Current Solicitations': www.ojp.gov/nij/funding/htm

National Institute of Justice (2003) 'NIJ Fiscal Year 2003: As of Monday June 9 2003': www.ojp.gov/nij/funding/htm

Neef, D. (ed.) (1998) *The Knowledge Economy*, Boston: Butterwoth-Heinemann.

Nelken, D. (ed.) (1994) *The Futures of Criminology*, London: Sage.

New York Times (2002) 'Protecting Speech on Campus', editorial (27 January).

Newburn, T. (1992) *Permission and Regulation: Law and Morals in Post-War Britain*, London: Routledge.

Newsam, F. (1954) *The Home Office*, Liverpool: Tinling.

Noaks, L. (1999) 'Cops for Hire: Methodological Issues in Researching Private Policing', in F. Brookman, L. Noaks and E. Wincup (eds) *Qualitative Research in Criminology*, Aldershot: Ashgate.

Norris, C. (1993) 'Some Ethical Considerations on Field-Work with the Police', in D. Hobbs and T. May (eds) *Interpreting the Field: Accounts of Ethnography*, Oxford: Clarendon Press.

O'Connor, M. (1980) 'A Decade of the *Australian and New Zealand Journal of Criminology* 1969–1977', *Australian and New Zealand Journal of Criminology*, 13, 11–21.

O'Leary, C. and Platt, T. (2002) 'Pledging Allegiance: The Revival of Prescriptive Patriotism', in P. Scraton (ed) *Beyond September 11: An Anthology of Dissent*, London: Pluto Press.

O'Malley, P. (1992) 'Risk, Power and Crime Prevention', *Economy and Society*, 21(3), 252–75.

O'Malley, P. (1996) 'Post-Social Criminologies: Some Implications of Current Political Trends for Criminological Theory and Practice', *Current Issues in Criminal Justice*, 8(1), 26–38.

O'Malley, P. (1997) 'The Politics of Crime Prevention', in P. O'Malley and A. Sutton (eds) *Crime Prevention in Australia: Issues in Policy and Research*, Sydney: Federation Press.

O'Malley, P. (ed.) (1998) *Crime and the Risk Society*, Aldershot: Ashgate.

O'Malley, P. (2000) 'Criminologies of Catastrophe? Understanding Criminal Justice on the Edge of the New Millennium', *Australian and New Zealand Journal of Criminology*, 33(2), 153–67.

O'Malley, P. and Sutton, A. (eds.) (1997) *Crime in Australia: Issues in Policy and Research*, Sydney: Federation Press.

O'Neill, R. (1994) *Crime Prevention Strategies: The New Zealand Model*, Wellington: Department of Justice.

O'Reilly-Fleming, T. (1996) *Post-Critical Criminology*, Scarborough, Ontario: Prentice-Hall Canada.

Orwell, G. (1980 [1968]) 'A Hanging', reprinted in *George Orwell: Complete and Unabridged*, London: Secker and Warburg/Octopus.

Osbourne, D. and Gaebler, T. (1993) *Reinventing Government: How the Entrepreneurial Spirit is Transforming the Public Sector*, New York: Plume.

Parenti, C. (1999) *Lockdown America: Police and Prisons in the Age of Crisis*, New York: Verso.

Parsons, T. (1964) *Social Structure and Personality*, New York: Free Press.

Pasquino, P. (1980) 'Criminology: The Birth of a Special Savior: Transformations in Penal Theory and New Sources of Right in the Late Nineteenth Century', *Ideology and Consciousness*, 7, 1–17.

Patton, M. (1986) *Utilization-Focused Evaluation*, second edition, Newbury Park, California: Sage.

Pavarini, M. (1982) *La criminologia*, Florence: Lemonier.

Pavlich, G. (1998) 'The Art of Critique, or, How Not to be Governed Thus …', paper presented at the International Institute for the Sociology of Law, Onati, Spain (13–16 September), unpublished.

Pavlich, G. (1999) 'Criticism and Criminology: In Search of Legitimacy', *Theoretical Criminology*, 3(1), 29–50.

Pavlich, G. (2000a) 'Forget Crime: Accusation, Governance and Criminology', *Australian and New Zealand Journal of Criminology*, 33(2), 136–52.

Pavlich, G. (2000b) *Critique and Radical Discourses on Crime*, Aldershot: Ashgate.

Pavlich, G. (2001) 'Critical Genres and Radical Criminology in Britain', *British Journal of Criminology*, 41(1), 150–67.

Parenti, C. (1999) *Lockdown America: Police and Prisons in the Age of Crisis*, London: Verso.

Park, R. (1915) 'The City: Suggestions for the Investigation of Human Behavior in the City', *American Journal of Sociology*, 20(5), 577–612

Park, R. (1925) 'Community Oganization and Juvenile Delinquency', in R. Park and R. Burgess (eds) *The City*, Chicago: University of Chicago Press.

Payne, G., Dingwall, R., Payne, J. and Carter, M. (1980) *Sociology and Social Research*, London: Routledge and Kegan Paul.

Pearson, G. (1994) 'Youth, Crime, and Society', in M. Maguire, R. Morgan and R. Reiner (eds) *The Oxford Handbook of Criminology*, Oxford: Clarendon Press.

Pepinsky, H. (1997) 'Crime, Criticism, Compassion and Community', *The Criminologist*, special issue, 2 (Winter).

Peters, M. and Roberts, P. (1999) *University Futures and the Politics of Reform in New Zealand*, Palmerston North: Dunmore Press.

Petersilla, J. (1991) 'Policy Relevance and the Future of Criminology: The American Society of Criminology 1990 Presidential Address', *Criminology*, 29(1), 1–16.

Pierson, C. (1996) 'Social Policy', in D. Marquand and A. Seldon (eds) *The Ideas That Shaped Post-War Britain*, London: Fontana.

Plato (1974) *The Republic*, translated with an Introduction by Desmond Lee, London: Penguin.

Poovey, M. (1995) *Making a Social Body*, Chicago: University of Chicago Press.

Poulantzas, N. (1978) *State, Power, Socialism*, London: New Left Books.

Pratt, J. (1997) *Governing the Dangerous: Dangerousness, Law and Social Change*, Sydney: Federation Press.

Pratt, J. (1996) 'Criminology and History: Understanding the Present', *Current Issues in Criminal Justice*, special issue, *The Future of Criminology*, 8(1), 60–76.

Pratt, J. and Priestley, Z. (1999) '*The Australian and New Zealand Journal of Criminology* Thirty Years On', *Australian and New Zealand Journal of Criminology*, 32(3), 315–24.

Presdee, M. and Walters, R. (1998) 'The Perils and Politics of Criminological Research and the Threat to Academic Freedom', *Current Issues in Criminal Justice*, 10(2), 156–67.

Price, D. (1997) 'Anthropological Research and the Freedom of Information Act', *Cultural Anthropology Methods*, 9(1), 12–15.

Prins, A. (1910) *La Défense sociale et la transformation du droit pénal*, Brussels.

Punch, M. (1985) *Conduct Unbecoming*, London: Tavistock.

Quetelet, A. (1842) *A Treatise on Man*, translated by R. Knox and T. Smibert, Edinburgh: Chambers.

Rabinow, P. (ed.) (1997) *Essential Works of Michel Foucault 1954–1984*, volume one, *Ethics*, London: Penguin.

Radzinowicz, L. (1961) *In Search of Criminology*, London: Heinemann.

Radzinowicz, L. (1988) *The Cambridge Institute of Criminology: Its Background and Scope*, London: HMSO.

Radzinowicz, L. (1994) 'Reflections of the State of Criminology', *British Journal of Criminology*, 34(2), 99–104.

Radzinowicz, L. (1999) *Adventures in Criminology*, London: Routledge.

Radzinowicz, L. and Hood, R. (1986) *A History of English Criminal Law: The Emergence of Penal Policy*, London: Stevens.

Rampton, S. and Stauber, J. (2003) *Weapons of Mass Deception*. London: Robinson.

Rapport, B. (1999) 'The Uses of Relevance: Thoughts on a Reflexive Sociology', *Sociology: The Journal of the British Sociological Association*, 33(4), 705–23.

Rawls, J. (1971) *A Theory of Justice*, Cambridge, Massachusetts: Harvard University Press.

Reckless, W. (1970) 'American Criminology', *Criminology*, 8(1), 4–20.

Reiner, R. (1988) 'British Criminology and the State', *British Journal of Criminology*, 28(2), 138–58.

Reiner, R. (1992) *The Politics of the Police*, Brighton: Harvester.

Rhodes, R. (1994) 'The Hollowing Out of the State: The Changing Nature of the Public Service in Britain', *Political Quarterly Review*, 65, 137–41.

Rhodes, R. (1997) *Understanding Governance: Policy Networks, Governance, Reflexivity and Accountability*, Milton Keynes: Open University Press.

RMIT University (2000) 'Position Description: Lecturer, Criminal Justice Administration, Criminology', www.rmit.edu.au/departments/hr/pds/3000267

Robson, J. (1975) *Criminology: Its Search for an Identity*, Occasional Papers in Criminology, no. 1., Wellington: Institute of Criminology,Victoria University of Wellington.

Rock, P. (1988) (ed.) *A History of British Criminology*, Oxford: Oxford University Press.

Rock, P. (1994) 'The Present State of Criminology', in P. Rock (ed.) *History of Criminology*, Aldershot: Dartmouth.

Rock, P. (1995) 'The Opening Stages of Criminal Justice Policy Making', *British Journal of Criminology*, 35(1), 1–16.

Rock, P. (1997) 'Sociological Theories of Crime', in M. Maguire, R. Morgan and R. Reiner (eds) *The Oxford Handbook of Criminology*, second edition, Oxford: Clarendon Press.

Romilly, S. (1978 [1806]), *Observations on the Criminal Law of England*, New York: Garland.

Roos, J., Roos, G., Dragonetti, N. and Edvinsson, L. (1997) *Intellectual Capital: Navigating the New Business Landscape*, London: Macmillan.

Rose, G. (1961) *The Struggle for Penal Reform: The Howard League and Its Predecessors*, London: Stevens.

Rose, G. (1964) 'The War against Crime in England and Wales', *British Journal of Criminology*, 4(6), 606–07.

Rose, N. (1996) 'Governing Advanced Liberal Democracies', in A. Barry (ed.) *Foucault and Political Reason*, London: UCL Press.

Rose, N. (2000) *Powers of Freedom: Reframing Political Thought*, Cambridge: Cambridge University Press.

Roshier, B. (1986) *Controlling Crime*, Milton Keynes: Open University Press.

Ross, S. (1998) *Ethics in Law: Lawyers' Responsibility and Accountability in Australia*, 2nd edition, Sydney: Butterworth.

Rothschild, M. (2001) 'Newspaper Publisher Shouted Down at Commencement for Defending Civil Liberties' (19 December): www.progressive.org

Rothschild, M. (2002a) 'The New McCarthyism' (22 April): www.progressive.org

Rothschild, M. (2002b)'Student Teacher Canned for Teaching Islam' (23 March) www.progressive.org

Rothschild, M. (2002d) 'Student Art Exhibit Censored' (28 February): www.progressive.org

Rothschild, M. (2002e) 'Another Prize-Winning Journalist Fired' (9 March): www.progressive.org

Rothschild, M. (2002f) 'The New McCarthyism' (January 2002): www.progressive.org

Rousseau, J.-J. (1984 [1644]) *Of the Social Contract, or, Principles of Political Right*, translated with an Introduction and notes by C. Sherover, New York: Harper and Row.

Rutherford, A. (ed.) (1997) *Criminal Policy Making*, Aldershot: Dartmouth.

Said, E. (1994) *Representations of the Intellectual*, London: Vintage.

Salladay, R. (2001) 'Fallout Continues from Interrupted Sacramento Speech', *San Francisco Chronicle* (19 December).

Sallmann, P. (1988) 'Cautionary and Congratulatory Tales of the Criminological Enterprise', *Australian and New Zealand Journal of Criminology*, 21, 195–201.

Salonga, R. (2001) 'YRL Employee Punished for Political Mass Email', *Daily Bruin* (4 October).

Sampford, C. and Wood, D. (1993) 'The Future of Business Ethics: Legal Regulation, Ethical Standard Setting and Institutional Design', in C. Coady and C. Sampford (eds) *Business Ethics and the Law*, Sydney: Federation Press.

San Francisco Chronicle (2002) 'On the Public's Right to Know: The Day Ashcroft Censored Freedom of Information', editorial (6 January).

Sapsford, R. (1996) *Researching Crime and Criminal Justice*, London: Sage.

Sarantakos, S. (1998) *Social Research*, second edition, South Yarra: Macmillan.

Savage, D. (2000) 'Academic Freedom and Institutional Autonomy in New Zealand Universities', in R. Crozier (ed.) *Troubled Times: Academic Freedom in New Zealand*, Palmerston North: Dunmore Press.

Scally, D. (2001) 'German Teachers Critical of Us Get 'Stasi Treatment', *Irish Times* (12 November).

Scammell, W. (1975) *International Monetary Policy: Bretton Woods and After*. London: Macmillan.

Scarpitti, F. (1985) 'The Recent History of the American Society of Criminology', *The Criminologist* (November 1985), 1–9.

Scherpenzeel, R. (2000) *2001 Directory: Computerized Criminal Justice Information Systems*, The Hague: European Institute for Crime Prevention and Control.

Schoenwald, J. (2001) *A Time for Choosing: The Rise of American Conservatism*, New York: Oxford.

Schumann, K. (1981) 'On Proper and Deviant Criminology: Varieties in the Production of Legitimation for Law', in M. Brusten and P. Ponsaers (eds) *State Control on Information in the Field of Deviance and Social Control*, Working Papers in European Criminology, no. 2, Leuven: European Group for the Study of Deviance and Social Control.

Schutz, A. (1979) 'Concept and Theory Formation in the Social Sciences', in J. Bynner and K. Stribley (eds) *Social Research: Principles and Procedures*, London: Longman.

Schwartz, M. (1997) 'Does Critical Crim Have a Core? Or Just Splinters?', *The Criminologist*, special issue, 1 (Winter).

Scraton, P. (2001a) 'Defining Power and Challenging Knowledge: Critical Analysis as Resistance', keynote address, Whither Critical Criminology in the 21st Century conference (26 February), University of Western Sydney.

Scraton, P. (2001b) 'A Response to Lynch and Schwendingers', *Critical Criminologist: Newsletter of the ASC's Division on Critical Criminology*, 11(2), 1–3.

Scraton, P. (ed.) (2002) *Beyond September 11: An Anthology of Dissent* London: Pluto Press.

Scraton, P. and Chadwick, K. (1991) 'The Theoretical and Political Priorities of Critical Criminology', in K. Stenson and D. Cowell (eds) *The Politics of Crime Control*, London: Sage.

Seddon, N. (1999) *Government Contracts: Federal, State and Local*, second edition, Sydney: Federation Press.

Sessar, K. and Kerner, H. (eds) (1991) *Developments in Crime and Crime Control Research*, New York: Springer.

Sharpe, J. (1996) 'Crime, Order and Historical Change', in J. Muncie and J. McLaughlin (eds) *The Problem of Crime*, London: Sage.

Shaw, C. and McKay, H. (1942) *Juvenile Delinquency and Urban Areas*, Chicago: University of Chicago Press.

Sheldon, W. (1940) *Varieties of Human Physique*, New York: Harper and Row.

Sherwin, M. (2001) 'Tattletale for an Open Society', *Nation* (21 January).

Signorel, J. (1912) *Le crime et la défense sociale*.

Sim, J., Scraton, P. and Gordon, P. (1987) 'Introduction: Crime, the State and Critical Analysis', in P. Scraton (ed.), *Law, Order and the Authotitarian State*, Milton Keynes: Open University Press.

Simon, J. (1987) 'The Emergence of a Risk Society: Insurance, Law, and the State', *Socialist Review*, 95, 61–89.

Simon, D. and Eitzen, D. (1990) *Elite Deviance*, third edition, Boston: Allyn and Bacon.

Simpson, C. (1994) *Science of Coercion: Communication Research and Psychological Warfare 1945–1960*, New York: Oxford University Press.

Sjoberg, G. (ed.) (1967) *Ethics, Politics and Social Research*, London: Routledge and Kegan Paul.

Sked, A. and Cook, C. (1993) *Post-War Britain: A Political History, 1942–1992*. London: Penguin.

Smandych, R. (ed.) (1999) *Governable Places: Readings on Governmentality and Crime Control*, Aldershot: Ashgate.

Smart, C. (1990) 'Feminist Approaches to Criminology, or, Postmodern Woman Meets Atavistic Ma', in L. Gelsthorpe and A. Morris (eds) *Feminist Perspectives in Criminology*, London: Routledge.

Smellie, P. (1996) 'Fight to Put Contract Research in Public Realm: Criminologists Risk Gag for Touching Raw Nerve of State', *The Australian* (7 February 1996), 23.

Smith, J. (2001) 'Local Press Distorts Washington Protest', International Action Centre (30 September): www.iac.org

Solomon, R. (1993) 'Corporate Roles, Personal Virtues, Moral Mazes: An Aristotelian Approach to Business Ethics', in Coady, C. and Sampford, C. (eds) *Business Ethics and the Law*, Sydney: Federation Press.

Squires, P. (1981) 'The Policing of Knowledge: Criminal Statistics and Criminal Categories'. in M. Brusten, M. and P. Ponsaers (eds) *State Control on Information in the Field of Deviance and Social Control*, Working Papers in European Criminology, no. 2, Leuven: European Group for the Study of Deviance and Social Control.

Stangl, W. (1981) 'Considerations about the Process of Everday Control over Science', in M. Brusten and P. Ponsaers (eds) *State Control on Information in the Field of Deviance and Social*, Working Papers in European Criminology, no. 2, Leuven: European Group for the Study of Deviance and Social Control.

Stenson, K. (1999) 'Crime Control, Governmentality and Sovereignty', in R. Smandych (ed.) (1999) *Governable Places: Readings on Governmentality and Crime Control*, Aldershot: Ashgate.

Stewart, L. and Brownfield, C. (2001) 'Photography Museum Director Resigns over Afghanistan Exhibition' (13 December): www.news-journalonline.com

Struthers, A. (1952) 'Crime in 1950: Note on the Criminal Statistics in England and Wales for 1950', *Howard Journal*, 8(3), 151–58.

Student Press Law Centre, (2001) 'Students, Teachers Face Free Speech Limitations after Terrorist Attacks' (21 September): www.splc.org

Sullivan, R. (2000) *Liberalism and Crime: The British Experience*, Lanham, Maryland: Lexington Books.

Sunstein, C. (1993) *Democracy and the Problem of Free Speech*, New York: Free Press.

Sutherland, E. (1940) 'White-Collar Criminality', *American Sociological Review*, 5, 1–12.

Sveiby, K. (1997) *The New Organizational Capital: Managing and Measuring Knowledge-Based Assets*, San Francisco: Berrett-Koehler.

Sykes, G. and Matza, D. (1957) 'Techniques of Neutralization', *American Sociological Review*, 22(6), 664–70.

Tarde, G. (1912) *Penal Philosophy*, London: Heinemann.
Tarrow, S. (1994) *Power in Movements: Social Movements, Collective Action and Politics*, Cambridge: Cambridge University Press.
Taylor, I. (1995) 'Critical Criminology and the Free Market', in L. Noaks, M. Levi and M. Maguire (eds) *Contemporary Issues in Criminology*, Cardiff: University of Wales Press.
Taylor, I. (1999) *Crime in Context: A Critical Criminology of Market Societies*, Boulder, Colorado: Westview.
Taylor, I., Walton, P. and Young, J. (1973) *The New Criminology: For a Social Theory of Deviance*, London: Routledge and Kegan Paul.
Taylor, I., Walton, P. and Young, J. (eds) (1975) *Critical Criminology*, London: Routledge.
Thomas, J. and O'Maolchatha, A. (1989) 'Reassessing the Critical Metaphor', *Justice Quarterly*, 6, 143–72.
Thrasher, F. (1927) *The Gang*, Chicago: University of Chicago Press.
Thucydides (1972), *The History of the Peloponnesian War*, translated by R. Warner, R., introduction by M. Finley, London: Penguin.
Tilley, N. (1993) 'Crime Prevention and the Safer Cities Story', *Howard Journal*, 32, 40–57.
Times Higher (2003) 'Research Appointments' (11 April), 57.
Titmuss, R. (1959) *Essays on 'The Welfare States'*, London: Allen and Unwin.
Titmuss, R. (1962) *Income Distribution and Social Change: A Study in Criticism*, London: Allen and Unwin.
Toffler, A. (1965) *The Culture Consumers: Art and Affluence in America*, Baltimore: Penguin.
Tombs, J. (2003) 'Evidence in the Policymaking Process', paper presented at the Department of Criminology, Keele University (7 May), unpublished.
Tombs, S. and Whyte, D. (eds) (2003) *Unmasking the Crimes of the Powerful: Scrutinising States and Corporations*, second edition, London: Peter Lang.
Trasler, G. (1962) *The Explanation of Criminality*, London: Routledge and Kegan Paul.
Troiden, R. (1987) 'Walking the Line: The Personal and Professional Risks of Sex Education and Research', *Teaching Sociology*, 15, 241–49.
Turpin, C. (1989) *Government Procurement and Contracts*, London: Longman.

United Nations (1947) 'The Economic and Social Council', *Yearbook of the United Nations 1946–47*, Department of Public Information, Lake Success: United Nations.
United Nations (1948) 'The Economic and Social Council', *Yearbook of the United Nations 1947–48*, Department of Public Information, Lake Success: United Nations.

United Nations (1949a) 'Prevention of Crime and Treatment of Offenders', *Yearbook of the United Nations 1948–49*, Department of Public Information, New York: United Nations.

United Nations (1949b) *Economic and Social Council: Prevention of Crime and Treatment of Offenders*, Report of the Meeting of Principal International Organizations Concerned with the Problems of the Prevention of Crime and the Treatment of Offenders Convened under the Auspices of the United Nations at the Palais de Chaillot, Paris on 15 and 16 October 1948, E/CN.5/104 (18 February), New York: United Nations.

United Nations (1949c) *Economic and Social Council: Report of the International Group of Experts on the Prevention of Crime and Treatment of Offenders*, E/CN.5/154 (9 August), New York: United Nations.

United Nations (1949d) *Report of the Social Commission (Fifth Session) to the Economic and Social Council, Lake Success New York 5–15 December 1949*, supplement no. 2, New York: United Nations.

United Nations (1949e) *Economic and Social Council: Action to be Taken on the Report of the International Group of Experts on the Prevention of Crime and the Treatment of Offenders*, E/CN.5/170 (28 October), New York: United Nations.

United Nations (1950) *Yearbook of the United Nations 1949–50*, Department of Public Information, New York: United Nations.

United Nations (1954) *First United Nations Congress on the Prevention of Crime and the Treatment of Offenders*, A/conf.6/inf.1 (15 November), Department of Public Information, New York: United Nations.

United Nations (1956) *United Nations Congress on the Prevention of Crime and the Treatment of Offenders*, Department of Public Information, New York: United Nations.

United States Government (2003) 'Promoting Innovation and Competitiveness: President Bush's Technology Agenda': www.whitehouse.gov/infocus/yechnology/tech2.html

University of Cambridge (1998) *Diploma/Master of Studies (M.St.) in Applied Criminology (Police Studies)*, Cambridge: Institute of Criminology.

University of Melbourne (2001) 'Crime and Policy Relevance', *Melbourne University Magazine*, 28–29.

Van Swaaningen, R. (1999) 'Reclaiming Critical Criminology: Social Justice and the European Tradition', *Theoretical Criminology*, 3(1), 5–28.

Vincent, N. (2001) 'Intimidation is a Form of Censorship', paper presented at Centre for Research on Globalisation (8 November), *Los Angeles Times*, posted on Centre for Research on Globalisation website: http://www.globalresearch.ca

Walgrave, L. (1995) 'Criminaliteitspreventie: Op Zoek naar Orde in de Chaos', in *Handboek voor Criminaliteitspreventie*, Diegem: Kluwer.

Walklate, S. (1998) *Understanding Criminology: Current Theoretical Debates*, Buckingham: Open University Press.

Wallace, J. (1988) *Moral Relevance and Moral Conflict*, Ithaca, New York: Cornell University Press.

Walters, R. (2003) New Modes of Governance and the Commodification of Criminological Knowledge, *Social and Legal Studies*, 12(1), 5–26.

Walters, R. and Bradley, T. (2002) 'The Managerialization of Crime Prevention and Community Safety: The New Zealand Experience', in G. Hughes, E. McLaughlin, and J. Muncie (eds) *Crime Prevention and Community Safety: New Directions*, London: Sage.

Walters, R. and Presdee, M. (1999) 'Governing Criminological Knowledge: State, Power and the Politics of Criminological Research', in M. Corsianos and K. Train (eds) *Interrogating Social Justice: Politics, Culture and Identity*, Toronto: Canadian Scholars Press.

Washington Post (2001) 'Resisting the Censor's Impulse', editorial (26 September) 2001.

Weber, M. (1922) *Economy and Society: An Outline of Interpretive Sociology*, New York: Bedminster Press.

Weiner, T. (1999) 'Lobbying for Research Money, Colleges Bypass Review Process. Critics Say Politics Distorts Priorities of Science', *New York Times* (24 August).

Weiss, (1975) 'Evaluation Research in the Political Context', in E. Struening and M. Guttentag (eds) *Handbook of Evaluation Research*, volume 1, Beverly Hills, California: Sage.

Whyte, A. (1950) *The Evolution of Modern Italy*, Oxford: Blackwell.

Wiles, P. (1976) *The Sociology of Crime and Delinquency in Britain*, volume two, *The New Criminologies*, London: Robertson.

Wiles, P. (1999) 'Crime Reduction Programme, Guidance No. 1 – Analysis of Costs and Benefits: Guidance for Evaluators', London (August), CRP-GN1: Home Office, Research Development Statistics Directorate.

Wiles, P. (2002) 'Criminology in the 21st Century: Public Good or Private Interest – The Sir John Barry Memorial Lecture', *Australian and New Zealand Journal of Criminology*, 35(2), 238–52.

Williams, R. (1977) *Marxism and Literature*, London: Oxford University Press.

Williamse, H. (1994) 'Developments in Dutch Crime Prevention', in R. Clarke (ed.) *Crime Prevention Studies*, volume two, New York: Criminal Justice Press. Wilson, H. (1953) *The War on World Poverty: An Appeal to the Conscience of Mankind*, London: Gollancz.

Wilson, J. (1974) 'Crime and Criminologists', *Commentary* (July), 47–53.

Wilson, J. (1975) *Thinking about Crime*, New York: Basic Books.

Wilson, P. and Nixon, C. (1988) *Practical and Policy Related Research Conducted by the Australian Institute of Criminology 1974–1987*, Canberra: Australian Institute of Criminology.

Wolfram, C. (1986) *Modern Legal Ethics*, St Paul, Minnesota: West Publishing.

Wootten, B. (1978) *Crime and Penal Policy: Reflections of Fifty Years' Experience*, London: Allen and Unwin.

Wright, R. (2000a) 'Are There "Perils of Publishing" for Critical Criminologists? A Content Analysis of Leading Journals', *The Criminologist*, 25(5), 1–4.

Wright, R. (2000b) 'Left Out? The Coverage of Critical Perspectives in Introductory Textbooks, 1990–1999', *Critical Criminology*, 9(1), 101–22.

Yin, R. (1991) *Case Study Research: Design and Methods*, Newbury Park, California: Sage.

Young, J. (1981) 'Thinking Seriously about Crime: Some Models of Criminology', in M. Fitzgerald, G. McLennan and J. Pawson (eds) *Crime and Society: Readings in History and Social Theory*, London: Routledge and Kegan Paul.

Young, J. (1986) 'The Failure of Criminology: The Need for a Radical Realism', in R. Matthews and J. Young (eds) *Confronting Crime*, London: Sage.

Zdenkowski, G. and Brown, D. (1982) *The Prison Struggle*, Ringwood, Victoria: Penguin.

Zvekic, U., Lixian, W. and Scherpenzeel, R. (eds) (2000) *Development and Policy Use of Criminal Justice Information: Proceedings of the Beijing Seminar*, Publication no. 53, Rome/The Hague: United Nations Interregional Crime and Justice Research Institute.

Index